Gina –

I hope you enjoy the read & lessons taught.

Chi

A Promise Kept

VERNON RAVSTEN
AN UNCOMMON MAN
FOR OUR SEASON

Bruce J. Couch
with
Robert M. Couch

ISBN: 0-75960-212-3

Bob Richards' audiotape transcript used with permission of Bob Richards

Letter from Danny White

I have been involved in sports as a player, spectator and coach nearly all my life to one degree or another. This experience has always given me great enjoyment and satisfaction.

As a player and participant, the guidance and direction given by coaches in the development of skills and innate ability was paramount to achieving the success I was blessed with in my years on the prep, college and professional fields of endeavor.

When I retired from activity between the sidelines and graduated to giving encouragement and direction pacing up and down those same sidelines, I recognized even more how much impact the position of coach occupies in the whole scheme of things.

I watch sports now and have a greater appreciation for those who participate on the field, floor, track or other such venue. I also value those responsible for developing the skills on display along with the implementation of a "game plan" to enable those demonstrated skills to result in the success of a "win."

Through the years, I have come to understand what a "WIN" is defined as in terms of life and living it to the best and fullest extent possible. It is more than points on a scoreboard and who has the most at the end of the game. With life, it's more in line with "how you play the game" than the point total involved.

This book tells the story of a small town football coach and high school teacher who had great impact on the lives of young men and women in their formative years in a little town on the banks of the Snake River in southeastern Idaho. Not only did he achieve success on the field, he gave those he came in contact with in the classroom and everyday life a vision of what was important in life in achieving true success and happiness in life's journey.

I would highly recommend your reading this decidedly entertaining and enlightening work. It tells of exciting football games, funny episodes from the lives of high school students in the mid 60's, poignant interludes between individual students/athletes and their mentor/coach and gives great life lessons in a manner easily understood and related with. These same lessons will bring peace and happiness to one's life along with a sense of purpose and direction.

I know you will enjoy reading A Promise Kept and will benefit by the time you spend and the things you learn from it. It's a fast and very enjoyable read. You'll come away laughing, maybe crying a little but all the while satisfied that your time has been well spent.

Danny White
Coach, Arizona Rattlers
Quarterback, Dallas Cowboys
Arizona Football Hall of Fame

Acknowledgements and Explanations

The following story is a result of many hours of labor by a couple of "authors" who are anything but that by profession and training. We are a couple of Idaho "near" farm boys, proud of our heritage and educated by the grit and hard work we were exposed to and expected to give growing up in Idaho Falls, Idaho. While not raised on a farm, we put in many an hour in bucking and stacking hay, picking and storing potatoes, working in the fields of the dry farms that cover the Eastern Idaho countryside, installing and moving irrigation pipe and generally growing up no stranger to hard work and the benefits derived therefrom.

We enjoyed many an hour of fun and recreational time swimming in the canals that flow through the area, tunneling in the hay stacks of the farms that dot the landscape, devouring apples from local orchards, sneaking raspberries from under the noses of the nuns at the local hospital garden area and generally having a good time growing up. We both graduated from Utah State University, whose attendees are proudly called Aggies. Both are currently vice presidents for the firms they work for. Our day-to-day efforts are directed to coordinating and focusing the activities of those we work with to achieve worthy and successful goals and objectives; leaders and trainers in our own right-coaches.

Coach-an almost sacred word in our lives because of the experience with the man this book is written about.

Many have helped in the compilation and editing of the manuscript you are about to read. Some discussion was had between the authors and one editor in particular in regarding the many sentences in the first drafts that ended in a preposition. While these have been eradicated in most instances, should you find one we missed, please consider the following true vignette we heard from a returning matriculated scholar educated in one of the venerated eastern "Halls of Ivy."

It seems that the Idaho graduate was walking across the "Yard" upon arriving at Harvard and approached a passing professor to ask, "Excuse me sir, but can you please tell me where the library is at?"

The staid, old educator looked over his rimless bifocals and, in a condescending manner, replied, "My young man, we here at Harvard never end a sentence in a preposition!"

Our friend from the land of the potato thought for a moment and then responded, "I understand sir, in that case, could you please tell me where the library is at, you JERK?" (Or words to that effect!)

While not being that emphatic about our shortcomings, we appreciate your understanding them and recognizing the spirit the following story is written <u>in</u>!

We have had fun remembering the many things we learned and the experiences that brought so much growth and depth to our young lives. We appreciate those who have contributed to the process of putting these thoughts and experiences together and the encouragement we were given by friends and family in starting, working through and finally finishing this work of respect and love.

There are many to thank, Keith for planting the seed, Heidy for her patience and encouragement, Diane for initial editing, Bobette for her time and effort in pointing out the errors in the manuscript, (If a man goes into the forest, speaks, and his wife is not there to hear it, is he still wrong?), Kari for her proof reading the work, Jenny for her many hours of help,team members for their recollections, school and town officials for their information, class members for their support and Coach Ravsten's loved ones for their memories and the background material they provided. Without all these and more, the memory of Coach Vernon Ravsten may not be revealed as the kind of individual and valued personality he was.

The world needs more information about the kind of men and women who are cut from the same cloth as Coach was. Too many "heroes" or role models nowadays are not what one would want our children to emulate when you look at the lack of character and seemingly total disregard for values they portray. Even the leaders we elect are so many times found to be lacking honesty and integrity and instead desire to be all things to all people rather than stand up for what is right and true. Responsibility is an unknown word in the lives of too many it seems. Someone else is always at fault or circumstances preclude acting the proper way in standing up for the right and true.

This work is an effort to show what can happen when a man stands up for what is right, says what he will do and has the courage and tenacity to do it. If our effort falls short, it is not for lack of desire. Please enjoy the following and look for the greatness in others out there who are sacrificing and helping the young people of today ground themselves in the principles and values that our founding fathers came to this land to develop and enjoy.

> **Note:** The story told hereafter is from the perspective of Bruce Couch who graduated from Skyline High School in June of 1968 after spending his Sophomore year at Idaho Falls High School and the final two years at Skyline once Idaho Falls High was split into two student bodies.
>
> Rob Couch, Bruce's older brother (and chief tormentor, if some erroneous accounts are to be believed-never mind the broken collar bone, intermittent spats of mild throttlings from Bruce's perspective and a little blood from an odd nose bleed here and there) graduated from Idaho Falls High School (IFHS) in 1963.
>
> Rob was there when Coach Ravsten assumed his duties as Head Football Coach in 1962 at IFHS and Bruce was there when the era closed with Coach's death from the effects of cancer in early 1968. Between the two of them

they have recalled their experiences and related the impact that interaction with this great man had in their lives.

Bruce tells the story, which is mostly about the final season of his football career, and what turned out to be the final year of Vernon Ravsten's life. It is interspersed with remembrances from Rob's experiences and interaction with Coach. These latter anecdotes are taken from Bruce's memory, as he attended many of Rob's football games and wrestling matches (being the rightful hero worshiper he was-besides, if he had not attended, a broken arm may have been the result, never mind the collar bone) or from input from Rob, himself, as he told the story to Bruce.

Each Chapter is headed by a quote that is thought to give insight to the content of the next pages of the story. The chapter is concluded with a short couple of paragraphs in an attempt to communicate what was learned in relation to the experiences from the preceding pages. They show the character development and value building expertise of our mentor, Coach Vernon Ravsten, as he helped individually to inspire, comfort, change, build or instill in young lives the ingredients of greatness that Coach knew would help us immediately and most importantly, into our future lives as adults.

As you read the book, look for these attributes and try to incorporate them in your life or the life of those you have stewardship over. We learned much from this great man and continue to honor him by adhering to and practicing the things he taught by precept and example. While this is a tribute to Vernon Ravsten, the reader can gain vicariously from the account by internalizing the values and motivational techniques he exemplified and taught.

Look for the message and understand the method.

Introduction

The legacy left by Vernon Ravsten is one of great import and example to those lucky enough to have known and as a result, loved him. He will never be a national hero or a renowned leader except in the circles in which he traveled. But the impact he had on the lives of young men and women while in their formative years undoubtedly will result in the greatness of leadership or impact of heroism being realized in the life of one or more of the students who were benefited by knowing and being taught by this great leader and teacher.

He exemplified, in the early 60's, the attributes and qualities of the modern-day proponents of PMA (Positive Mental Attitude) and hard work---motivation and success principles that are so popular today. It is certain that, had he been 20 years later and been of a mind to, he could have written the books on these subjects that have reached the zenith of their appeal in the late 80's and into the new millennium. Keep in mind that Vernon Ravsten's era was during the days of "doing your own thing" and "if it makes you happy, do it." Selfishness was the norm. Doing unto others before they do it unto you was more the axiom of the day than the current teamwork approach popular in today's business and relationship trainers.

Vernon Ravsten, however, did not live to see the day when the principles he thought so important would be put into print and widely read in the offices and homes of America and the world abroad. He, rather, taught these principles on the football field, in high school classes, in religious meetings, on lonely roads in the farmlands of

Idaho, on wrestling mats and in everyday encounters with life as they occurred.

His personality and style touched many, many lives. One could not know the man and not love him and respect the great individual he was and the sacrifice he made for the good of others he came in contact with.

This book does not pretend to open his life and examine all aspects of his personality and style, nor give an all-encompassing overview of his life in general, but rather, to indicate in some detail how his talents, the loyalty he engendered and the principles he stood for affected the lives of a group of young men involved in athletics and the concurrent development of character and success.

An editorial was published in *The Post Register* concerning the 1967 football team he coached to an undefeated season:

> "The Skyline High football team in 1967 was the best in the state last year. It was not just endowed with unusually versatile talent. There could have been several teams with equal talent. Even the team's poetic precision was not its remarkable characteristic. It was the thrilling determination that the players exhibited in every game that has set this team apart from the great teams of the Idaho Falls' past. The Skyline Grizzlies were the on-the-field heartbeat of a coach the players loved and admired as few coaches in the history of high school coaching in this state."

The young men and women in the two high schools he taught and coached in were not the only ones to recognize his great value and the service he gave to others. Vernon Ravsten was a good neighbor, a valiant son, a quality friend, a worthy husband, a good church member-one who served others, an excellent father, a great teacher, an envied leader, a patient mentor, a great man, a skillful coach.

This is a true story about 'COACH' Vernon Ravsten.

Chapter 1

"...If one advances confidently in the direction of his desires, and endeavors to live the life which he has imagined, he will meet with success unexpectedly in common hours."
Henry David Thoreau

It was November 11th, 1966, and I was brought back from my semi-conscious state by my mother's voice.

"We're here."

I had not noticed that the car had ceased its motion and Mom had pulled up as close to the Skyline Grizzly dressing room as she could get. It was time for me to go through that door and transition from a typical 17-year-old high school junior to a linebacker for the high school football team I was on. I had been engrossed in thought and was brought back to earth by her voice.

"Make sure you zip up your coat before getting out of the car. Are you sure you're going to be warm enough?" Typical motherly concern for her second born son.

I mumbled something about it not being cold (didn't everyone take the opposite tack when confronting parental guidance during those years-it was cold) along with a 'Thank You' for the ride as I exited the car and made for the door. I'm sure that she had expressed the same sentiments and concerns as she dropped my brother Rob off at a different door but in like circumstances some 4 or 5 years before. He played center and defensive end for the Idaho Falls Tigers, the team we were about to play in a few short hours.

It was a team by the same name but definitely a different team in terms of many things, not the least of which was the name of the head coach-Vernon Ravsten. He had been Rob's coach in his high school career and was now mine even though we played for different high schools.

One thing, which was not different, was the weather one experienced in Idaho in the late fall. November in Idaho is a time for sitting by the fire and reading a good book. The potatoes are all out of the ground and safely stored in cellars, away from the numbing cold that reaches deep into the ground and turns it into concrete. The wheat has long since been harvested and the golden stacks of straw await their spreading in the mangers and corrals of local farmers to bring some comfort to the animals that are forced to brave the winters, the likes of which only come to the northern tier of states.

The sugar beets are being turned into the tons of white granules that are required on the tables of the masses. Among other uses in Idaho, they ladle it onto their hot mush in the mornings to make it palatable enough to eat on those cold winter mornings before venturing forth into the below-zero temperatures that are the norm from December through the shortened month of February.

It is a well-known fact in Idaho that February is only 28 days long because the populace could only stand that many days at the end of a normal Gem State winter. Any more and the state would be vacant. Enough already!

November also brings the end of the football season that started back in August with "two-a-days" (two practice sessions of 2-3 hours duration) that brought pain and suffering to the bodies of young men desiring to show their prowess on the gridiron. The 50 or 60 some boys who showed up in mid August had visions of wearing the crisp uniforms of their respective high school if only they could make it through the first four or five days it took to first strain every muscle and then work out the collective lactic acid that accumulated in large doses in every extremity and region of the body.

Usually by the end of the first week of practice, a candidate could begin to focus on making the team rather than just being able to move his legs in coordinated fashion or raise an arm above his head, ignoring the pain that came with the conditioning exercises that were so obviously necessary. As with the eternal round of life, or so it seemed, August's pain came 'round again to be November's suffering, albeit from a different source.

November's pain came from the frozen ground as one collided with its unyielding surface while performing assignments on the football field. Sports Illustrated once ran an article about the rigors of playing on artificial turf and how hard it was in comparison to the "Real Thing." Even though Idaho football games were all played on real grass fields (The "Real Thing"), they couldn't have been less yielding than the artificial fields spoken of in that article.

Running backs didn't go down in the latter part of the season, not because they were so strong, but because they didn't want to hit the ground. Tacklers and their pads would give somewhat, but the frozen ground was cold and hard and extremely rigid. It got so cold sometimes in the waning days of the season, that if you were on the bottom of a big pile-up after some run up the middle for short yardage, and it took an inordinate amount of time to get everyone off the pile, you could be frozen to the ground by your sweat soaked uniform fusing with the frozen tundra.

The final game of the 1966 season was one of those days. It was cold. The mercurial temperature at about 25 degrees. On the ride from home, I looked out of the car window and saw the wind blowing the dust and leaves through the gutters on the way to the stadium. That was another beauty of living in Southeastern Idaho-wind. They call Chicago the Windy City. I don't know who "they" is, but "they" never visited Idaho Falls. The wind blew everyday in I.F. (the preferred moniker of the town we all called home), from the mountains in the east and northeast in the morning and from the desert in the west and southwest in the afternoon.

They assured me that there was an easily explained

meteorological explanation for the situation-something to do with the differing ways the sun heated first the desert and then the forested mountains, or some such wizardry. The only thing I knew was that the wind was always in my face as I rode my bike to work in the mornings and home in the evenings during summer vacation from school. Kind of like the way my Dad always told us about the hard times he endured as a kid walking to and from school, uphill both ways! The wind in Southeastern Idaho was not a fish story of the same genre'-I know! The only time it was calm was from the time you went to bed until the time you got up in the morning.

In November, that meant that when it was 25 degrees outside with the normal "breeze" blowing, it felt like 40 below zero! Who cared what the thermometer read, it was cold! The wind did have its good side to some. It's said that the snow does not melt in Idaho. The wind just blows it around until it wears it out! As cold as it stays in Idaho, one may well imagine a snow covered ground year round if the wind didn't wear the white stuff out. Actually, it's not that cold in Idaho-just feels that way!

I had closed the car door and started for the dressing room as Mom's final words registered in my consciousness, such as it was.

"Dad will get off work a bit early and we'll be there for the opening kick-off."

I knew that meant that they would be there only if the advertising in the local newspaper, The Post Register, was all put to bed and absolutely correct. Dad was the Advertising Manager for the paper and if the Outdoorsman's ad was wrong or Food King's ad was missing a special, Dad would be there until it was right. Advertising revenues paid the bills and it was his responsibility to insure that local advertisers were always filling the coffers. Even so, it was rare that my folks were not in the stands at an athletic event in which I participated.

As I pulled the large, steel door open, I could see guys

walking around in various stages of dress as they prepared for the upcoming game. Some were just beginning to take off their street clothes while others had fully dressed in the uniform of the day---shoulder pads, thigh and knee pads, tail bone and kidney protectors, forearm "shiver" pads worn below their elbow pads, all covered with the blue and white jersey and football pants so coveted back in August when this had all begun. Others were being attended to by trainers or coaches who were taping knees, fingers, ankles or other suspect and vulnerable joints that either had in the past failed in some measure or were suspect to in the future without such pre-emptive care.

We had a few hours before the game, so I sat down on the bench in front of my locker and began the process of changing from a woolly bear of the great outdoors to a gridiron gladiator. As I pulled up my football pants, I looked over and saw Kenny Barnes, our quarterback, sitting in the trainer's room with his right foot stretched out on the table. Coach Jacoby was taping his ankle. Kenny was a junior that year and had had a good season, statistically speaking. He had a great arm and was very accurate with his aerial strikes.

As everyone on the team arrived and continued the process of shedding the cocoon that protected one from the blustery weather outside, to the shell that would hopefully protect one from the rigors and blows of the upcoming 48 minutes of game time, the tension in the air grew. The locker room got measurably quieter as we got closer to game time. I thought about how cold it was outside and how my hands would hurt as I hit my opponent's helmet with an open hand to ward off the oncoming blocker. Playing middle linebacker, I got a lot of opportunities to do that. I was glad I'd brought some gloves with me to keep my hands warm.

I finished putting on my uniform slowly, because I wanted to make sure everything fit just right. Escapees from cocoons are usually butterflies and butterflies continued to churn in my stomach. I could feel the pants snug on my legs. The support of the thigh, knee, kidney and tail pads gave a strange feeling of security. A feeling, I suppose, that only a football player could relate to.

I pulled on my T-shirt, put on my socks and wrapped my ankles with adhesive tape over the socks. Some guys taped their ankles directly on the skin, but I found it much more comfortable to tightly wrap the tape over the athletic socks I wore under the blue and white game socks that we donned only for official contests.

I walked over to the trainer's room and Coach Jacoby wrapped my right shoulder with an elastic bandage, finishing up with a few strips of tape. Somehow this helped to stop the burning sensation I got whenever I hit someone really hard with my right shoulder. I put on my shoulder pads, pulled my jersey on as far as I could and yelled at one of the other linebackers to come over and finish the job. Bob Nelson walked over and jerked really hard on the back of the jersey and it came down over my shoulder pads and fell down to my waist. That's the way it always was, a hard jerk on the back of the jersey. I sometimes wondered if football players had some weird, hidden longing to see if they could jerk a jersey hard enough to decapitate their buddy. I quickly tucked it into my pants and put on my shoes, making sure they were good and tight and the laces were double tied so they wouldn't come loose. I grabbed my helmet and walked to an open space along the wall and sat down to contemplate what the next couple of hours might hold.

Coach Ravsten came out of his office a few minutes later and yelled, **"Okay you guys, this is the last game of the year and the biggest. Turn out the lights, sit down, relax and think about your assignments today. Go over in your mind what you have to do and how you're going to do it. See yourself accomplishing what you're supposed to do."**

The locker room became very quiet as everyone lay down on

the floor or on a bench or sat against the wall somewhere in the locker room. Those still dressing did so quickly and everyone started communicating in whispers. As I lay there, I thought of the opponent I was to key off of and follow. This was going to be a tough game. In fact, by all accounts, we were not supposed to win, but we were going to give it all we had. I felt very relaxed and comfortable even though I was lying on a concrete floor wearing all of my pads and helmet. You got used to it after all that practice on the frozen field outside. And besides, it was warm in here!

After about ten minutes, Coach Ravsten came out of his office with Coaches Doug Leathem and Brizee. Coach Jacoby was still taping one of our running backs in the trainer's room. Coach Ravsten stood about six feet, was well built and weighed about 190 pounds. He had sandy blond hair, thinning a bit, but still nowhere near balding. He wore glasses most of the time. He was not the Clark Gable of the day, but was ruggedly handsome and always neat and crisp in his appearance.

"Okay boys, gather around here," Coach said in his, mild yet very firm, voice. We all got up and gathered on the benches in front of him.

"This has been one heck of a year," Coach began. "In fact, I would say this has been the most frustrating year I have ever coached. You have the size and the talent to be eight and one instead of one and eight. But we've learned a lot together this year from our adversity and I've been very proud of some, as I have seen you develop character you didn't show before. In the final analysis, that's the most important thing a coach can do; develop character in the lives of thc athletes he coaches.

"But, dang it guys, I hate to lose. Anyone can give up, not live up to the potential within you, and lose. But it takes a real man to go out there and beat that guy across from you. We are not losers, not a one of us here. We are winners and that is what I want you to do today. Go out there and show this town that this is the best football team in this city. You can do it, I know you can.

"I know, just as each of you do, that we are the underdogs today. In fact, *The Post Register* says we will lose by 21 points! This is a new school, Skyline's first year at everything, and we are setting the traditions that will give this institution the innate character that it will have through the years of its existence. Think back to just one year ago when those guys up there in the other dressing room were our teammates and we were all in the same school, Idaho Falls High School. If we had not been divided, we would all be playing together today against some other team. Now those guys up there are our opponents instead of our teammates."

This was our first game against the Idaho Falls Tigers, Halloween High, as Coach was so fond of calling it, in reference to the school's orange and black colors. It seemed natural then for him to refer to it in those derisive terms even though just one year ago he had been the head coach and a very popular Psychology instructor at I.F.H.S. Skyline High had been formed from Idaho Falls High School and we were both meeting in the same school facilities on a split schedule until our new school could be built. I.F. went to school in the morning and we went in the afternoon.

Idaho Falls is a small city in southeastern Idaho on the banks of the Snake River. There are some waterfalls on the river from which the city takes its name. In its earliest history it was known as Eagle Rock. The city sits on the river and at the edge of the volcanic desert from which thousands upon thousands of acres of rich farmland have been and still are being reclaimed from nature's idle grasp.

These acres support grain, hay and other crops, but none so profitable and popular as the Idaho potato. Millions of acres of potatoes grow in the surrounding environs, from the desert on the west to the foothills in the east. All up and down the beautiful

Snake River Valley grow these wondrous tubers that end up on the dinner plates of so many people as the premier potato in the United States and even the world at large.

They say the volcanic soil around the area is the reason for such big, high quality potatoes being grown here, but I suspect the real reason for growing potatoes rather than any other crop was the fact they are the only thing nature could conjure up that would withstand the wind blowing up and down the valley. Those big potatoes under the ground were about the only thing that could keep the greenery on top from being blown away. JR Simplot and Ore-Ida may argue that point, but I have my own thoughts on the matter.

At the time, Idaho Falls was also the home for many naval personnel who were learning how to be first-rate submariners on the desert to the west of the city. Now you may ask, how can anyone learn to operate submarines in the desert? Below that desert lies one of the largest underground sources of water in the USA, if not the world. No, there were no submarines lurking beneath the desert lava, but that water supplied the cooling liquid required for the dozens of nuclear reactors being operated and researched by the then Atomic Energy Commission and Department of the Navy.

They said there was a BIG tank out there large enough to dive a real submarine in, but I never saw it. There was, however, the largest airplane hanger in the world out on the Arco desert, as we knew it. I had seen pictures of it with a small airplane making a turn, while flying, inside the hanger! The government was doing research on the feasibility of constructing a nuclear powered airplane, but in the end had only the building in which to build it.. I guess you do need a building to hatch your ideas in, something like the chicken and the egg question. Which came first? In this case, the government laid one giant egg with nothing inside.

Idaho Falls had a third high school that catered basically to the outlying farming communities. Bonneville High School was known as the "Farm Boys" while we were the "City Slickers." In reality, both Idaho Falls and Skyline High Schools had their fair share of "farmers" attending classes. But the Bonneville Bees were THE farmers and the other two schools were THE city boys. Prior to the splitting of I.F.H.S., the big rivalry had always been between I.F. and Bonneville. But that was history. The big game now was I.F. versus Skyline and you didn't let anyone try to tell you otherwise!

Coach continued, "Their record is much better than ours and I fear what might happen out on the field today." Coach was getting pretty excited as he paced back and forth in front of us. He really loved the game and he showed that same love for the boys that played it for him.

"We can go out there and get our butts kicked or we can go out there and kick their butts. That, boys, is entirely up to you. When you go out on the field today you are on your own. The coaching staff has done all we can do and have taught you all you need to know, tutored all the skills you need to exhibit. Now it is up to you. When you come off that ball the first time, I want you to pop that guy across from you and make sure you hit him harder that he hits you. It won't hurt. You all know that. Make sure he thinks this is going to be one long day for him.

"I've told you this many times and I want to make sure you all remember that if you cheat out there on the gridiron and don't give 100%, I can guarantee you will do the same in life. Learn now how to give of yourself, learn how to work with each other and to support and encourage each other. Do these things now and you will have learned how to be successful throughout your life in whatever endeavor you attempt.

"That is a miniature of life out there on the field," as he pointed in the general direction of the football stadium beyond the walls of the dressing room.

"Give your all, reach down deep inside yourself and give your all. You will then walk off that field, win or lose, and feel good about yourself and what you've accomplished. Cheat out there and I guarantee you will feel badly about yourself.

"I want each of you to go out there today and have a lot of fun. It's the last game of the year and I think half the town is out there to watch and see just how good or how bad we really are. I'm very proud of how many of you have grown so tremendously during this year. Some of you have grown from boys to men and I feel good about that. And I'll feel a lot better about it when we go out winners today. Now go out there and show this town what kind of men we're developing here and what kind of traditions we expect to foster and continue."

Coach finished his pep talk, which was really much more than that because he believed so much in what he'd just said. He then asked all of us to kneel down for a prayer. Tom Wood, one of the captains, had earlier called upon one of the players who now said a quick prayer. Then forty boys jumped up and started yelling. The excitement and feeling in the air was enough to bring tears to my eyes.

"Come on, let's get 'em! Let's do what we know we can do!" came booming from all of the players.

Tom opened the door and led us out onto the field. As I left the locker room, I could feel the chill. I had forgotten all about how cold it was going to be out on that field today, having been warmed within by the glowing enthusiasm that Coach had engendered within each of us in the preceding moments. We ran out and lined up to warm up with side straddle hops. I looked up into the stands and saw that there weren't very many people there at this point. Coach had said he expected to see half the town out here for the game, but you'd have to be half crazy to be in the stands this early in that cold air.

We finished our basic warm up exercises and then separated into our individual drills. The I.F. Tigers were coming out onto the field now to warm up. I was always nervous at that point, but even more so today. In fact I felt nauseated. I was really looking forward to the kick-off, because that was when the nerves would go away and emotion would take over. Warm-up drills finished and we all walked to the sideline to await the kick-off.

I looked up into the stands to see if I could see Mom and Dad, but there were now too many people to be able to find them. In fact, the stands had more people in them than I had ever seen out to a football game in Idaho Falls. People were jammed together in every corner of the seating area. I suppose that there were at least two good reasons for that-one to survive the cold by sitting next to another warm body and another to see the game. This was going to be a big one.

Lessons Learned:

Coach Ravsten taught us the value of confidence in our approach to the activities we participated in regardless of their nature-sports, school, social or religious activity, etc. That confidence was a result of hard work and learning the intricacies of the project we were involved with. Many of the skills we learned were on the football field, but Coach always emphasized the fact that football was just a little slice of life in general and the principles we learned on the practice field could easily be translated into our approach to life and how to succeed.

He realized that few of us would even go on to college sports, let alone make a career of professional sports. Yet the confidence built in each young man through consistent effort and proper reinforcement, was carried over in many a young man's life to benefit both him and those he associated with after leaving the tutelage of Coach Ravsten.

When we left the practice fields as victors or as those who knew we had given our best and were confident in that knowledge, we did a better job in living lives in the challenging and difficult world in which we live. We had the confidence to know that if we gave our all, we could come out victors, no matter the arena.

Chapter 2

"A man has made a start in discovering the meaning of human life when he plants shade trees under which he knows full well he will never sit".

Elton Trueblood

Vernon Ravsten began his career in Idaho Falls by assuming the duties of head football coach at Idaho Falls High School in the fall of 1961. My brother, Rob, a junior that year, was on the first team Coach led at Idaho Falls High School. He played center for the Tigers on offense and defensive end for the defensive squad that year and during his senior year of 1962-63. In those two years, Rob grew to love and appreciate him in much the same way we did who were lucky enough to grow for three years under his tutelage.

The diversity of his personality with his great sense of humor was established very early during his initial days at I.F.H.S. During those first dog days of August practice in 1961, Coach was forming the offensive team he wanted for a particular drill. He looked over his roster, being unfamiliar with all the boys names and the positions they played (or wanted to play), and called each individual by his last name as he decided on the alignment he wanted walking down the line. When he got to the middle of the formation, he studied the clip board for a moment, studying the names that were listed for the position of "center" and then called out, "Crotch, get over the ball at center."

Well, there were only two guys on the team who were unconscious enough to want to play center and one of them was my brother. He was, however, not so unconscious as to not recognize that Coach was calling him to hike the ball in this particular formation even if Coach had butchered his name.

Now there's an adage that we in our family had adopted early in our youth having the last name "Couch." I'm not sure what people thought about the name, but nearly everyone would try to pronounce it any way but the way they would if they were asking you to sit down on that overstuffed piece of furniture that nearly everyone in the USA has in their own front room. You name it---Coach, Cotch, Cooch, Catch, Crouch, Conch---we'd heard it all. Folks would add letters, change letters, drop letters, whatever. They could not bring themselves to say, "COUCH." So we just figured, "Okay, call me anything, just don't call me late to dinner," and left it at that.

This particular butchery, however, deserved a bit of corrective action, even if you were trying to make the team and didn't want to embarrass your new coach-who would, in not too many days distant, post a list of NAMES of those who would go on to vie for a first string position on the varsity football team. Rob stepped forward to the position indicated over the football.

As he did so, he mentioned with the utmost respect, "That's Couch, Coach, not Crotch."

"I know," replied Coach, "just get over the ball, Crotch."

It was never determined for sure, but only assumed, that the new coach had so changed the name of the player to fit the position of center as the position on the offensive team around which all activity pivoted much like the human body pivoted around that area just below the belly button.

In any case, the nickname was not lost on the other 50-60 young men on the field that day and my brother bore that moniker for the balance of his high school career-"Crotchman, Idaho Falls Tigers."

I was thankful for two things (among many) in my football days:

1) There were four years between my brother and me and,

2) I didn't play center.

The nickname mostly died with his graduation. Thankfully.

This experience revealed at an early stage the humor and good naturedness that Coach possessed. He had many other nicknames for others on the team or would have a joke to tell or a prank to play on an unsuspecting victim at an appropriate time. There was always a sense of propriety and integrity, never demeaning or disrespectful but mindful of one's feelings and sense of being.

He exhibited this great trait along with a devotion to young people and their success among others that made him fun to be around. He was recognized immediately as a premier instructor in the academic classes he taught during school hours and one was considered privileged to be in his class no matter what the subject matter---health, PE, or psychology. The classes were tough and the material up-to-date.

Coach was pursuing his doctorate in psychology at the time and brought the latest information and knowledge to his classroom. He made learning fun and exciting, as well as beneficial and meaningful to those who were willing to work hard and learn. He was always willing to listen to dissent when some point of knowledge was in question. Rather than assume that the book answer was the correct one, he would entertain any argument and debate as long as the student could intelligently put across his point.

One classroom dissent involved a discussion of the attributes and limitations of a condition called "Congenital Hip." Coach had explained the physical ramifications and resultant accommodations the body of the one afflicted with such a condition would intrinsically make to be able to carry on with life.. At the conclusion of this explanation, one of the students in the class, a member of the football team to boot, raised his hand and stated that there was no way that what had been just explained could ever be possible.

The rest of the class period was spent debating the differing points of view.. This carried on into the next day's class period with much more clarification and detail exposed by both sides than was in any way deserving of such a relatively inane subject. The point was that Coach allowed intelligent debate and dissent if the one so responding was respectful and willing to go further in his discovery process.

Many extra hours were spent in the library and research done to justify the point, or trying to. More learning and skills were developed in this kind of process than ever would be experienced by just sitting and accepting all that was being said at the front of the class knowing there was no room for conflicting ideas.

Minds expanded, intelligence was enhanced and students had a great time in the learning process. I saw it happen both in person, as a student in his classes and even vicariously---the student in this particular incident was my brother! I believe to this day that Rob thinks he was right and Coach was in error. But I know that like numerous others so lucky to be instructed by Coach, he was magnanimously benefited by the interaction between student and teacher, counselor and petitioner, coach and athlete.

On the other side of the coin, unintelligent or improper behavior would bring a swift and pointed response that would get your attention immediately, be it in the class, on the playing field or in everyday life.

There were three basic "classes" of students in our high school days and I speak not of sophomore, junior and senior. Rather, there were the athletes/leaders, the partiers/ruffians and finally the precursors to the "silent majority." The first group consisted of the guys that played on the various athletic teams and the girls that hung around with them. These were the days before female athletics. There were no such teams in Idaho. The only athletically associated activities the girls could participate in were cheerleading (there wasn't a single guy that would even think of participating in that activity in those days), the drill team and the Pep Club. All of these latter activities revolved around athletics and the guys and girls so involved generally were found together in social gatherings as well.

Closely associated with this group were the leaders-the student body officers and student council members. Many of these individuals came from the former sub-group (athletes) but there were some that did not participate in athletics but did enjoy and contribute to the leadership of the student body. All of these individuals meshed and got along very well.

The partiers/ruffians seemed to have a chip on their shoulder and something to prove to the world. They were the smokers and drinkers who enjoyed hanging out somewhere to do just that-smoke and drink and little else, or so it seemed. They had an aversion to authority and seemed to be insolent and have a "better than you" attitude. They did not support or participate in any extracurricular activities other than the ones they threw together on their own. Clubs, sports, student government and the like were activities that held no interest for them. They just bore the burden that life had shackled them with and got through the day. These first two groups were like oil and water, never the twain to mix.

Then there were the members of the third group. They were there everyday and did the thing they did best-got good grades, won the prizes at the science fairs, worked after school at the local theater or grocery store, played instruments in the orchestra, painted beautiful pictures and displayed other such talents that the world so desperately needs in every age. They didn't make any waves and you'd never know they were around but would definitely know if they weren't.

They gave the backbone to the society at high school and life in general. They weren't concerned with being recognized for their efforts and went through each day with perseverance and drive to produce excellent results in nearly all they did. The "Silent Majority."

One day a young man from the ruffian/partier classification

decided it would be the "cool" thing to fly the proverbial "bird" at the popular instructor as he was stopped in front of him at a stoplight. For what reason, no one knows.

Now you have to understand the maturity level of some Idaho drivers in those days. We lived in a state that was agrarian by nature. The mechanization of the farm required that every hand be licensed as early as possible to drive the vehicles that brought the harvest in from the fields to the marketplace of America. That being the case, you could get your driver's license at the age of fourteen (14) in those days. Now that would strike fear and terror into hearts of many today, but in the early 60's in Idaho you could legally drive during daylight hours if you could prove you had a full year of teenagery under your belt! Back to the streets of suburban Idaho Falls-

As soon as the young man had made the crude gesture to Coach (who had his two sons in the car with him), the mental giant gunned it and turned right. Now Coach was a student of the wiles of man and a believer in the integrity of the laws of the land. He couldn't decide if the one finger indicated the youngster's age or IQ but decided to find out. If it were his age, how could he possibly be driving a vehicle on the roads of Idaho Falls? And if it were his mental age, Coach wanted to know how he passed the driving exam to get his license. In any case, not wanting to be left in the dust of the rapidly escaping culprit, Coach also turned right (never mind the left hand turn signal, please) and followed the boy through the streets of Idaho Falls.

Finally, in desperation, after failing to shake the following teacher, the boy pulled over to the curb and jumped out of the car deciding he'd outrun the old geezer on foot. He didn't count on the fact that Coach stayed in great shape with the rest of his athletes. No sooner had the kid reached the top of the fence between the two houses he was running toward, than the long arm of the Coach latched on to his pegged pants and he was not so gently eased back to imminent punishment.

No one knows for sure exactly what happened then (as the view of the two boys left in Coach's car was obscured at that point and they were the only witnesses present) but the finger waver was no doubt the recipient of some rectifying discipline at the hands of the Tiger football coach and instructor. He wore as a badge of dishonor, a cast on his hand with his middle digit permanently straight out from the hand for the next six weeks as a broken bone healed.

Now, there is surely some out there reading this who are horrified at the thought of such assumed "abuse." It must be noted that no one at the time, youth or adult, gave the incident a second thought-other than it was appropriate and proper. All who saw the cast and knew the story (and it got around rather quickly) recognized that it was inappropriate to show such disrespect and lack of intelligence. The punishment was quick, just and accepted by all.

There is a law, irrevocably decreed, that all behavior be rewarded or punished according to the stipulations and standards in force/declared. Well, at least there used to be such a standard in life. Nowadays it seems that no one wants to stand up and be counted for the values and pillars upon which good life is founded. Coach did not believe that these standards be modified nor ignored and he taught that belief by word and action. We all knew where he came from and what he stood for and admired and respected him for it. The community at large felt likewise-about Coach, yes, but more importantly, about that general philosophy that there was acceptable behavior and unacceptable actions and you suffered the consequences you brought upon yourself if you crossed the line. There was no one there to make excuses for you if you did something bad.

This was not today but was a day when you bore the consequences of your actions and everyone understood that. In this case, there was no call for censure or demands for resignation. There was no parent beating down the doors of the administration hollering for the head of a man who had "abused" an "innocent" youth. People in that day or perhaps that area recognized responsibility and consequences and accepted the fact of living with the decisions you made in life. No one gave this little scenario a second thought-if the truth be known, even the cast wearer.

Coach taught us the value of making good decisions and standing up for what is right. There was no acceptance of bad behavior. There was no treatment that was without respect.

And there was no ignoring poor performance.

Rob remembers one game his senior year in which his team had displayed an atrocious disregard for the fundamentals of football, let alone the points of expertise they had been taught and were adept at performing. The game had ended with the Tigers at the short end of the score that Friday night, the fans (including me) had gone to the warmth of their homes and the team had dejectedly left the field, walking heads down back to the dressing room.

Rob had just managed to get himself to the parking lot separating the practice fields from the gymnasium and locker room. Cramps in his legs kept forcing him to stop every couple of feet all the way across the practice field on his way back from the stadium after the final gun ended the disgrace of the evening.

Just as he was crossing the wire rope at the end of the parking lot, he looked up to see his team rushing out of the doors and running back out onto the playing field wearing their practice jerseys. No one spoke a word as the team ran past him and only when one of the assistant coaches came by and told Rob to get inside and change into his practice uniform did he understand what was going on. The team was going back out to correct poor performance and reinforce proper technique. That was probably the meanest and most productive practice session of anyone's season according to what Rob told me later.

Since the stadium playing field was the only one with lights, they were out there banging heads until the athletic director came out and told Coach the residents of the surrounding community were complaining about the lights being on after midnight. There wasn't a problem of noise because no one was uttering a word, other than the coaches giving instructions, and they were almost whispering. They would have been out there still if the athletic director had not finally gone over and turned off the lights himself.

But it turned a team that was capable of winning the conference championship, but sporting a so-so record, into one that won the most important remaining game of the year.

The last game of Rob's high school season in the fall of 1962 was against Pocatello High School, then the biggest rival, aside from Bonneville, that Idaho Falls faced each year.

That particular year the game fell on the same day that the ACT tests were given to seniors who desired to go on to college. The test was administered beginning at 8 a.m. on a Saturday at Idaho State University in Pocatello where the game would be played that afternoon in the college stadium. After the seniors on the team were finished with the exam, they hurried over to the stadium to dress and try to shift gears from logarithms and sentence structure to blocking assignments and play diagrams.

Coach had been ill for the last couple of games in 1962 and was not expected to be at this final game. He had been diagnosed as having hepatitis and the doctors had told him to stay in bed at home in Idaho Falls. The assistants, Doug Leathem, Rod Smith, Cecil Flint and Dale Leathem were filling in for Coach in this final game of the season.

The first half was a struggle for both teams and ended with the score Pocatello 14, Idaho Falls 12. I.F. had a place kicker, Mike Bell, who was a freshman and kicked like a freshman. He had a hard time with extra points and had never kicked a field goal except in practice. He had missed both of the extra points after the two touchdowns in the first half.

The team went into the locker room to get its half-time adjustments but somehow it didn't have the same impact since the headman had not been there in practice or games for the past couple of weeks. Not that the other coaches were not good or talented, or that their hearts were not in it, the team just needed the personality and fire of Coach Ravsten, their mentor and leader.

The whistle blew and the second half began. As the third quarter came to an end, the Pocatello Indians had managed to score two more touchdowns and were driving for their third of the second half. Sure enough, just after the teams switched goals in the second half and began the fourth quarter, Poky pushed it across to make the score 35 to 12. All seemed surely lost as the defense came off the field and stood along the sidelines for the ensuing kick-off.

As they were standing there, a buzz went up and down the sidelines, "Coach is here!"

As unlikely as it was thought to be, someone said, "Let's win this one for Coach."

I was sitting in the stands that day with my parents watching Rob play. I saw Coach Ravsten bundled up in a fawn colored overcoat with a brown fedora hat, the kind that President Kennedy shunned and by so doing ultimately killed the hat industry, walking up the stairs toward the press box.

If he felt as bad as he looked to me, it was a wonder that he was not in bed.. His skin had a funny coloring and he was stooped and in obvious discomfort as he negotiated the steps to the relative comfort of the press box.

People greeted him as he walked up the stairs and many said, "Vernon, what in the world are you doing here? You should be home in bed. You look terrible." People in Idaho were known for their bluntness and sometimes lack of tact.

But Coach just looked at them and said, "I need to be here with my boys."

As he passed by me, I returned my attention to the Idaho Falls players on the field below. For the moment, their attention was on Coach as he walked into the press box. It's hard to explain, but there was a new spirit that suddenly entered the football stadium. You could actually feel it and the result of that feeling was soon to be displayed on the playing field.

You've heard the old story of "Winning one for the Gipper," and it seems old hat now. But at that time no one in the potato fields of Idaho had ever heard of the gipper or if they had, thought it must be some sort of snow tire. Be that as it may, the team came alive and wanted to win this one for their coach who had gotten up off his sick bed and traveled a distance to see his boys play their last game of the season-for many of the seniors, the last organized game of their lives. This fact was not lost on the Idaho Falls head coach and he exercised this recognition with his presence at the ISU football stadium that particular beautiful fall afternoon.

"Win this one for Coach," was the rallying cry that Pocatello could not overcome---at least for the moment. It wasn't so much a cry but a determination in the hearts and minds of the players that seemed to turn the tide of the game. I.F. took the ensuing kick-off straight down the field and in short order had six more points on the board. Rather than risk the boot of Mike Bell again, the extra point was run in successfully to make the score 35-19. Those were the days before running in the extra point resulted in two points being put on the board. It didn't matter if you ran the ball over the goal line or kicked it through the uprights, you got one point.

Pocatello couldn't do a thing on the next series and punted the ball to I.F. The Tigers again wasted no time putting another seven points on the scoreboard, but there was no time to waste either. There was less than five minutes on the clock and Poky was still ahead by nine points. The Indians got the ball on the kick-off and succeeded in getting two first downs and eating a large share of the remaining five minutes.

I was sitting in the stands watching my big brother and the rest of the team play the game of their lives. Rob played offensive center and defensive end. The defense was on the field at this point and he was sitting on the bench, I supposed resting for the upcoming offensive series. All of a sudden I watched number 51 run into the game and replace one of the defensive ends. Rob, number 51, was back in the game.

He was in there for a few plays when the defensive coach, Cecil Flint, began what I would call an old fashioned Indian war dance. I mean this guy was hopping mad. Seemed somewhat normal, what with the fact that Idaho Falls was playing the Indians and the Fort Hall Indian Reservation was just up the road, but...

Coach Flint sent in the player Rob had relieved to replace Rob and as Rob came to the sideline, the defensive coach was waiting for him. I felt sorry for Rob as I watched the coach screaming at him.

As it turned out, the problem was that as Rob had been sitting there on the sideline watching Pocatello moving the ball, he had gotten so excited and worked up that he had put himself into the game without being told to by Coach Flint. When the coach saw him in the game, he went crazy! Rob was out for the next few plays and then the coach put him back in, I guess because Coach Flint recognized Rob was so willing and excited to be in the game and was doing a good job while in there.

The defense was finally able to force Pocatello to punt. The Tigers got the ball on their own 20 with less than three minutes to play. Now with the sophisticated offenses of today's teams, one would not be surprised to see a quick score leaving lots of time on the clock for another attempt. But this was not today nor did sophistication enter into the game that day, just nitty-gritty, old fashioned football, enhanced in this instance with guts and desire to do something for someone who meant so much to the guys in the black and orange uniforms---Coach Vernon Ravsten.

The offense again came through with a score, but an expensive one in terms of time. Mike Bell again sat on the sideline and Russ Radford ran the ball into the end zone for the extra point to make the score 35-33, still in the Indians' favor.

The biggest favor for Poky, however, was the clock that showed only 42 seconds remaining in the game. Pocatello was doing some early celebrating on the sideline assuming they could easily run those 42 seconds off the clock after receiving the ball on the kick-off.

They weren't counting on the intensity and desire of the team on the other side of the field. That team had been taught by Coach Ravsten that there was never a time to give up and that if you had the desire, you could achieve wonders. They did not always live up to their potential but that was not the case this afternoon.

On the ensuing kick-off, Rob hit the receiver so hard that he fumbled and Montie Davis jumped on the ball for the Tigers. Still, there was not enough time in nearly everyone's mind. Rob had hit the ball carrier hard, which was good, but he hadn't hit him quickly enough, which was bad. There were now 54 yards between the spot of the ball and the demarcation line between the field of play and the Indians end zone that the Tigers must cross to achieve the victory they so anxiously desired. And precious few seconds left in the game.

Rob always did do things half good and half bad it seemed!

Anyway, the offense got out on the field and managed to get the ball to the Pocatello 23 yard line before the clock showed eight seconds to play and the sideline markers indicated fourth down with five yards to go. Things were not looking good to say the least. I.F. took their final time out and discussed the situation on the sidelines.

The assistant coaches initially had this super strategy and fancy play, but it was finally decided after much discussion, (as much as you can do during a time out), to let Mike Bell try a field goal for the win. This is the same Mike Bell who all had watched as his two extra point attempts in this game went wide and the last three extra points made as he sat on the bench. Furthermore, Mike had never kicked a field goal in a real live game.

For some reason the players argued for the kick and their argument resulted in Mike running out onto the field about as prepared to kick that field goal as a dentist is prepared to extract the tooth of grizzly bear in a phone booth.

The Poky players were really celebrating now and were even being a bit derisive of Mike as he prepared to boot the ball through the uprights. They're a little slow in Pocatello, but not enough time had elapsed for even them to forget the first half's performance given by Mike's foot.

They didn't count on Mike's heart this time, however. Rob snapped the ball and Steve Kuharski expertly placed it on the ground in the exact spot desired. Mike's foot contacted the ball a split second later and it started its long journey toward the uprights some 40 yards away.

Now 40 yards is a heck of a long way for a ball to fly and especially so in this instance. The time of flight seemed inordinate. There was nothing for anyone to do but watch. The ball was veering to the left, as was the case in Mike's previous kicks. But it looked like it might have just enough range. The question now was, would the azimuth hold out while the range wound down? In the end, the ball just did sneak by the left upright and over the bar.

The resulting celebration cost the Tigers a penalty for delay of game and they had to kick-off to Pocatello from five yards further back, but who cared? The final score was 36 to 35 and Idaho Falls had defeated an arch rival, but more importantly had won the game as a gift to their Coach who meant so much to them and had made the sacrifice to come down to see them play their last game. It was a successful end to an otherwise mediocre season, but a great way to finish.

Later Coach was diagnosed as having a form of jaundice. He missed some school but was relatively soon back at his teaching post and helping to coach the wrestling team.

At the end of the football season in the fall of 1962 Coach approached Rob with the idea of joining the high school wrestling team. Not thinking much of the impending challenge and thinking he was in good shape after having spent four months on the football team, he accepted the offer.

During the first session on the mat, however, he was brought quickly to a realization of the differing levels of being "in shape" in athletics. He went out on the mat that first afternoon and had to be dragged off after only two three-minute rounds. Wrestling is a sport that quickly separates the men from the boys and Rob decided he'd just as soon stay a boy for a while. He decided to give up the glories of cauliflower ears, mat burns and the strain and demands of such a "lessor" activity in his estimation.

Somehow Coach got wind of the notion Rob had of not being at wrestling practice until further notice (forever, if the truth be known). Rather than trooping past the athletic offices and gymnasium the next day, which was the normal route out of school after sixth period, Rob decided to go down to the basement and through the cafeteria, past the DECA school store and up the back stairs to the exit and freedom. No more abusing the young athlete's body for this guy!

But Coach had other ideas and was at the top of the back stairs just around the corner from the exit door. As Rob's hand hit the fire bar to exit, Coach stepped out and "convinced" (that's a nice way to put it) him to change his plans and finish out the season on the wrestling team.

It was always amazing that Coach seemed to know everything and be at the right place at the right time to affect for good the lives of those he so loved to serve and mentor. I suppose that is the reason he was knowledgeable and in the right place and the right time with the right thing to say or do-because he loved the young people he worked with. He took the time to know and be and did not rely on others or circumstances to dictate action but made things happen himself.

Although Rob had had no previous experience on the wrestling mat, he found himself at the end of the season in the Idaho Sixth District Wrestling championship match in the light heavyweight division. The District Meet was being held in the little town of Driggs, snuggled in the shadows of the Teton Mountains in eastern Idaho.

Driggs was a farming community that didn't have enough students to field much of a football team, so they concentrated on wrestling. Their guys were used to hefting 85-100 pound hay bales all day long in the haying season and were an awesome force on the wrestling mat. Their claim to fame was the success of their grapplers. Rob's opponent in the championship match was a guy named Bob Cherry of the Driggs team.

Since the meet was held over a two-day period, the team was staying in a small (so what's big in Driggs?) hotel in town. While waiting for the championship matches to be held on Saturday evening, the team retired to their rooms Friday night. As the evening wore on, Rob decided to get a drink out of the vending machine at the end of the hall and around the corner.

Just as he rounded the corner, Coach jumped out into the middle of the hallway in a particular and specific stance. Rob's immediate reaction was to grab Coach and "tie him up" in wrestling terms. Somewhat confused and embarrassed, he quickly released Coach and apologized. But Coach would have none of that.

He asked, "Who takes a stance like that on the wrestling mat?"

It didn't take but a moment for Rob to realize that his opponent for the championship match to be fought the next evening always assumed that stance in the initial "up" position.

Now he had a perfect take down move and possible way to pin his opponent.

How long Coach had waited for Rob to come down that hall or how long he would have remained waiting will never be known. But the incident indicated the immense dedication Vernon Ravsten had to his boys, his profession and to success itself. The next night in the light heavyweight match, Rob immediately got a take down and went on to the state championship matches in Boise that spring. The lesson from the previous evening had been successfully put into practice.

Travel back and forth to all athletic events we participated in was by bus. Sometimes we were even lucky enough to get a Greyhound-type coach and ride in the lap of luxury, in comparison to the short-haul school bus (Yellow Fellow) trips.

The trip to the Idaho State Championship Wrestling matches in Boise in the early spring of 1963 was made in a stretch "weenie-dog" bus. These vehicles were the precursor to the limos of today. While about the same length as the stretch limos of today with their darkened windows and television sets, some even with a hot tub in them, this Teton Stage Lines bus (or any other for that matter---Stage Lines were the operative words here!) had none of the above. It held twelve people on four bench seats accessed by four doors on each side of the vehicle. There were four wrestlers, including Rob, going to the state meet that year and the coaches (Ravsten and Leathem) drove them over in the bus.

It was a 300 plus mile trip from Idaho Falls to Boise and it started out with the two coaches in the front seat and the four boys spread out from the second to the back seat. The trip started out peacefully enough. It wasn't long, however, until the rambunctiousness and noise convinced the coaches that the further they were from the source of the noise and confusion, the better. Eventually the boys all moved to the back seat, which gave some relief to the adults, but only for a short time. The horseplay and noise eventually reached a crescendo level.

Coach Ravsten was driving and slowed to a stop at the side of the road about two miles outside a small "wide spot in the road" so familiar in the farming country of Idaho. You could just see the outline of the country store and gas pumps under the signature cottonwood trees down the road. These little places afforded the resident farmers and weary traveler the opportunity to gas up, buy a pop and a candy bar and continue on with the day or trip as the case may be. They also served the local housewives as a place to replenish the essentials for the daily menu until a weekly "trip to town" could be made.

Coach Ravsten lured the athletes out and away from the bus and then jumped behind the wheel and drove off, looking at his watch.

"We'll be leaving the store up ahead in 15 minutes. Here's a dime," he yelled back to the surprised wrestlers as he dropped four dimes from the window, "for those of you who don't make it on time and need to call your parents to come and pick you up!"

It didn't take a moment for the four of them to pick up the dimes and begin running down the road to the store. They all made it just in time to jump back inside the vehicle as Coach drove off for the last leg into Boise.

After the run to catch the bus in the allotted time, the confusion and noise was absent as the boys slept the rest of the way. He was a master of the school of motivation and control of young adults and always commanded the respect and love of those who were lucky enough to associate with him. He utilized all in his great bag of tricks and accepted methods of developing and nurturing relationships and leadership principles to win the admiration and devotion of his students and their parents and the citizens of the community.

Lessons Learned:

Selflessness was a value that was pre-eminent in the life of Coach Ravsten. He would sacrifice all to guarantee that his charges would learn to do their best and develop the character that would stand them in good stead when called upon to face the challenges of life.

He was that way in his classroom activity, fulfilling his church assignments, on the playing fields, in the home, wherever he was called to serve.

He had learned the great principle of knowing that when you are in the service of your fellowman, you are only in the service of your God. He taught that principle to others and they were greatly benefited by the results of his service and his enlightened guidance to help others to reach that same understanding.

The sum is greater than the whole because of the synergy developed by the combined efforts of individuals working together to accomplish a worthy goal. To help others was his greatest goal and achievement in life as an individual. That he taught others the same virtue left the world a better place to live in. Those who had the benefit of learning and applying those principles from Coach, helped to make the path they trod in later life that much better for countless others in turn.

Chapter 3

"What counts is not necessarily the size of the dog in the fight-it's the size of the fight in the dog."

Dwight D. Eisenhower

Back to our last game of my junior year in November of 1966.

As mentioned earlier, the chill of the day had set in in force and now that the sun had set, even the feeble warmth of the bright sun was absent. Anytime after September in Southeastern Idaho you would not be surprised to see snow on the ground, although it would be rare to have a snowstorm of any magnitude before late November. But I do remember one July 4th when it actually snowed-didn't last long but it was there.

What was not rare was the current temperature-it was cold! Especially standing on the sidelines along the west side of the stadium across the dark cinder track from the base of the stands. I looked across the field that was still a reasonable color of green despite the coolness of the weather. The football field was not used for anything other than games. We had practice fields for the daily sessions of preparation and learning the rudiments of the game. We would use the playing field at times on a Thursday before home games when we would run through light, no pads exercises to solidify the game plan for the up-coming game, but nothing extensive. The field had a nice crown on it and it was in very good condition; if only it weren't so blasted chilly! That feeling would disappear as soon as the first kick-off was signaled by the official's whistle. Adrenaline would then fire the internal boilers, if nothing else would, to keep you warm.

As I looked across the field, I saw my brother Rob on the far sideline. He had figured out some way to help run the yard markers for the officials. He was easily recognizable since he was probably the only guy in Idaho Falls, if not the entire state, that wore a bright yellow ski parka. Even though he had on the zebra striped officials vest, you could see the yellow nylon, bright as the noonday sun, blazing away underneath it. He was always good at getting what he wanted. Running the chains for the referees was a great place to see the game and enabled one to keep moving and help the blood circulate.

All I wanted was to get out on the field and start playing so I could get warm and get rid of this sense of uneasiness. I was really nervous now and between that and the cold, I couldn't stand still.

Coach called us all around him and said, "Okay guys, this is it. For you seniors there is no tomorrow. Do your best and give your all. Kicking team, get out there and keep them inside the 20 yard line."

I was on the kicking team so I ran out onto the field and took my position. Waiting for the National Anthem, I could hear the wind blowing by the holes in my helmet. It was a very biting wind and I could imagine how miserable the people sitting in the stands must be. The way the playing field was oriented from north to south, there was no blocking the eternal winds that always blew in Idaho from north to south or south to north. It never blew from the east or west where the stands were and which would have done some good in deflecting the ill winds. We were through practicing for the season, but the wind was toning up for the up-coming winter season, not that anyone thought it needed any practice!

Even with the cold and discomfort I was feeling, I knew it would disappear with the first whistle of the game signaling the kick-off. Along with that realization came the same feeling I always felt as I stood on the field for the rendition of the Star Spangled Banner. A chill always went up and down my spine as I saw the flag go up that pole at the north end of the field as our

National Anthem was played. Nowhere else in the world could this same happening occur. Yet it happened in hundreds of communities every Friday night all over America. The freedoms we enjoy were great and appreciated by all gathered in that arena to some degree of consciousness or another. As far as I was concerned, it thrilled me to be a citizen and be able to enjoy the competition and gathering.

In contrast to the crowds I see today when the National Anthem is played at an athletic event or at some other civic gathering, everyone in the stands and on the field that day stood bareheaded with hand over heart to show respect and thankfulness for the blessing of living in the great nation we do. Today you are in the minority to show such deference and respect for the symbol of freedom and accompanying lyrics that celebrate the freedoms we enjoy, purchased with such a heavy price over the years.

People today do not recognize the greatness of the blessing it is to live in the USA-at least in comparison to the hardy and patriotic citizens of our home town by the falls of the Snake River in Southeastern Idaho. We were a thankful and respectful people who loved America and the opportunities it afforded.

As the school band finished the National Anthem, a large roar went up from the teams and the crowd. Suddenly I wasn't cold at all. The whistle was blown and we kicked off. I was running down the right sideline to cover my area of responsibility as fast as I could go when I was hit from the side and went down. I quickly got up and saw the ball carrier going to the other side of the field. I began running after him diagonally back across the field and saw four of our guys take him down on the Idaho Falls 23-yard line. We huddled up quickly and got ready for our first defensive play of the game.

On the first couple of plays, Idaho Falls was able to move the ball easily up the field and it initially unnerved us. But then the defense settled down and forced the Tigers to punt the ball from their own 32-yard line. We got the ball in reasonable field position at our 30-yard line but our offense wasn't able to move the ball either, so we punted from our 38-yard line after gaining only eight yards.

It seemed like the first quarter of the game was a punting contest with neither team able to move the ball with any consistency. The game was played around the 30-yard line at one end of the field or the other. It was three plays and a punt for both teams since the offenses couldn't seem to get untracked and consistently move the ball. Both offensive teams were playing as cold as the people in the stands looked and the weather actually was. At least on the sideline we had some of those turbine gas heaters to keep us "warm."

Of course you couldn't be caught standing in front of one for too long for a couple of reasons. There was a bunch of guys desiring the warmth that was coming from them and it was not considered "cool" to hog the warm air that was coming from the outlet vent of the tubular heaters. Then there was the fact that they were mostly reserved for the quarterback, running backs and receivers-oh, and yes, the center, one of the few times there was a benefit to being a center! It was wisdom to keep the hands of those who were to handle the ball warm and supple enough to hang on to the pigskin and not fumble it away to the opposition. So we other guys had to sneak a bit of warmth whenever we could. Actually, with the little exposure we got to the heat, it was better to stay away from the heaters altogether since the contrast was so great it would only make you feel worse. I generally stayed clear.

Just before the first quarter ended, the Tigers pushed the ball down to our ten-yard line. The defensive team was bending and we had to reach down deep like Coach had taught us and stop the advance right here. Luckily, we were able to stop them and take over the ball on their failure to convert on fourth down.

Idaho football is not known for all the nuances of the game

we see today such as the field goal. Few teams were lucky enough to have a kicker that could kick an extra point, let alone for the extra yardage that was required to push a ball from somewhere out on the playing field to the goal line and then the final ten yards from there to where the goal posts were located. Not to mention that the ball had to go between the uprights which were only twenty-three feet four inches apart and over the bar which was ten feet above the ground. The Tigers were no exception-they didn't have a field goal kicker and failed to get the fourth down conversion so the Grizzlies took over the ball on downs deep in our own territory.

The offense gave it all they had, but after three plays we had to punt. Our quarterback also did the punting and got off a pretty good punt putting the ball down to the I.F. 45-yard line.

Their defensive line did a good job of blocking at the line of scrimmage, which gave their punt receiver the opportunity to take the ball on the run. He made some pretty good moves and we made some real sad attempts at open field tackling resulting in them getting great field position at our 35. The game was still being played around the 30-yard lines but this was not the right 30-yard line as far as we were concerned! And concerned we were.

On the first play of I.F.'s next offensive series, their quarterback, Cook, came around our left end for ten yards. On the next play they came at us up the middle for three yards. We knew we could stop them on runs inside the defensive ends because we'd been doing it all day long. The Tigers had also figured this out, so Cook rolled out to his right and lofted a pass into the arms of their split end as he sprinted down the right sideline and then cut back to his left toward the middle of the field.

Our pass coverage had normally been pretty good, especially close to the end zone with the limited amount of field we had to cover. But we "dropped the ball" on this play and got too many defenders too far to our left, what with the flooding of that side of the field the Tigers accomplished on this particular play. The receiver got behind our last defender and slipped into the end zone untouched for six points. I was really upset because I knew we should have stopped them. We were suddenly behind 6-0.

In the huddle there were some sharp words exchanged about missed assignments and the price of rice in China, among other things less mentionable. We were on edge and we had to get rid of these feelings to be able to function, as we knew we could and had to in order to win this all-important game.

They came up to the ball, which was sitting with its nose on the two and a half-yard hash mark right in the middle of the field in front of the goal line for the extra point try. They ran their big fullback at us but we stopped him right at the goal line with about 18 bodies wearing black and orange and white and blue uniforms in one big pile that straddled the goal line. The officials determined, and rightly so, that he didn't get across the line with the ball. As we walked off the field, I felt a little better since we were able to stop the extra point. But I was still frustrated that we had allowed them to score in the first place.

The receiving team was coming onto the field as we ran to the sideline and they muttered some half-hearted congratulations in passing while we shouted encouragement for the run-back effort. It was obvious they felt about as happy about the touchdown as I did. I wondered if the temperature had anything to do with the attitude of the guys, as some of them looked awfully cold out there. The cold had now left me and I didn't even think of it anymore. But it seemed like some of the guys hadn't yet warmed to the task at hand, neither physically nor, more importantly, mentally.

I heard the whistle blow and could see the ball flying through the air toward our receiver, Craig Lords. He took the ball at the five-yard line, ran left and faked a hand off to Leonard Rios. Lords continued to the left with the ball hidden on his left thigh and turned the corner. The blocking fence was fairly well set up and the majority of the orange and black uniforms were on the ground. Finally someone pulled Lords down from behind, but not before he got out to the 40-yard line. Perhaps the "fire" had finally been lit.. We were all excited, jumping up and down and screaming our lungs out. The offense tried the middle a couple of times but there was nothing there but black and orange.

On third and six, Kenny Barnes, our quarterback, rolled to his right and hit Hurley for 18 yards down the left side. It was a great cross-field pass that caught them looking. On the very next play he threw a strike to Dahley for another 13 yards and another first down. Coach called another two running plays, but we lost a yard on each play and it was third and 12.

Barnes took the ball and rolled to the right. He was directing traffic with his left hand and could see both Dahley and Hurley open down the middle. The defenders were following the lead receivers down each sideline supposing that they would be the likely targets since the clock was becoming a factor in this first half and we had only one time-out left. I suppose they thought the ball would go to one of them where, if caught, the receiver could easily step out of bounds and stop the clock. Barnes saw the coverage and where his open men were. He zipped the ball right into Dahley's arms on the run. Jim gave a great effort to get the ball down field a few more yards, finally ending up at the eight-yard line.

We all went crazy on the sideline, but there were only 21 seconds left in the half. Barnes quickly called time out and came over to the sideline to talk to Coach. I could hear Coach telling him to flood the middle and delay to each corner of the end zone, hitting the one who ended up free. Barnes ran back out on the field and called the play in the huddle. As the offense moved up to the line, you could sense their determination.

On the snap Barnes took the ball and dropped straight back, looking for someone to break into the open. The middle linebacker was blitzing, but was picked up by our fullback and knocked to the ground just before he got to Barnes. Kenny couldn't see anyone open and was getting ready to throw the ball away when Hurley made a quick move back toward the middle of the end zone, temporarily getting free from the excellent coverage the Tigers were executing in the end zone.

The middle linebacker was up and coming at Barnes again with his hands held high. He leaped at Barnes just as he lobbed the ball over his outstretched hands. Hurley streaked to where he saw the ball would fall and dove to make an incredible catch at the back of the end zone with a defender reaching over his back trying to knock the ball away. Pass interference probably should have been called, but it made little difference since he made the catch and there were now only eight seconds left on the clock.

We quickly and easily kicked the extra point (we actually had a kicker that could normally accomplish the task). If the truth were known, most of the team members on both sides were as surprised as the people in the stands were shocked as they looked at the scoreboard, Skyline 7, Idaho Falls 6.

And to be honest, I was somewhat surprised myself.

After the kick-off and one quick play, we all ran to the locker room. The fans on our side of the stadium were really going crazy, because they hadn't really had that much to cheer about the whole year. Now here we were, leading after the first half in the most important game of the season. Of course, there was still another half to go and it was who won that half that won it all, and we all knew that.

In the locker room Coach went over our assignments and we made a few small adjustments. Except for the lapse in our pass coverage in the second quarter, defensively everything was working about the way we had hoped it would. The offense was another story and Coach spent most of the time during the half-time break going over offensive plays on the chalkboard, emphasizing responsibilities and the perceived weaknesses of the

Tigers' defense. The coaches had been doing their normal great job and had observed some possible areas we might take advantage of in the second half. A couple of guys were getting re-taped or having bumps, bruises or sprains looked at in the training room. It had been a tough game physically for both teams. There had not been a lot of flair or flash, but the players on both sides knew there was a real contest in progress.

The Skyline Grizzlies had the option to kick or receive to start the second half and, of course, chose to receive. The Tiger kicker booted a line drive that didn't get too high or go too far, but went like a bullet and landed between the two Skyline receivers. They didn't get a chance to touch the ball as it hit the frozen ground and bounded into the end zone and over the end line.

The first series of downs after the second half kick-off at began at the 20-yard line Barnes hit Dahley for 17 and then eight yards in quick succession. The offense had listened during the interlude between halves and was proving the coaches' strategy correct, moving the ball almost at will.

Well, for two downs anyway. On the next play, the blitzing middle linebacker sacked Barnes.

In the huddle Barnes was less than pleased and said, "Let's try that play again, but make sure that middle linebacker doesn't get through this time."

On the snap of the ball, the middle linebacker again got by the center as he was tied up with the nose guard in a vicious battle for rights to the center ground of the line of scrimmage. It looked like another sack for I.F., but just in time our fullback knocked the intruding linebacker on his backside with a great blind side block. Barnes ducked another oncoming lineman and looked all over the field as the receivers ran their routes and attempted to get free of the defensive pursuit. He rolled to the right and saw Revello wide open down the middle running slowly at the 15-yard line.

The defensive backs had followed the other receivers deep

toward the end zone and the linebackers were intent on dropping Kenny for a loss. Revello was all alone. Kenny quickly rifled the ball downfield and into the arms of Revello who side-stepped a defensive back who had picked up on the lapse in coverage and was coming back from the deep coverage, albeit a bit too late. Revello slipped into the end zone untouched.

We all went nuts on the sideline, as did the Skyline fans in the stands. This wasn't supposed to be happening! We missed the extra point (the Idaho non-kicking syndrome strikes again), but we were on top 13-6! The kick-off team ran onto the field intent on keeping the return behind the 20-yard line. The kick was a good one and the I.F. return specialist, who had done such a good job all year long for the Tigers, returned the ball just past the 20, well below his average.

This was the first series for the Skyline defense after the half and it took a couple of first downs by Idaho Falls for the Grizzly defense to wake up to the fact that the Tigers were thinking they could still win this thing. Finally we settled down and forced the Tigers into a fourth and eight situation at our 42-yard line, from which they punted.

Revello took the ball on our three-yard line in the left corner. He could see a couple of tacklers bearing down on him like wild buffalo, but decided he could slip to the other side of the field and get away from them. As he retreated into the end zone on his way to daylight on the right side of the field, the sunset on his little scene of glory and he was caught from behind for a safety. (He said later that he forgot there were nine other players wearing orange and black on the field at the time!) The score quickly changed to 13-8, still in favor of the Skyline Grizzlies, just as the third quarter ended.

We began the fourth quarter by kicking to them after the safety. Their return artist wiggled his way out to the 32-yard line on the runback. The Tiger offense started a ground attack that began to frighten us with its intensity and success. We couldn't seem to be able to stop them for anything less than four to five yards at a crack. They were averaging a first down every two to three times they hiked the ball. We were not slowing them down and they didn't even come close to being forced to punt. The safety they had scored had changed the momentum of the game and we were having a very difficult time stopping them-actually, we weren't!

We suddenly found our backs to the wall with the Tigers at our nine yard line, first and goal. They tried a reverse on the first play but we got a lucky break. Instead of second and goal at the three, it was first and goal from the 25 because of a clip by an Idaho Falls lineman.

In the defensive huddle there was a definite sense of relief because we were relatively sure we could stop them from scoring a touchdown and maybe even a field goal because of their weak kicking game.

The first two plays from the 25 got them only to our 18. We were feeling quite confident now. On third down their All-State tailback took a pitch on the run and headed to the right. Our pursuit was excellent and it looked like we were going to sack him for a loss at the 19 or 20. He was running out of real estate and there were an ever-increasing number of white and blue jerseys converging on the scene.

Suddenly, he pulled up and lofted a "pass" over all of our heads to the split end slanting across the field from the other side. He was waiting all alone in the end zone for the ball, which looked much like a wounded duck as it made its way to his hands. Wounded duck or not, we were, just that fast, behind 15-13 after the extra point was scored around left end.

I looked at the clock and saw eight minutes and 41 seconds left in the game as we made our way to the sideline and the receiving team got set to take the ensuing kick-off. Not a lot of time, but enough, I hoped! We took the kick-off on the seven-yard line and returned it to the 29.

Barnes, with a little help from his friend on the sidelines, Coach Ravsten, was very methodical as he engineered the offense down the field. Running plays were sandwiched between some great pass receptions to keep the defense honest and off balance. There were no standout or razzle-dazzle plays, just some excellent execution of the kind of football we had been practicing all year long.

At the I.F. 34, however, we got stalled with a fourth and eight situation. This would likely be the end if we didn't get a first down. There was no time left to punt and hope for an early turnover. The drive had been successful in yardage gained, but also had eaten up a lot of the remaining time on the clock. This was it.

Barnes called time out and came over to the sideline to talk to Coach. After a few minutes he went back onto the field and called the play. The offense lined up and I could hear the Tiger defensive players yelling to each other, "Watch this and Watch that." They knew as well as we did that this play would certainly win the game for them if they could stop us from gaining the eight yards required for a first down.

Our center snapped the ball after a long count that didn't have its desired effect of drawing the defense offsides. The Tigers were playing disciplined football under the tutelage of Dale Leathem and his team of assistants, many of whom, like the opposing players, had been on the same team with us just a matter of months before-all directed by Coach Ravsten.

Barnes rolled to his right. He was looking downfield and saw that Dahley, the primary receiver on this particular play, had a half a step on the defender, but he wasn't really open. Kenny couldn't see anybody else with better chances for a reception, so he threw the ball straight down field just over the head of Dahley, hoping he would be able to run under the ball using his speed.

Dahley saw the ball coming his way and gave it everything he had to get where it appeared the ball would come down. From the arc of the ball and Dahley's position on the field, it didn't look like there would be any way a catch would result. All I had learned in Mr. Herd's trig class told me the angles were all wrong and the distances were too great.

And that telling came easily since we were so close to the room where Mr. Herd, another stellar teacher in the District 91 High School system, opened young minds to the mysteries of trigonometry. Under the stands that the fans were jammed so closely into on the West Side of the field, were classrooms, one of which was Mr. Herd's permanent teaching post.

Efficiency demanded a high utilization of space and budgetary dollars and when the size of the original Idaho Falls High student body demanded more space, the Board of Trustees acted. Rather than pull in some trailers, like is the solution relied on by so many school districts today to provide for needed classroom space, they decided to build a new stadium seating facility on top of the required classrooms. It worked great. The new teaching stations were provided for and the fans of football and track events had a great vantage point from which to witness the relevant contest.

But Dahley obviously hadn't paid attention in Trig class. Just at the last moment he leapt forward, stretching his hands and arms as far as they would go. The ball landed on his outstretched fingers and he immediately tucked the ball away as he fell to the ground, the defender falling on top of him.

Now there were two questions. One, will they call it a catch? And two, if so, where will they spot the ball? Both were crucial. A huge roar went up from the crowd as the official signaled reception and first down with what looked like a yard to spare.

Barnes, (again with a lot of help from his friend), now changed the attack and kept the ball strictly on the ground, alternately handing off to Revello and Tom Wood as we rolled down the field to their two yard line.

The offense waited in the huddle for the play to come in from

Coach. It was to be a fullback dive to Wood who was a lot like an oil tanker, once he was moving, it was hard to stop him cold. He usually played offensive guard and defensive tackle, but for short yardage Coach used him to carry the ball up the middle a good deal of the time.

Tom took the ball on a quick count and smashed into the end zone for the score. The scoreboard now read Skyline 19, Idaho Falls 15. There were two minutes and 46 seconds left in the game now, and some were thinking we had this one in the old gunnysack. (Some may think in terms of "being in the bag," but in Idaho the term was "gunnysack". All the best potatoes in the world were conveyed at least a portion of their way to market in a gunnysack. It was a fixture in the minds and lives of residents of Southeastern Idaho. Everyone had some kind of a relationship with a gunnysack.) Now if we could just stop them, perhaps we could tie a rope around the top of the gunnysack in which the Tigers now found themselves. No one wanted to let the Tigers out of the sack but they had another idea altogether.

We kicked off to the Tigers, just wanting to prevent a run back. They managed to get the ball out to the 36-yard line on the kick-off and use only seconds in doing so. We had to hold them. We were playing a prevent defense, assuming the only way they would attempt to score in the time remaining was through the air. A lot of us were playing deep to make sure nothing got through. They were able to move the ball down field with short passes underneath our deep coverage and, with six seconds left in the game, were on our 25-yard line.

There was time remaining for just one more play. We were far from that confident feeling we had had about ten minutes earlier when we had them on our 18-yard line, thinking they wouldn't score on us then. We knew this play was for all the marbles and it would be into the end zone. This one play would either make or break our season and the season for the Idaho Falls Tigers, too.

In the huddle, I called a middle linebacker blitz with everyone else dropping deep to cover all of the possible receivers. On the snap, I slanted off to my left and ran through the line untouched between the guard and center and toward their quarterback. He saw me coming and rolled to his right. I thought that I was going to get him and end the season in a blaze of glory for both the team and myself. I was going to make the final tackle of the game and prevent the Tigers from scoring the winning touchdown in the final seconds of the most important game of the season and Skyline's brief history to date. But just as I got ready to grab him, I was creamed from my blind side by one of their backs that had stayed in to block. I never saw him coming.

As I was going down on my left side, I looked up to the scoreboard to see the oversize light bulbs on the clock turn to two big zeros indicating that the game was over as far as the time was concerned. But as everyone knows, the game cannot end in the middle of a play-it has to come to a "natural" end.

I looked up to see their quarterback step back a few steps and look around for someone to get open. By the time I had gotten to my knees, he let go with a bomb to the deep left corner of the end zone. I scrambled to my feet just as a big roar went up from the crowd.

Now, all fans in Idaho Falls sound alike and I couldn't distinguish a Skyline roar from an Idaho Falls roar, so I wasn't too sure whether to be elated or downcast. Just then I saw Bingham, one of our defensive backs, running out of the end zone with the ball tucked under his arm. He had intercepted the ball and the look on his face was one of great determination and resolve. He was going to score again for us! He was one of our senior defensive backs and this was his last game and last play. He gave it everything he had and got out to about the 30-yard line before being run out of bounds by the Idaho Falls quarterback, who was just as determined that we not add insult to injury.

The game was over and we had done what no one in the town thought we could do. And rightfully so, I suppose, based on our record up until that time. In any case, we were all elated as we ran into the locker room, laughing and hugging each other. We gave the coaches a big yell and then threw Coach Ravsten into the shower.

As I took off my uniform, I thought of next year and the great team we should have. Most of the team members were juniors that year and I was positive and naive enough to think that this game was the start of something big.

What a glorious day it had been and I knew next year would start off where this one had ended.

Lessons Learned:

There was never a doubt about what was required to achieve rewards in Coach's world. Hard work was the maxim to be observed. It was many times difficult to grasp an academic tenant, master a wrestling technique, understand the reasons for executing a play on the football field or change a habit that was not in accordance with accepted principles.

It didn't matter the lengths one had to go to in achieving the established goal. If consistent, long-term effort was required, so be it. He was there with us until the job was done

He recognized and taught that sacrifice was giving up something good for something better. We were all better for having expended the effort required to improve our performance, grow in ability and magnify our talents by the virtue of hard work.

Chapter 4

"The quality of a person's life is in direct proportion to their commitment to excellence, regardless of their chosen field of endeavor."
Vince Lombardi

The morning after the game dawned clear and cool but without the "breeze" we were so used to. Actually, with all this talk about the climate and conditions we faced, it was really nothing that anyone really concerned themselves with since that was the way it was and no amount of talking or complaining could change things one iota. We did complain a bit at times but generally one just accepted the weather for what it was.

Being born and raised in Idaho Falls and never venturing further than about 300 miles from there until over nineteen years old, I remember going to a place away from Southeastern Idaho for an extended period. After being there for some time, I got to thinking that there was something about this particular place that I really liked yet could not put my finger on the exact reason for feeling that way. Then it came to me. The wind didn't blow here like back home! It was an accepted fact that wind was a part of your life in Idaho Falls and I just assumed that the wind blew everywhere. It was a great experience to wake up every morning and not have the prospect of wind in your face the balance of the day as in Idaho. Since that time, picking a place to live has had as an important ingredient, the absence of wind. I hate it.. Snow, rain, fog-whatever, just don't let the wind blow.

The fact that I rode my bike north from home to work each day just as the wind was coming up about 10 a.m. and home again around 7 p.m. was probably the thing that set my teeth on edge against the wind. I had a job in the summers working for the Bureau of Land Management (BLM) on a fire crew and we worked a shift from 10 to 7 since that is when most of the fires would be discovered-none early in the morning. The wind would come up and blow in my face as I pedaled north in the mornings and then would switch in mid-afternoon to blow from the south and continue until about 8 p.m., after I had cranked into our driveway on the south side of town that evening. Wind in my face both ways! I know this phenomenon has been alluded to earlier, but it is such an evil wind, it bears repeating.

Working at the BLM during those summers was a treat in that I got another opportunity to see Coach in action in another arena. He and a couple of the other coaches had summer jobs working as Crew Bosses for 25 man Sho-Ban Indian crews from the Fort Hall Indian Reservation just south of Idaho Falls. While the crew I was on manned a tanker truck which carried several thousand gallons of water which the 2- to 4- man crews would spray on range fires out on the desert west of Idaho Falls, the crews that the coaches headed up used their expertise in wielding pulaskies (a combination of a hoe and an ax) and shovels on the fire lines. These crews only got paid while they were fighting a fire but the coaches were "permanent party" and were paid throughout the summer fire season while they were away from their more scholarly duties as academic teachers and athletic mentors.

"Sho-Ban" came from the combination of the names of the Shoshone and Bannock Indian tribes, which were the inhabitants of the Fort Hall Indian Reservation. The 25-man crews were all Native Americans who were very skilled and hard working individuals and who loved the coaches, especially our beloved head football coach, Vernon Ravsten.

These crews would respond to the fires that would start in the sagebrush and dry grasses, as lightning would strike the desert floor during the frequent electrical storms that occur in the area. Coach would lead these men out to the fires and develop strategies that would get the fires out in an efficient manner, all the while considering the safety of the individuals he was responsible for.

A range fire is an unpredictable and very dangerous situation as are all fires that are out of control, and it took one with wisdom as well as courage to get the job done. It didn't take long for the crewmembers to recognize that they were being led by someone who cared for them individually as well who had the ability to determine strategy to get the fires out.

In the middle of one of the summer fire seasons, there was a lull in the thunder and lightning storms that normally occurred, yet there continued to be a regular number of fires spotted from the lookout on the Big Southern Butte, 40 miles west of Idaho Falls, on an almost scheduled basis. The officials at the BLM could not figure this odd situation out and decided to put an airplane in the air and patrol the desert and see if they could discover how these fires were starting in the absence of the natural ignition that occurred with the lightning strikes.

>From these spotter flights they discovered the regularity and source of the fires. It seemed that a few of the fire crewmembers had become addicted to "firewater" and the actual fires were funding their purchase of the bottled liquid conflagration. Once the money from fighting the fires ran out and left no cash to purchase more "heat," the renegades would go out on the desert and start a fire knowing they would shortly be called on to put it out. They would then be paid and have another bankroll to provide for their liquid entertainment.

When this was discovered it descended upon Coach Ravsten to drive down to the reservation and inform the recalcitrants that their wayward ways had been discovered and they were no longer welcome as members of the otherwise respected fire crews. I was requested to go down and help Coach replace some equipment that had been damaged in a recent fire on this same trip he had to go and terminate the guilty parties.

It was an experience to remember to see how he spoke with the individuals involved and made them understand the error of their ways while treating them with dignity and respect. Even though those so involved were very much affected in a negative manner in regard to their ability to continue to earn the good money that they would otherwise be making in this summer fire season, they were not individually treated in a manner that would destroy their self-respect or sense of worth. They knew they had done wrong in a very serious manner, yet went away from the encounter with Coach feeling they had been fairly treated and rightfully terminated. He was a master in human relations..

On the way back to the BLM yard north of Idaho Falls, we stopped at the trading post on the reservation to get a drink and an ice cream sandwich-it was hot, maybe 82 degrees in the shade! I was driving and Coach said that he would jump out and get the treats while I waited in the truck. And waited, and waited. There were no other vehicles around the store so I couldn't figure out what was taking Coach so long to get the goodies and come back out so we could get home before the gate to the yard was locked at 7 p.m.

I was just climbing down from the cab of the truck when I saw him coming out with just one can of pop and one ice cream sandwich. I figured what with the heat of the day there must have been a run on "coolers" and was satisfied that the elder should have the benefit of whatever was left. All I really wanted to do was get back to the yard and climb on my bike for that trek against the wind back home-right! There must have been something else going on that evening that escapes me at the moment, but I was content to get back on the road, with or without my own treats.

As I settled back into the driver's seat and started the engine, Coach climbed into the passenger seat and reached over and turned off the engine. He said, "Couch, you have to go in there and get your own pop and ice cream," as he handed me a dollar bill. "Bring me back the change."

Things were reasonable then in terms of price (you could get a pop and an ice cream and come away with change from a buck!). But I figured Coach was being more than unreasonable making me go in and get my own treats. But I had learned that you do what you are told by your elders at the knee of my parents (too many times over their knee!) and besides, who was going to disobey the man who was the lynch pin to your future on the football field, unreasonable or not?

I got down from the truck and made my way across the dusty parking lot, across the wooden porch that surrounded the post on three sides and into the store. I wasn't looking right or left, but made a beeline to the back of the establishment where the coolers were located. This equipment is never at the front of the store, but always at the back. Must be some marketing ploy that escapes my understanding.

I selected my drink of choice, a bottle of RC Cola. I always chose Royal Crown Cola for two reasons, both absolute and very defensible even in the face of the market leaders, Coke and Pepsi. RC came in 16 ounce bottles while the competitor's biggest container at the time was 12 ounces and RC tastes the best by far. It always wins the "blind" taste tests even today.

A vanilla ice cream sandwich was chosen from the chest freezer at the other side of the store at the back. I quickly made my way up the aisle to the cash register area. As I rounded the head of the aisle where the candy was positioned and proceeded to the register, I saw the reason for Coach's lengthy stay inside the trading post.

There, sitting on a high stool was the most drop dead gorgeous girl I have ever seen before or since (and I'll deny these words were ever penned should my wife ever come across them!). She was an Indian Maiden of such beauty; one can scarcely describe it so I shan't. It took me probably five minutes of searching to find the dollar bill that Coach had given me and which I had put in my shirt pocket on the way across the parking lot. There was not a chance that I was going to look in that pocket until I absolutely had to.

I could finally stall no more and handed her the bill. I dropped the change (I told you things were reasonable in those days) and took my time picking it up. The bottle opener seemed to be bent or something since I had a difficult time getting the top of the Royal Crown bottle and she finally had to operate it for me. Since my ice cream was rapidly turning to liquid mush in my overheated hands, I figured I'd best make my way back to the truck and see if I could still see anything beyond the vision of what I had just beheld.

I climbed back into the driver's seat and looked back over my shoulder in hopes that maybe I had developed some x-ray eyes to perhaps penetrate the rough hewn walls of the establishment-no luck. As I turned back around and started the truck, I caught Coach grinning from ear to ear out of the corner of my eye.

Nothing was ever said by either one of us. I was too overcome by the event and he recognized his position as mentor, leader, coach, religious teacher and adult. I recognized my position as having beheld a vision of loveliness unchallenged by any model living or conjured up by the mind of man or woman.

I also recognized that Coach had seen the same vision, yet had maintained a proper sense of dignity and respect for the girl, for the situation, for him and for me. It taught me a great deal. Coach was worthy of emulation in so many ways in so many situations. It was a blessing to be tutored by his words and by his actions.

Besides, I thought as I looked back one more time at the trading post door in hopes she had to sweep off the porch or something-Coach had made me go back in myself and get my own "treats."

Where were we? Ahh, yes....the day after our victory over Idaho Falls in that all-important first meeting between the two teams.

We all went back to the school that beautiful Saturday

morning to turn in our uniforms and tie up loose ends. Besides, we were all so high from the experience of less than 12 hours before, we had to get back together to savor the moment. Every team member had some play to re-live and usually some point or another to exaggerate on, (why else participate in this form of "Monday morning quarterbacking"?) and bumps, bruises or sprains to display and treat as medals of valor and signs of victorious gladiators returning from battle.

One of those "loose ends" was to vote for team captains for the coming year. I wanted to be a captain so badly I would have agreed to play in the "pits" on the offensive line, even center if that would somehow insure I could achieve that honor. Now that I think of it---maybe I didn't want it that bad. (I was not as dumb as my brother Rob who played center his entire high school career along with defensive end. Later in college he switched to offensive guard and defensive end-I guess that high school diploma was what it took to make him realize that center was not the place to be, pivotal or not! I watched him get beat up in the center of the line many times as teams would try to rattle the snapper by paying particular "attention" to him in the hope of getting him punchy and messing up the snap, perhaps causing a fumble.) But I did want to be selected as a captain pretty darn bad!

There was really not much chance of it happening, though, based on the popularity/glory factor that always had an influence in high school football. The guys playing the more visible positions on the team were usually the ones to be chosen to lead the team---positions like quarterback or running back. Besides, there were a lot of great guys on the team. But one could dream and hope.

I remembered Rob telling me some years after we had both graduated from high school and had put that part of our lives behind us, (if there really is such a thing as guys putting the great memories and experiences we had "behind us") about his experience in this same situation. As I mentioned, he played center and defensive end for the Idaho Falls Tigers. Neither position was one that received a lot of attention from the fans-only opposing defensive linebackers, middle guards or offensive blockers. Playing those positions rarely found you anywhere but at the bottom of the pile after successfully opening a hole for the running back or knocking down the leading blockers so the defensive back could get a clean shot at the opposing running back. But they were obviously critical positions to the team, just not to the normal fan. How that affected the selection for captain of the team, I'll never know, but in high school athletics it certainly did.

Anyway, in Rob's senior year he was selected to start as first string center on offense and first string defensive end and as such was on the list of candidates for team captain. The vote was taken in his last season just before the first game of the year. Three captains were to be selected by popular vote. At the end of the count the three stellar running backs for the Tigers that year, Steve Kuharski, Russ Radford and Charlie Marquez were selected with my brother a close fourth.

He told me in that moment years after that time in his senior year-one of those rare moments of reminiscing in such a melancholy manner between two brutes of the gridiron who would otherwise never admit to such emotion-of being crushed when told of the result. He had missed the honor by just one vote. He asked the three duly elected captains to intervene on his behalf with the coaching staff to allow another captain that year, four instead of the traditional three.

Now, that's got to take a bundle of humility, to go to your friends and ask for such a great favor, but the honor was without peer in those days of adolescence and limited vision. To be the captain of the football team was a real honor and much sought after. Being the friends that they were, they did try, but tradition held and the original three acted as captains in the fall of 1962.

The yearning on my part was just the same. I guess some things never change and would venture to guess that they're the same even today as teams gather to choose their peer leaders for the gridiron bashes of the ensuing year.

Everyone put their choice down on a slip of paper and gave it to one of the coaches. Your "ticket" to vote was the handing back the personal playbook we had utilized during the past season. No play book, no vote. Coach knew that everyone wanted in on this all important process, so being the great tactician he was, legislated that you would not vote for your captain if you had not turned in your player's manual first.

I suppose that with the splitting of the school into two different groups, I..F. and Skyline, it became more important to shield your plans from the opposition. No one was going to give a book to a Pocatello puke or a Bonneville farmer, but you never knew what alliances were still out there between bosom buddies that were only on differing teams at the whim of Idaho School District 91 administrators, not of their own free will and choice. Coach covered all the bases even if this was football, not baseball, and got all his playbooks back and safe from the eyes of the opposition.

You must remember this was before the advent of the copy machine. You could rest assured that if you got your original material back, your ideas and plans (plays in this case) were safe. One did not go down to the local Kinko's and make a copy for your buddy. In those days, mass copies were done on a mimeograph machine that resulted in those purple lettered sheets that you sniffed for the first few moments after being handed one, enjoying the unique smell that only a mimeograph copy had. Eat your heart out Xerox!

I figured I was worth at least one ballot so I handed my playbook to Coach Jacoby along with my slip of paper voting for myself and then waited to see what happened.

As I was waiting to turn in my uniform (the managers had

been waiting on us all year long and now it was their turn to be waited upon and they were making up for it all at once, or so it seemed), Coach Ravsten walked up to me and said; "Couch, wrestling practice starts Monday morning. Be dressed down and in place at 9:00."

I didn't know how to wrestle and, besides that, I wanted to start working on the weights. But there was no talking Coach out of it. Coach simply looked at me and said, "I did the same thing for your brother, Rob, and it was the best thing for him and it will do you wonders, too. Besides, I want you to wrestle. So be there at 9:00 a.m."

From my brother's experience, which I remembered well, I knew there was no real choice. So.....

Monday morning Coach was leading the wrestling team in exercises and I learned very quickly how demanding a sport wrestling is. I thought I was in pretty good shape from football, but I found out differently in a big hurry. For days I ached in places I didn't even know could ache, like my ears, the back of my neck and the top of my head to the bottom of my feet, including all regions in between. It was the hell of the first few days of "two-a-days" that started the football season in the fall, only worse. Probably because you were not mentally prepared to suffer once more like you did in September where you paid for the indulgences of the summer vacation. You had already gone through that pain and suffering once this school year and then an additional two and a half months of practice and games. A football player was supposed to be tough!

But, like the initial pain of fall, this more pervasive and all encompassing pain of winter eventually subsided and one could finally chew without discomfort, roll over in bed without moaning and, most importantly, walk down the halls in school without looking like some invalid.

The girls would never understand your supposed "wimpiness" and the guys who had never wrestled would think you a real pansy if you let on in public how you really felt physically. So you hid your pain as well as you could and kept "a stiff upper lip." Heck, it was sore anyway-just as well keep it stiff!

Wrestling is a great sport as it combines the team aspect of activity with the individual performance that you have to contribute to the sum total of team effort. Only the help of the coaches as they teach you the skills of the sport in practice and their shouted instructions as you are engaged on the mat during a meet can be given. It's all up to you individually to win the match and contribute to the point total, which will determine the winning team for that particular meet. Loose the match and you contribute nothing.

The initial pain and suffering of the early season soon gave way to excitement and anticipation for the first real match between someone other than those you practiced with on a daily basis. Workouts were tedious but valuable in learning the various moves and holds. They were also critical in gaining the strength and stamina necessary to go for six full minutes if required to win the match and help your teammates win the meet.

A few weeks into the wrestling season (which coincided with the round ball season, otherwise known as basketball), we had our football banquet. On the appointed Friday night I went to the banquet room of the Westbank Hotel where the affair was held this year. My parents accompanied me as they were invited to participate in the honoring of individual effort and team success.

We had a good meal and everyone was having a good time associating with each other and reliving the great times we had spent during the past year on the practice field, in the locker rooms, on the busses, on the playing field and in the classes and halls at school. There is a great bond that develops between team members all striving to do their best and growing to mold themselves into a unit that can perform in a unified manner that achieves success. And besides, the food was great (and free), the pains of the preceding season had long been forgotten (along with the definition of Bernoulli's Principle learned in physics last semester and other such crucial academic maxims)-and it was great fun!

All of the football awards were given out at this banquet and it was good to see outstanding effort rewarded. It felt GREAT to stand up and get your high school football letter. All athletic letters are special and these were no exception. On top of the special nature of all such awards, these were the very first athletic letters awarded for Skyline High School and we felt an extra measure of satisfaction and pride as we accepted our white "S" embroidered on a blue background. Everyone already had their dark blue letterman's jacket with leather sleeves or their dark blue letter sweater just waiting at home for these letters to be sewn onto them, and I was no exception.

I don't think there was a mother of a football player who wasn't up late that night sewing on these letters so they could be proudly worn the next day to school---the very first day that they would be seen in the history of our new school. We were very proud to have that opportunity to be the first ones to receive these coveted awards, badges of honor and symbols of strength and "power."

Coach stood up and said a few words about the past year and how frustrating it was for most of the season, but how sweet it was to win that last game and finish winners in more ways than one. He talked about how proud of us he was, not because we won the game, but because of the character we had shown in finishing the season's last three encounters.

"That is what football is all about," Coach went on. "It is to teach you how to be a man. I would like to read you something that Theodore Roosevelt once said. This says exactly what I feel about the importance of football. It is called Dare Greatly.

'It is not the critic who counts; not the man who points out how the strong man stumbled, or where the doer of deeds could have done better. The credit belongs to the man who is actually in the arena; who errs and comes short again and again; who knows the great enthusiasms, the great devotions, and spends himself in a worthy cause; who at the best knows in the end the triumph of high achievement; and who at the worst, if he fails, at least fails while daring greatly; so that his place shall never be with those cold and timid souls who know neither victory nor defeat.'"

Coach got a little emotional at the end as he finished by saying, "This is why I coach. This is why I love it so. For you see, every day of the season we all climb into the arena and face reality. None of you are timid souls, for we all know the despair of defeat and we have tasted the sweetness of victory. I appreciate you all for the effort you give and for the opportunity you have given me and the rest of the coaching staff to share these emotions and enjoy the growth we've experienced this season. Let's build always on what we have achieved so far in our lives and make the future a reflection of those efforts. Let's give all that we can to make whatever we endeavor to do, an unqualified success."

Coach sat down to a standing ovation from all in the room. There wasn't one person there who didn't love that man and respect his devotion to doing what was necessary to walk the path he had chosen to walk in this life. He was a great inspiration and we would have followed him anywhere.

Things were winding down for the evening and everyone was sitting and talking with one another. I was talking with Craig Hickman about the prospect of an early snow and the chances of getting on the slopes for some snow skiing when I vaguely heard Coach come to the podium and say something about the captains for next year. Not counting much on my chances, I continued the conversation with Craig in lowered tones and heard Kenny Barnes's name being applauded as the offensive captain for the up-coming season. That was great and I also applauded the decision of my teammates. Kenny was a great leader and had great athletic ability. He'd make a great captain.

Coach then began the announcement of the defensive captain for the next year.. I heard what he said, but was not able to respond very quickly when he said, "Bruce Couch, will you please stand as the defensive captain for the Skyline Grizzlies in 1967!?"

When it finally registered and I stood, my father reached over and gave my arm a quick little squeeze. I could feel how proud he was and saw the same pride on my mother's face as I glanced her way. I felt GREAT! I knew this was going to be a great experience and a lot of fun! Little did I realize the added responsibility and work that would go along with such an honor. True to life, those things that are worth anything cost you something in return..

As I reflect on that period of my life and the effect the selection of captain of the football team had on me, I can honestly say that it had incalculable impact on any success I have experienced in my life since then.

When I was in the fourth grade, I remember taking one of those hated slips from my teacher home to my folks. I couldn't think of what I had been caught at now but figured I must be guilty of something-I usually was. As it turned out, it had nothing to do with behavior but with developmental progress, whatever that meant.

My teacher got with my parents and decided that it may be the best thing for me to hold me back and repeat the year. It appeared that I was not performing up to standard and after some consideration, they decided that by repeating the learning objectives of that fourth year at Longfellow Elementary, I would be better prepared to continue in my quest for knowledge-not that I had any idea I was on a quest!

Nowadays the percentages of high school graduates that hold a diploma and cannot even read at a fourth grade level is mind boggling. In those days you didn't slide by as one obviously does today. There were standards to achieve and I was not meeting those standards.

At the time, I was only 10 years old; being held back was a big deal. As time went on and I got older and "wiser," that hiccup in my schooling continued to be a source of self-doubt and an inferiority complex, I suppose.

In many activities I felt less than adequate in meeting the expectations that were there. If ever I did not "measure up" in my own estimation or someone else's, I laid it to the fact that I must just be slow and less than able. Why else would I have been held back for a year of my academic career?

There was no reason in reality to feel that way, but as each year passed, the hole I was digging for myself was getting a bit deeper. As I look back now, there is no question that the act of having me repeat the fourth grade was the best thing that could have happened to me. I did not end up crossing the stage at graduation time first in line as the class valedictorian-far from it, but I did do reasonably well in school from the fifth grade on. Had those in authority not made that decision when I was 10 years old, I know now that the final 8 years of my education would no doubt have been shear hell from a learning standpoint. Hindsight is obviously 20/20 but I'm cognizant of the benefit it was despite the self-inflicted self-image problem I had. Besides, if I had not been held back, I probably would not have had this experience with Coach.

That all ended with my selection as Defensive Team Captain for the 1967 football season and the encouragement I received from Coach. It was as if a light had been turned on and I could see everything more clearly now. Not like I was totally in the dark or anything, it was more like I was reading life with the illumination of one of those 3-way lamps on the lowest wattage. All of a sudden someone came along and turned the switch to the 250-watt setting and there was - light!

My whole attitude and demeanor changed. Again, not dramatically, but it certainly gave me much more confidence and incentive to move forward and improve my life's situation. There was not a huge change overnight, but the expressed confidence from my teammates and especially Coach, allowed my self confidence and self worth to grow and blossom as time and effort marched on.

The event allowed me more contact with Coach and thereby made possible the interaction that helped me to achieve much of what I have done to date in my life. Now, I don't want to lay too much at the feet of this occurrence, but know that it did result in Coach building me and my ability to further develop in life's everyday churning toward the accomplishment of reasonable and worthy goals and objectives. The foundation was laid at that time and I will be eternally grateful for the fact that I was selected and so honored at the banquet that evening.

On the way home, my parents told me how proud they were and I told them how much I appreciated having them support me the way they did. They came to all our games and wrestling matches no matter where or when they were held. It was great to feel that support.

Just allowing me to play would be enough considering the fact that some parents wouldn't let their kids participate because they were concerned that they might get hurt or for the amount of time that these activities took from an already busy, young life. But my folks were always there, involved, supportive and interested in the growth that comes with both our successes and failures, of which there are many instances of both in our lives.

Beyond the normal thrills and other feelings associated with athletic endeavors, I had learned much about myself and other people during the past year. Football was great, Coach was an inspiration, the team was outstanding and I was one of the captains for next year! I received a lot of congratulations from people in the neighborhood and enjoyed the added attention.

What more could a guy ask for?

On Monday I quickly came back down to earth at wrestling practice. I was on the Junior Varsity (JV) squad due to the fact that I did not have the skills to beat out the guy in front of me on the roster in my weight class of 136 pounds. In wrestling, you are placed in a category depending upon your maximum weight, i.e.; you could wrestle in the 136-pound class as long as you did not weigh any more than that amount.

I stayed on the JV squad for most of the year and learned a great deal more about myself than I recognized at the time now that I look back on that period. I suppose that I did recognize some inner workings during that time, but the main cognitive activity at that moment was working on the weights to build strength and improve stamina for football.

One day Coach came up to me at practice and asked me to move from my 136-weight group up to 141 for a varsity match. I liked the idea of being able to eat more and not having to watch your every bite trying to maintain weight, so after a millisecond's consideration, I agreed. I played football at between 155 and 160 so I had lost a lot of weight to get down to below 136.

Coach told me we were going over to Burley (a farming---what else? ---town in south central Idaho) for a meet. Burley's competitor at 141 pounds was a two-time state champ and our 141 pounder, Dale, couldn't beat him. But Coach thought Dale could move up a weight class and beat their 148-pound guy.

"You don't have to beat this guy," Coach went on. "We don't expect that. But just don't get pinned."

The scoring in a wrestling match is as follows. If you win a match by a pin, holding your opponent's shoulders to the mat for a count of two, you individually contribute five points to the team total. If you win by amassing more points than your opponent gets by the end of the third two-minute round, you contribute three points to the team score. These latter points are earned throughout the match by getting takedowns, holding your opponent in a "precarious position," getting a reversal or some other category that shall for the moment remain unexplained. If you were going to lose (heaven forbid!), don't get pinned because you would give the opposing team two more points than if you had just been out-pointed. Strategy.

I wished Coach hadn't told me my opponent was a two-time state champ. I was so worried about the match, I couldn't think of anything else and dreaded going over to Burley. But worry or not, the dreaded day quickly came and we took the long bus ride halfway across the state.

We all weighed in when we got there, but no one mentioned to Burley officials that I was going to be the one to wrestle their varsity 141 pounder. There is no requirement to hand in a "line-up" card for wrestling meets. Even before the meet started and each individual went out and shook the hand of their opponent, I didn't go out. Rather, Dale did in the 141-pound class. This was really going to be interesting. My stomach was in knots as I sat there waiting for my turn to be sacrificed. Strategy.

The 136-pound match finished and it was my turn. I walked out onto the mat.

Their coach stood up and started yelling. "This isn't who is supposed to be wrestling now," he shouted.

Coach Ravsten walked over and a big argument ensued. Burley's coach had assumed (and you know how that turns out all too often!) that Dale, who had wrestled all season to this point in the 141 class, was the one who would wrestle their state champion. As I was standing there on the mat, I looked across to the guy I was about to wrestle. All I could think of was how bad I had to go to the bathroom, and this for about the tenth time in the past hour. But it was too late now.

The argument ended and they decided to let me wrestle, darn it. The ref blew the whistle and we began. I was trying to stay away and at the same time look aggressive so I didn't get any stall warnings (that can cost you a point---one more lesson on scoring for the non-wrestlers in the crowd). This was a real trick.

Suddenly he came in, grabbed my leg and I went down. I immediately stood up and he pulled me down. So I stood up again. Up - down, up - down we went for the rest of the first period. The only thing I could think of to do was stand up, so that was all I did. It's amazing what a little intimidation (fear) will do for your otherwise trained body. At the conclusion of the first two minutes, the score was only 2-0 in his favor, and I felt really good about that! But I was still scared half to death and I could hardly think straight.

I won the coin toss and chose "up" because it was so hard to ride your man the last period. (Another brief digression for those of you who are not from Iowa-the great state of wrestling. The first period of a match, both wrestlers are on their feet trying to get their opponent on the mat for a takedown and two points. Once you are on the mat, you try to get your opponent's shoulders on the mat for a pin and if you are on the defensive, you try to stay off your back and prevent a pin and try for a reversal so you can pin him..

A coin toss determines who chooses up or down for the second period. The loser of the coin toss gets his choice for the third period. One chooses "up" if he wants to be in the offensive position and down for defense. There are strategies for both choices, which will again be left unstated for the moment, and maybe forever as far as this work is concerned.) Again, I chose "up" and we got ready. The ref blew the whistle to start the second two minutes. I rode him (stayed on offense---on top) for about 30 seconds before he reversed me and got two more points for that action.

What the other guy didn't know was that I was fighting for my life. The second period ended the way the first had, that is, with me standing up and him throwing me to the mat every few seconds. I never got completely away from him to constitute an escape and earn one point so the score remained 4-0 in favor of the Burley wrestler at the end of the second period.

There were just two more minutes to go in the match, which seemed like 100 years at this point. The ref blew the whistle and I tried to stand up again; up-down, up-down we went. There was just one minute to go now and I could see the end in sight. I just wanted to get off the mat. Suddenly he grabbed my arm, flattened me out, threw a quick half nelson on my neck and rolled me over on my back.

It happened so fast I didn't have time to react at all. I arched my back and got up on my head to keep my shoulders off the mat, but I was just too tired and I couldn't keep it up. He pinned me with 50 seconds left in the match.

I felt very disappointed and felt I had failed but was relieved at the same time. I was so afraid Coach would be upset with me, because it looked like his strategy was going to fail. I looked up to see Coach was laughing as I walked over to him and my other teammates at the edge of the mat.

"Good job," Coach said. "You just needed to run for a few more seconds and you would have had him."

I thought Coach would have been somewhat disappointed, but I could see by the way he was acting and talking that he wasn't.

He put his arm around my neck and said, "You did your very best, I can see that. And I can't ask any more of anyone. I'm proud of you."

As I walked to the bench, I suddenly realized again that there truly was life after that match. Boy, did I ever need that at that particular time. I knew I had done my best, but I sure needed the praise from Coach. As I sat there watching Dale begin his match, I looked at Coach and realized how much he loved his work and why. Yes, he loved to win. But the most important thing to him was to develop young men and he was doing a great job of it.

Wrestling ended soon thereafter. I learned a great deal during that time, both in the sense of the sport and about myself and reactions to certain circumstances. I also got into the best physical condition I had been in my life. If you work at wrestling, even your tongue will get stronger! I was looking forward to the weights so I could get even more strength for the sport I loved the most. Football.

The first day of formal weight training felt great. Much different from the first day of wrestling! I was very glad wrestling was over and I could go to work on specific strengthening exercises for football. Coach was there every day and took roll at 9:00. If you were late, you had to go out into the gym and run laps on the stairs, which everyone hated.

Coach sat everyone down and said, "All right, listen up everybody. This year we are going to change the workouts. You will all work on your legs on Monday, Wednesday, and Friday. Then on Tuesday and Thursday you will work on your upper body. We don't want any knee injuries this season and we are going to be faster than last year. On Tuesday and Thursday I want you out in the gym after workout to do some running exercises we will show you later. This will improve your agility and your speed. Now you are to be here every day and I will take roll. If you aren't here you had better have a good excuse. If you are late, there are the stairs. Now let's get busy."

The last comment about the stairs got everyone's attention. We all looked over at the north side of the gym to see the stairs rise from the lower bleacher area of retractable seating, to the top of the building. No one ever ran the stairs on the south side of the building for some reason. Perhaps it was because they were over the girls' dressing room and one didn't want to be associated with girls-at least in the sense of athletics.

Running the stairs was excruciating and as such rapidly built strength. The last thing you wanted was to fall so you quickly developed an added agility, if not mental awareness, of where your feet were supposed to be at every step so you wouldn't fall and hurt yourself badly. We all ran the stairs because it was good training but no one wanted to run them an additional time

The leg exercises were terrible! We spent two hours each day working out and my legs got so sore I had a difficult time walking. It was easy to see who was working out just by standing in the halls and watching everyone walk by on their way to class. You could see the very distinct, stiff-legged walk of a diligent weight trainer. Every day there was a great turn out for the training with about 40 boys on the weights. A synergistic effect was being created in the weight room as you saw everyone working so hard.

Coach had a number of sayings hanging around on the walls of the weight room.. One he used a lot was, "The man who aims at nothing is sure to hit it." After about a week of working out Coach pulled us all aside one at a time and asked us to set a goal for our personal training. As he and I talked, he asked me what my objective was. I said I really didn't have one, other than to work as hard as I could and get as strong as possible.

"Coach, I really don't know what I should be aiming at," I said.

He asked me how much I weighed then, which was about 150 pounds. "Okay," he said, "You should be bench pressing (lying on a bench and bringing a barbell down to your chest and back up again for several repetitions) 300 pounds by the time you graduate."

Well, that floored me because at the time I was benching about 180 pounds and struggling at that! Three hundred pounds seemed miles away. But I set the goal and went to work. I quickly noticed it did make a difference in my workouts. I worked harder because of the objective I was striving to achieve.. I worked longer and concentrated on exercises that would help me attain that goal.

Every few weeks we took some time to measure progress and see how we had grown physically. Coach had a file on each one of us and we would measure our biceps, forearms, chest, waist, thighs and calves to see the progress we had made. Then every two months we had a weight-lifting contest, which really generated some excitement and competition between us. It was a lot of fun. The contest was structured so that the less you weighed, the more points you got for the weight you lifted. A 120-pound kid could get as many points for lifting 150 pounds as a kid who weighed 200 pounds got for lifting 240 pounds. I was lucky enough to win the first two contests we had. But it was really tough with everyone working so hard.

Every day, as we walked out of the weight room, we saw a sign hanging by the door that simply said, "10-0." This, without a doubt, was the most far-reaching goal we had. This was our objective for the coming football season and had been the goal Coach encouraged for each of his teams. But no team had ever been able to achieve that goal. A lot of people talked about an undefeated season, but it took a great deal of dedication and determination. Dedication and determination were two words Coach talked about constantly those days. One day in the weight room he became quite philosophical and quoted the saying by Roosevelt about how the critics really don't matter, because they never get in there and get their hands dirty. Most people don't ever learn what these words can mean in their lives. We all wanted to achieve the 10-0 goal and felt we could and were all working very hard to that end.

One day while I was working out, I realized Coach wasn't actually laboring with the seniors like he had been in previous years. He was walking around the room helping and coaching but he wasn't lifting with us. That night at the dinner table I mentioned that to my father and he simply said that Coach was getting a little older and couldn't do the things young men do forever. I didn't buy that because Coach was only 38 and I knew how much he enjoyed the competition with the boys. He loved to get in there and challenge someone to out-lift him. Most of the time we couldn't.

One morning I got up and went to workout and Coach wasn't there at all. He was sick. He wasn't there the next day either and an assistant coach came in and announced that Coach had contracted hepatitis again and would be out of school for a number of weeks.

So that was why he wasn't lifting with us, he was sick. The bad thing was that Jean, his wife, had just had a baby and they couldn't bring the little guy home because he might get hepatitis, too.

Coach called me at home after school one day several weeks later and asked me to come over to his house and talk to him about workouts. I had been going to weight training every day but many of the other players had eventually stopped. Coach knew this from previous discussions with me and he wanted to talk about the situation.

I drove over to his house the next day and knocked on the door. Coach's oldest son, Chris, came to the door and let me in. I sat down in the living room to wait for Coach. After a few minutes his wife showed me into the bedroom. Coach was lying in a bed with a playbook in his hands and the roll for workouts next to him.

"No one is coming to work out any more," Coach said to me.

"Well, attendance is not as good as when you were there," I agreed.

"Life is funny and you really see what people are made of when there isn't someone there to watch over and prod them on, promises are easy to make, but difficult to keep," Coach said as he looked down at the roll he had set up for weight training.

"I want you to continue to take roll every day and let me know who isn't working out. I will contact them," he said.

I was somewhat uncomfortable as I sat there and talked with Coach because I knew how hard it was going to be to talk to some of the guys and get them to work out when Coach wasn't there. As we discussed the situation, I noticed how yellow his eyes were and how even his skin had a yellowish cast to it. But coach said he would be back to school in a few weeks and I was certain we would then really get back to the program again.

For the next few weeks I kept roll at each workout and then would call Coach every few days and let him know what was going on. Coach told me one day that he would be back to school the following Monday. I really looked forward to that because it would take some of the pressure off me and I really wanted to see him at workouts again. I knew what his presence would mean to the team members and their activity. Captain or not, I was no replacement for Coach Ravsten.

But the next Monday Coach didn't show up. When I asked one of the other coaches about it, they told me he had had a relapse and wouldn't be back to school for the rest of the year.

"Well, no big deal," I thought, because there were only a couple of weeks of school left anyway.

Coach called me a few days later and asked me to come over again and talk to him about training. As I drove over to his house, I began wondering how we were going to work the summer training sessions.

When I got there he was again in bed and I immediately noticed how much more yellow his eyes were and that the color of his skin was worse. He looked tired but was in good spirits as I sat down on the bed next to him. I handed him the roll and he looked over those who had and had not been attending and sighed.

"It doesn't look much better than the last time you were here," he said. "I really don't know what else to do."

"Nor I," I mumbled.

"Well, we have about two weeks of school left now so let's keep pushing and get as many excited as we can and then hope they will keep coming during the summer."

We made some small talk about how he was feeling and I made a comment that he would make one heck of a Chinaman.

Sensitivity was not a required course at Skyline High! I left with the roll book tucked under my arm.

The next few days at workout were worse than they had been for quite some time from an attendance standpoint. It seemed the only two there on a consistent basis were Jamie Bauchman and myself. Most of the others had about given up for the year. Spring fever was afflicting our team members and even I was glad to see Friday and the weekend come and have a chance to do a little "messing around."

That Saturday night we had to practice square dancing at the church for a program we were to put on in a few weeks. I really wasn't very happy about the whole thing, but I decided I would tolerate it. One of my friends made some smart remark about some innocuous thing and the next thing you know we had managed to get into a bit of a tussle over it, but nothing too serious. Stress and tension were taking a toll.

The next day at church, my Bishop who is the leader of our church, cornered me as I came in a little late. We sat down in the back of the foyer and discussed what had happened the night before. He expressed his disappointment at my activity. I, of course, was defensive and could see little consequence for the incident.

After we had settled our differences he said, "Do you know about Coach Ravsten?" (Coach Ravsten was a member of the same church I attended and was a leader in the church, but he attended a Ward, or congregation in another part of town.)

Well of course I did. "Everyone knows he has hepatitis, I replied.

"No," he said. "He doesn't have hepatitis. He has cancer, and the doctors have given him only two weeks to live. It's cancer of the liver, that's why the doctors were fooled at first, thinking it was only a case of hepatitis."

I don't think I would have been any more shocked if a doctor had told me I had cancer. I was numb and felt somewhat sick.

As I went in to Sunday school class, I saw Craig Hickman who was my neighbor and good friend. He also played football with me and I could see from the look on his face that he had heard, too. I didn't listen to anything in church that day (some would say that I didn't listen much any day, but that was not true.) I was just too shaken by the news of Coach's condition.

There were all kinds of questions in my mind. What was going to happen to us as a football team? What was going to happen to Coach and what was going to happen to his family? Why did this have to happen to such a good man who did so much good for so many people? I guess being in church was the best place to contemplate these questions about life, its purpose and its fairness. But I couldn't come up with an answer for the fair part, because it just didn't seem fair at all.

Everything was quite subdued around the entire neighborhood that day because the word was out and we had a number of kids in the immediate neighborhood on the team. Most of those in the neighborhood were members of our church and all shared the grief of this terrible news. Friends and neighbors shared the same concern once they came to know about the situation. There was concern for what Coach Ravsten would have to go through in the next days and weeks to say nothing of the trials that his young family and beautiful wife and companion would be going through and have to face in the future.

On Monday morning I got up as usual and went to work out. I got there a little early as usual and there were some guys in attendance that had not been there for quite some time. Word of Coach's condition was all over town and a lot of guys were showing up to see if anyone knew anything new. A condition report was issued later that day at school from Coach Ravsten, himself, through an assistant coach that he was OK, and that he was planning to be there for the upcoming season!

The next day at workout I was surprised to see even more

guys there and they weren't just asking questions this time, they were working on the weights. By Wednesday, it was just about like old times even though Coach was not there. The weight room was crowded and there was a different feeling of commitment among the players.

The "10-0" sign on the wall suddenly took on a new meaning and became very special to everyone on the team. It became a slogan, which was repeated many times during workouts, in the halls of school and shouted from one car to another as we dragged Main Street. A change had come over all of us that I cannot explain. It was as if in a moment we had all matured many years and stopped looking into our own lives, our personal cares, goals and problems.

We now looked to help and worry about one man as if it would make a difference. But it was all we could do. Our thoughts, feelings and love went out to him and we, as a team, seemed to take on his problems and cares as much as we could. But that was nothing in comparison to what he was going through.

On one of the last days of school there was a bunch of us in the weight room working and talking when Jamie Bauchman made the comment that we had to give this coming season to Coach. We had to give him that 10-0 season he had always wanted. Bauchman spoke in words but communicated something more, much more, which sunk deep into the heart of every team member there. We all promised to give our all, so we could obtain that most difficult goal of an undefeated season, for a man we loved.

There was a tremendous change-taking place among the players. Now the weight room was crowded, not because Coach was there taking roll or because I prodded them on in my inept way, but from a dedication and a promise to a man who meant so much to all of us. The attitude changed from personal, immature, self-centered glory to one of an outpouring of love and sacrifice for a man who lay in a bed in a home on the 400 block of 22nd Street in Idaho Falls, Idaho. It was expressed in a fashion we felt to be one of the few ways we could show him how much we cared. In a matter of days a bunch of boys grew up more than a lot of people grow up in their entire lives. A few simple words had changed our attitudes as Bauchman had said and we internally committed to,

"This is for Coach."

Lessons Learned:

Excellence was the goal of all effort. There was no quarter given for half-hearted effort or sloppy work. You had to perform up to standard and those standards were lowered.

Each was judged according to capacity and it was recognized that all were not equally endowed. That being the case, all were not held to the same standard if the situation allowed, but were expected to reach the heights that they had the capacity to achieve.

It was always understood that doing your best would be acceptable as long as it <u>was</u> your best and not a half-hearted effort that was beneath your capability.

By reaching for the stars, we sometimes missed and hit the moon, but the moon was a far more excellent destination than the place from whence we started the journey.

Chapter 5

A Promise Kept

***"This above all; to thine own self be true,
And it must follow, as the night follows the
day, Thou canst not then be false to any man."
William Shakespeare***

Spring in Idaho comes in fits and spurts, and seemingly never gets the job done. It is a frustrating time of the year. There may be a thaw in the latter days of February and some of the litter that has accumulated over the winter season appears peeking out of the snow banks, a lot like the pretty, little, purple crocus flowers that are much more appreciated. You decide not to wear your ski parka to school one day because of the recent "heat wave" and come out of the south door of the gym that afternoon to be greeted by a blistering wind, 30-degree temperatures and snow flurries-and a frozen nose by the time you arrive home not being dressed for the occasion.

One such Idaho spring came after a lengthy period in early winter where the temperatures were bitter cold, but without the attendant snow fall that is normal in an Idaho winter. The length and depth of the cold spell without an insulating blanket of snow resulted in the ground being frozen solid to some depth far beyond the norm. Then it began to snow and we got our normal compliment of snow for the winter to satisfy everyone's skiing or other winter activity desires, as well as the required snow pack in the mountains that supply the water for irrigation and culinary water during the ensuing summer months. No one thought much of the early winter anomaly or what it might result in with the advent of spring.

February came and the not unusual warm-up occurred. The run-off from the melting snow filled the canals and rivers in the area and then it turned bitter cold again, freezing the accumulated water in the normally empty canals and low running rivers. Again, no one gave it much thought until the temperature once more shot up and stayed up for several days. The snow melt coursed into those same ice-choked rivers, streams and canals that would normally carry the water into the lakes that dotted the area to be used in watering the crops during the summertime.

It wasn't long before this valuable and necessary liquid commodity became a serious and damaging threat to the little town by the falls. The frozen ground could not absorb the water that was melting far faster than was usual in the springtime. The canals were unable to carry the volume due to ice jamming up under bridges and culverts being clogged with the frozen variety of water that would otherwise, in not too many months distant, be tended and managed down row upon row of potato plants or pumped into endless courses of aluminum pipes that brought the life-giving water to the cash crops in the fields of eastern Idaho.

The water was coming off these same now frozen fields looking like the rapids of the North Fork of the Snake River. But instead of undulating quickly over the submerged rocks and boulders in shallow mid-river, this water was doing the same thing over the unprepared and frozen dirt of the fields surrounding the city of Idaho Falls and other nearby towns. Instead of flowing into reservoirs prepared to store this water for the crops in the summer, basements became storage vaults for muddy, cold water.

This was an unknown occurrence; it didn't flood in Idaho. The only water that got into a basement in an area where everyone had one, got there primarily because someone left the sprinkler on in the back yard too long and the window wells filled up and then ran into the basement. That never happened once at our house-four or five times maybe, but never once! That was why Dad would not put carpet in the basement bedroom where my brother and I slept through those cold winter nights and pleasant summer evenings. We had to be satisfied with the "warmth and comfort" of green and white asphalt tiles.

That was one reason it was so difficult to get out of bed on cold winter mornings. It was the opposite of walking on hot coals that you see the natives do in the Pacific isles but just possibly as dramatic. Once "awake" and on your feet they would freeze on the floor as you made your way across the room to the stairs and on up to the warmth and satisfaction of breakfast above.. If breakfast didn't always smell so good in the mornings, we probably never would have gotten out of bed until the crack of noon as was our habit absent any pressing engagements such as school, work, skiing, swimming or some such other enjoyable activity.

Back to the water problem. People in Idaho weren't used to natural disasters occurring but rose to this occasion in excellent fashion. Schools and businesses were closed and everyone joined ranks in filling sand bags and strategically placing them to keep the water within the banks of the canals that criss-crossed town, trying to get the water into the Snake River instead of into people's basements. There were irrigation contractors, farmers and other businesses that provided pumps for people to utilize in getting the water out of their basements in the event they were unsuccessful in keeping it out in the first place. And there were many in that situation.

A man we knew who owned an irrigation company provided three of us on the football team a large pump on wheels and told us to go house to house in the area east of Idaho Falls and pump peoples' basements out. There was never a thought of billing anyone for the time or use of the equipment. Many basements were pumped out without the owners of the house even being there-they were somewhere else helping their neighbors.

It was not a huge disaster in the same category of those that affect the people who live along the banks of the Mississippi River, nor of the magnitude of the destruction that occurred some years later in Southeastern Idaho when the Teton Dam broke and devastated the lives of hundreds of people and ravaged the land as the water made its way to the natural channels downstream of the dam.

But in both these instances, there were no psychologists in the schools when they re-opened after the mess had been cleaned up. There was no National Guard called out to protect the valuables of the citizens whose homes were open to anyone who should come along. There was little, if any, reliance upon the government to come in to provide relief in the form of grants, loans or such aid.

These people were responsible and strong and relied on their own strength, the help of their neighbor (known or unknown), the integrity of their fellowman and the values of hard work, honesty and service to come through these and other such challenges of life and the hand that was dealt each individual. No crying, no complaining, no standing in line with your hand out, just a sense of self reliance and grit that enabled lives to be put back together in short order and press on with life. And a good life it was.

After the flood, spring was no different than others in the past in that it lasted a long time. Freezes and thaws intermingled with the chore of cleaning up after the long winter and the dirt and trash that was otherwise hidden in the snow banks covering the area. Most people think of spring as a "re-awakening" and look forward to the end of the interminable winter. I thought of spring as kind of a miry season of the year. Dirty brown grass, papers and bottles seemingly everywhere, mud in vast areas. But it did bring the end of school which was definitely a plus looked forward to by every red-blooded student of the Idaho Falls School District.

School ended the last week of May. One other unfortunate thing that sprouted during the spring season were the typical, beer parties celebrating the end of school for all and graduation for the seniors. I suppose the only silver lining to this situation was that these parties did not involve drugs or other such associated vices.

Drugs in those days was putting an aspirin in a bottle of coke and watching it fizz as it dissolved. It was never explained to me what the affect such a drink had on the guzzler of the concoction, but I'm certain it didn't have much, if any, effect on anyone other than perhaps prevent heart attacks in the lives of the teenage participants (if you're to believe the current propaganda disseminated by the legal drug barons).

Even though I did not drink, I attended one of these with some of my friends.. A lot of the guys drank thinking it the cool thing to do, I suppose. I could never understand the rationale behind such activity which, in my experience, only involved making of oneself a general fool who, after speaking into the ceramic microphone for the better part of the night once getting home, would awaken with a splitting headache and miserable attitude, all the while wondering what stupid thing one had done or said that would come back to haunt you in the future. In any case, I was always the designated driver (before there was such a thing officially dreamed up by the liquor industry to moderate the sting of the drunk driver's' wreak of havoc on the roadways of America).

At the end of the party I had to help one of my good friends get into his car and drive him home because he was too inebriated. He said to me as I put him in the car, "Couch, this is the last time I am going to drink until after football season because Coach has asked us not to drink." This became the attitude of all those who did any drinking and to my knowledge all of them kept that pledge during the season. I guess every journey starts with a single step and the honoring of the commitment to maintain training rules was admirable.

Two weeks after school was out I got up at 6 a.m. to attend the first weight training session of the summer. I was a bit uneasy because I knew Coach would be there and I was nervous about seeing him for the first time since we had found out he had cancer and told that it was terminal-that he had only two weeks to live. Of course, he had obviously outlived that prediction and had a prediction of his own-that he would be there for the next season.

While we all believed everything that Coach told us, there was that unspoken quandary in our minds of who to believe in this instance-no one joked about such a serious matter. Nor would anyone talk of the alleged doctor's report of the amount of time Coach had left in this life. This feeling was reinforced by his physical appearance. He had lost a lot of weight and his color was still on the severely pale to yellow side of the spectrum.

Anyway, I got there a little early this particular day and walked into the weight room and found Coach sitting on one of the benches waiting for us to arrive. He was dressed in his standard garb for such occasions, gray sweats, athletic coaches' shoes and a whistle was dangling from a lanyard around his neck.

I walked over and said, "Coach, it's really good to see you. How are you feeling?"

"I'm feeling real good. The doctors have me on this new experimental cobalt pill and it helps. Don't worry; I am going to be around for a long time. I can beat this thing."

Well, I certainly hoped so and knew that all who were associated with him were pulling for him in every possible way. There just didn't appear to be anything that we could do and that brought the frustration level to a new high.. From what I have read, the male is of the problem-solving demeanor-don't bother us with the facts of the matter; let's just get to the crux of the deal and get the problem fixed. This was not a solvable situation by the admission of the medical fraternity let alone a bunch of teenage football fanatics with the limited resources we possessed, either inwardly or outwardly. And it was the inward deficiency that weighed on each of us even though we probably didn't recognize it at the time.

I told Coach I was working construction for the summer and would be coming in the evenings to work out rather than early every day. After a hard workout on the weights, my employer for the summer may have been a bit perturbed at my lack of enthusiasm on the job, so I thought it only the right thing to do, to work out after work. Besides, I wouldn't have to get up quite so early. I had just wanted to talk to him for a moment that first morning and let him know I would be there for the evening sessions.

"Just remember, you are the leader of this team and you must set a good example," Coach said.

A couple of other guys showed up and walked into the weight room. I turned and headed out to work.

The job I had was a good one to stay in shape, too, because I worked in a metal manufacturing plant and I had to do a lot of heavy lifting. That evening after work, I arrived at the weight room with my work clothes and boots on..

The weight room was a mess with weights all over the place. The three benches for bench press had bars on them and the folding doors that separated the weight room from the wrestling room were closed. The smell of guys working hard to improve their strength and stamina was strong in the air, an aroma that seemed to stimulate and make me want to get to the weights. I stripped off my shirt and began with my favorite exercise, the bench press, work boots, jeans and all.

There were quite a few guys in the room then and Coach walked in looking exactly how he had earlier that morning. He made his rounds to all the stations where guys were working out saying hello and giving encouragement to all. Most of them had not seen him for a long time and I could see they all initially felt somewhat uncomfortable, as I had. It didn't take long to overcome the discomfort as we instantly recognized that the same spirit and personality was residing in that emaciated tabernacle draped with the familiar trappings of coachdom we knew so well. Just seeing Coach there and experiencing that same great spirit that was still within him made everyone feel good within a very short time. Coach was still at home even if the house was a little (a lot) the worse for wear.

As I was sitting on the edge of the bench press resting, I

looked over at Coach as he was looking down into some kind of a book or manual. Right above his head was the sign he had so carefully made-"The man who aims at nothing is sure to hit it." I thought of another saying that Coach had put in our playbooks-"Who can ask more of a man than giving all within his span? Giving all is not so far from victory."

As my eyes went around the room, I noticed other sayings that meant so much to me. They were on bright colored paper, neatly printed by Coach, and then stuck up on the wall with some masking tape. Then there was the sign that meant so much more now than it had just a few weeks ago. The sign, which summarized everything the other signs, conveyed, "10-0."

Coach walked over to me and sat down. He actually looked pretty good considering all and I just couldn't believe he was going to die; it didn't seem possible.

"You look contemplative," Coach said.

"Just a little tired, I guess," I said.

"Well I am proud of you and the example you are setting as the captain of the team. Always remember you are a leader and must set an example for others to follow. Many of the players will take their cue from you. Make sure you come every day."

Coach paused for a minute and we both looked around the room at all of the guys working out. Coach looked back at me and said, "You know, I love this. I think we are going to have a very good team this year and I look forward to the season starting."

I noticed someone just walking in the door and turned my head to see Craig Lords come into the room. It was the first time he had seen Coach in weeks and I could see from the look on his face that he felt much the same as I had when I first saw Coach earlier that morning. But Coach quickly made him feel at ease. It really was a great inspiration to see Coach there. I finished my workout and as I walked out the door I put my hand up and touched the big "10-0" sign. A promise had been made.

I jumped on my green Schwinn, ten-speed bike with its yellow cross bar and rode home. The yellow paint was there to cover the worn off paint from hanging newspaper bags on the bike. I had inherited it from my brother who was now a big college guy at Utah State University.

We both had delivered The Post Register from those carrier bags to the townspeople on 24th and 25th Streets during our early youth. Before I got my own route, on a day when I was substituting for Rob (seemed to me that I was doing more of the delivering than he was at that particular time, but...), I returned from one evening's chore and parked the bike in the garage for the night. He let me use the brand new bike as an incentive to do the delivering for him. It was worth it to me. My bike was an old red one that was a hand-me-down from some cousin.

The next morning Rob discovered some serious scratches on the cross bar when he took the bag off the bike, revealing the damage. I had no idea that there were any scratches on the bike-had I known that I was responsible for marring the new two-wheeler; I would have got on the bus to my grandma's house in Logan, Utah!

I was smaller than he was, being four years younger, and had to drape the newspaper bag across the cross bar instead of over the handlebars. The metal hooks on the green newspaper bags with The Post Register stenciled in white on them, scratched the paint off the bike and resulted in my life hanging in the balance for a moment or two. My mother saved me from certain death at the hands of my brother as she stepped between us and suggested that we merely paint the cross bar with a contrasting and unique color.

The suggestion was accepted and Rob ended up with the only emerald green, Schwinn ten-speed with a bright yellow cross bar in town, maybe the world-kind of matched his ski jacket, now that I think of it! I never hung the bags on the cross bar again.

After the fifteen-minute bike ride from the high school home,

I quickly showered and went upstairs to have the dinner my mother had kept warm for me. I ached all over, but I enjoyed that feeling. I watched a little TV and at about 10:00 went into the kitchen to have my nightly brew, one quart of milk, two raw eggs, one banana, a little honey to sweeten the taste and a little powdered milk all mixed together in the blender. I never did figure out the why of the powdered milk, but...

I took it into the living room to drink as I watched the news and then was off to bed. I knew tomorrow would be another day of work and then back to the weight room for an hour and a half or two. I repeated this same schedule almost every day throughout the summer.

A number of the guys were working construction out of town and I was pleased to hear they were staying in shape by running and doing push-ups, sit-ups and other such exercises. There appeared to be a wholesale commitment to the undefeated season that we had decided would be our goal for the upcoming season.

Around the first of August we got the bug to play some football, so we took a ball to workouts and after lifting, went out and threw the ball around. It stayed light for a reasonably long time in the summers in Idaho, and that gave us the opportunity to fanaticize with action on the practice fields behind the gym.

June and July were hard months on Coach. He lost a lot of weight in his face, his skin began to take on an even more pronounced yellowish-green look and I could tell he was in a great deal of pain. We were all wondering if he was really going to make it to the first game, let alone hang in there for the whole season.

One day I noticed a number of band-aids on Coach's fingers. The pill he was taking stopped the growth of the cancer, but it also stopped all other cell growth, so if he cut himself it would not readily heal. He also had a tough time with saliva in his mouth. The medication he was taking also dried up bodily fluids so he was always drinking pop or sucking on ice. That was the only time Coach did not practice what he preached. He told us not to drink carbonated drinks but he did. I figured we could forgive him this weakness-no-necessity.

One week before fall practice started, the guys who had been out of town started coming back and joining in the weight training sessions. One evening Fred Finlayson showed up. I was doing some running outside. He yelled across the practice field to where I was and said, "10-0, Couch! We're going to do it!" Fred had been working out of town and had kept in good shape by running. He'd also kept the goal and commitment in mind we had made to go undefeated in the coming season even though he'd not been around any of the other guys. The goal was alive in us all.

The day before official fall football practice started, all the prospective players met on the track at the stadium for the initial annual tryout. The tryout consisted of running one mile in less than eight minutes. "If you don't make it, then you are out," Coach told us.

About 65 guys lined up and Coach yelled, "GO." We all took off in a mad rush. I hated to run. That's why I was out there the prior week when Finlayson had voiced his determination to meet our combined objective-to get ready for this annual trial. The first two laps weren't too bad, but the third started to hurt a bit, and by the fourth I was uncomfortable.

I hated to run; I think I already said that. I knew I could finish well under eight minutes but felt, as captain, I should be one of the first to finish. So I really poured it on the last lap and managed to finish among the top ten. "Finish" was the operable word-I felt like I had been eaten by a wolf and pooped off a cliff.

As I sat there at the finish line, Coach was holding the stopwatch and yelling at some of the offensive linemen who were really pretty good-sized guys. I could see they weren't going to make it and Coach was yelling at them to hurry. Ron Blacker, one of our best linemen who weighed about 230 pounds, was about 200 yards from the finish when eight minutes came up on the stopwatch. Coach clicked the stopwatch off and urged Ron on to the finish.

As he crossed the line as the last player of the group, Coach pretended to depress the stopwatch button, walked over to Ron, who was about to die from the run, and showed him the time. He had ostensibly made it with just two seconds to go! We all got a good laugh out of it. Coach loved working with us and we loved working with him.

On Saturday we all showed up at the dressing room to get our equipment. First string from the prior year got to go through the equipment line first to get the best pads and helmets. While Idaho Falls was not in the poverty belt by any means, the school was not blessed with an overabundance of new equipment each year either. Some of it had been around for years. So when you got in the front of the line you got the newest stuff available. It felt good to have some good equipment that fit the way it should. New or not, you were feeling just great at being about to start a new season of high school football. On Monday practice would begin.

Monday morning I got up at 7:00 and dressed in cut-offs and a T-shirt. I felt a bit of apprehension as I walked up the stairs to get something to eat before leaving for practice. At the top of the stairs I could see my mother in the kitchen fixing breakfast for me. My parents had always been very good in their support of my athletic endeavors. It was always good to know they were there in the stands supporting and yelling for the team and me. But the support went far beyond that as was evidenced by Mom being up early, ensuring I had something substantial to eat before going out to practice. I had not asked her to do that; she was just a great mother and fulfilled her role as one without peer.

I finished breakfast, went out to the car and drove down the street to pick up a few of the guys in the neighborhood who played, too. The leaves were just beginning to turn their resplendent autumn hues on some of the trees. If you looked at the foothills to the east and south of town, you could see the quaking aspens beginning to turn yellow as they mingled with the verdant green backdrop of the pines on the distant hills. I loved the fall. It is my favorite season of the year and would be even if football was played in the summer or spring-it was just a great time of the year. And today was such a nice day, already warm (of course, anything over 65 degrees was warm in Idaho!) and sunny, but I knew it would soon be hot in a football uniform.

Everyone was on the practice field by 8:00 waiting for the coaches to come out and start practice. Just a few seconds later I saw the coaches (Ravsten, Leathem, Rasmussen, Brizee and Jacoby) coming out of the door and walking to the field. Coach Ravsten was carrying a three-legged milk stool. The seat portion looked like a miniature saddle without the horn and was made of fine-tooled leather. It was really nice looking, light tan in color and about knee high.

As I saw Coach coming toward us with his stopwatch around his neck, I thought how much weaker he appeared than any of us had thought. Would he be able to make it through the season? I could see the same question on the faces of the players as we stood there watching the coaches. But Coach was not a quitter. He had said he would beat this cancer thing completely and wouldn't let any negative thoughts enter his head. And he didn't want anyone saying anything to the contrary.

Yet he didn't look good at all.

The coaches arrived on the practice field and Coach Ravsten yelled, **"Okay captains, get the troops warmed up!"**

Barnes and I moved to the front of the group and I yelled, **"Okay everyone, line up. Ready, side straddle hops. Let's go!"**

We were on our way to another season, which, if we had anything to do with it, would go down as one of the most memorable in the school's brief history, and probably in the history of Idaho Falls football. As we did the exercise we chanted, **"1-2,1-2."** Then suddenly, the team was chanting, **"10-0, 10-0."**

I looked over at Coach sitting on his stool watching us and he had a smile on his face. I got a little lump in my throat as I watched 65 guys voice their dedication to a man who meant so much to each one of them. There was electricity in the air that was hard to explain. What it was, I don't really understand. A love, a respect, a dedication and commitment? I really don't know. Probably a combination of all of them, but it was very strong and you could physically touch and feel it.

We stopped the exercise and a roar went up from the guys, a very intense roar. I felt excitement and intensity and knew this was going to be a very good year. We all knew.

We started slowly, no real hard hitting, but a lot of mental work and a continuation of conditioning for the upcoming season. The offense worked on their plays and the defense, on our counters. Technique was stressed and we continually went over the basics. The coaches harped on just the right stance and how, when you tackle, you hit just so. We were taught time after time how to push blockers off. We spent a great deal of time learning how to read the opposing team's offensive plays and how to react best to different situations.

During all of this Coach sat on his stool watching with a look of deep concentration. After a pre-determined amount of time he looked at the stopwatch hanging from his neck, grabbed his whistle and blew hard, signaling that that particular drill was over and we moved on to the next. Every once in awhile he got up off the stool and came over to show someone a better way of blocking or tackling. He still had amazing strength and more important, determination.

We had two practices every day during this period, the first from 8:00 a.m. to 10:00 a.m. and again in the afternoon from 4:00 p.m. to 6:00 p.m. This way we missed the hottest part of the day, but it still got plenty hot (for Idaho). After practice we all ran in and waited in line at the drinking fountain. We stood there tired and hungry, dripping wet from perspiration and ever so thirsty. Coach made sure we all took a salt pill to keep us from dehydrating.

By Friday of the first week we were running some offensive plays with the first team offense. The first team defense was holding the dummy bags so the offense could practice their blocking. It was really hot and boring just standing there and I wasn't really into it too much. One of the blocking backs came around the end on a sweep and knocked my bag and me down. Coach yelled at me and said to wake up and get in the game. It made me feel kind of bad because I was being lazy and inattentive.

After practice I thought of something Vince Lombardy once said, "Fatigue will make a coward out of all of us." I determined within myself to stay in as good a mental shape as I was physically and to give more of myself. Coach and the team deserved more from me.

We had spent a week going through drills and plays. Normally, this would be the time when the aches and pains of the first days of conditioning would finally be wearing off as we got our bodies back into shape after a summer of lazing about. But since we had all been so dedicated and consistent with our summer regimen on the weights, we hardly noticed the increased activity we were all experiencing with the advent of football season and the otherwise hated, "two-a-days." We now had been through 12 practice sessions without any real hitting and everyone was getting a little anxious to get into it.

On Monday we started practice the same as the previous Monday. But as we warmed up, I noticed everyone was doing a bit more stretching than usual. We all knew there would be some good contact today and we wanted to be ready for it. The chant of "10-0" had become the norm for our warm-up sessions and there continued to be that real feeling of togetherness and commitment like nothing I had ever felt before.

After warming up, Coach sent the offense over to one side of the practice field and the defense to the other. The offense was running against second and third string guys. The defensive unit was going through tackling and push-off drills. These drills got very intense and mean at times because everyone was watching, so you put out 100% on every play. With all of the players standing there along with the coaches, we saw some real good hitting.

It was time to show your stuff and make your case for making your spot sure on the first string roster or bumping the guy ahead of you off and taking his place, as the case may be. No one was out there to ride the bench and hold the dummy bags for the season. Everyone wanted to be on first string and the level of competition was beginning to become fierce. We could all feel it and loved it to a man. No one loved it more than the coaches did. They got into the feeling as much as the players themselves-it was contagious.

Coach had the defensive line going through a drill where they hit their man on the side of the helmet, and by so doing, turned his head, trying to move him in that direction and out of the way so they could penetrate into the backfield.

The linebackers were all together and Coach came over and said, "We are going to try a new drill this year that I call "Bull in the Ring." This is the way it works. All of you make a big circle."

Eleven of us made a large circle about 10 to 12 yards across. "Okay, now one of you get in the middle."

I jumped into the middle, wondering what we were going to do. This captain thing was beginning to take on a new dimension of always being the first one at every juncture, not always knowing what was coming next. I sometimes thought it might be better to just hang back a bit and see what was up.

Coach had a look of anticipation on his face as he said, "The rest of you count off. Now all of you change places with someone on the other side of the circle to mix up the numbers."

Coach was smiling because he loved a good hard-hitting drill and he had a bit of deviousness in him if the truth were known. I was beginning to think this was going to be a real dandy.

"Now, here is the object," Coach explained. "The guy in the middle is a linebacker, all of you are blockers and your job is to take out the linebacker. The linebacker is to take out the blocker without giving any ground and remain in position to make the tackle. When I call your number I want you to charge into the circle with the objective of taking out the man in the middle. The man in the middle won't know where you will be coming from because all of your numbers are now mixed up."

I was standing there in the middle when Coach yelled, **"Number five,"** who, as it turned out, was off to my left. I saw him coming at me hard. I turned with my feet spread wide, back straight and knees bent as we had drilled in past practice sessions. The first challenge went well for me; I stopped him without giving much ground at all and I was ready to make the tackle.

I was feeling quite smug when suddenly Coach yelled, **"Number eight."** I started to look for the next guy, who as it turned out, was right in front of me.. He hit me, but I was not in a good enough position and down I went. I jumped to my feet just as I heard Coach yell, **"Number two."** I whirled around to see where the next one was coming from and just picked him up in time to make the proper moves and defeat the onslaught. This went on through all ten numbers and was a very tough drill. I was getting really tired. But I felt pretty good after going through all ten blockers and doing well with most of them.

I looked at my arm as I took my position in the circle and another guy moved into the middle. I could see a nice big bruise and some blood running down my arm. This was a mean drill, but I enjoyed it because it was so intense. By the time we finished "Bull in the Ring" we felt like death warmed over.

Coach looked pleased, sitting there on his stool, and was smiling and laughing as he blew the whistle. "Good work boys," he said. "Remember, if you cheat and don't give your all in practice you will do the same in the game. If you cheat, you only cheat yourself and you will never feel good about yourself. All I want of you is to do your best. That is what is most important.."

It had been a rough Monday, but a good one. It felt good to be hitting again and, boy, had we ever hit! I knew we would all feel it later that night and even more the next day. Tuesday was about the same as Monday and then on Wednesday, just before practice was over, Coach got all of us together and said, "Okay, first string offense up to the ball."

The offensive line moved up and over the ball. "Okay, you guys are on the five yard line, let's see if you can push it in." The offense had a look of confidence as they huddled up to call a play because they had been working against second-string guys the whole time.

"Now let's have first string defense on the other side of the ball and let's see who has the most heart here!" Coach yelled.

There was a big roar as we ran up to the ball and huddled up for the defensive play call. I called goal line defense (seemed to be the most appropriate call to make seeing the situation we were in-that's why they choose me as captain, I guess-my intuitive abilities!) amid the yelling and cheering from the sideline. There was an abundance of excitement and our defensive unit was very proud of our presumed ability. The proof would now be in the pudding-our first real test prior to a game situation. We walked around and patted each other on the rear end, encouraging each other to do the job.

As the offense came up to the ball, Coach yelled out, **"Now here are the rules. If they score on you, defense, you have to give them a piggyback ride to the fence and back. If the**

offense doesn't score, then they have to give you a piggyback ride. Okay, here we go."

Another big yell went up from those on the sideline. The coaches were very interested to see how each of the units would react. There was a tremendous amount of pride on each side of the ball and, with everyone watching, there was going to be some real head banging. On the first play they ran a fullback dive and we stopped them cold with about a one-yard loss.

The defense jumped up yelling and slapping each other around. We called goal line defense in the huddle again (an obvious sign of leadership on my part). On the next play they got about three yards. On the next two we stopped them for little or no gain. That was four plays and we assumed (there's that word again) we had won a ride on the backs of the offensive unit, but Coach said he hadn't said how many plays were to be run before he called it finished. He gave them two more tries and they finally scored on a sweep around the end.

The defense complained long and loud to Coach, saying that it wasn't fair, but he sat there smiling and said, "Who said life was fair?"

So we had to give the offensive team a ride. But I could see Coach was very pleased with the defensive unit. There was a real feeling of oneness on the defensive unit like nothing I had experienced. All eleven of us were good friends and we played as a single unit, something we had not done the year before. This little experience did even more in a way to solidify our sense of purpose and reliance on each other.

Coach was a master of molding young men and getting them to work as a team, all the while bringing out the best in the individual and thc group as a unified force. Little things like carrying the offense was not offensive, but a great team-building exercise. Those little experiences were scattered throughout our association with Coach.

As practice started on Thursday, Coach told us we would

have a full scrimmage on Friday and a lot of people would be there to watch, including people from the paper, and he wanted us to look sharp and act like gentlemen. We had another rough practice working on special teams, punts, punt returns, kick-offs and kick returns. Everything seemed to be working very well and from my perspective all felt ready for the big scrimmage coming up on Friday afternoon.

Friday morning we spent most of the practice on mental preparation because of the scrimmage coming up that afternoon. We walked through plays and discussed what we should do in different situations. After practice we all showered and went home to rest and think about the scrimmage.

As we came in to dress for the scrimmage, I noticed some people gathering at the fence to watch. That was an anomaly for Idaho Falls. We had some fans, but not normally to the extent that they would come out to watch a practice session. This was not the Green Bay Packers! Coach said there were even a few people out there with cameras. I figured they were from the newspaper.. It seemed that even the community was perhaps catching a bit of the excitement and enthusiasm we had as team members.

During the scrimmage everything went very well and we all felt good about the way things were progressing. Just before showering and dressing after the scrimmage, Coach told us how good he felt about our play that afternoon and asked us to keep up the good work. He mentioned we would all take Saturday off, which got a big yell out of everyone. We were tired of the two-a-day practices.

So the hot, tiring practices were over and school would begin on Monday morning. We would be on the "practice before scholastic endeavor" schedule from Monday on for the next ten weeks.

"10-0" was the rallying cry that we all knew and believed was possible and even probable as we looked forward to the upcoming season.

Lessons Learned:

Integrity is a principle and value that had to be adhered to in all activity.. To be counted upon to do what you said you would do, no matter the consequences or conditions, was expected.

If you had talents that were not being utilized or you were holding back and not giving your all in the athletic arena, you found yourself sitting on the bench, or in the worst case, off the team. This was regardless of the comparative level of performance exhibited.

It mattered not that you, at half speed, could outrun your opponent at full speed, you were expected to put forth your very best effort and perform with the ability you had been blessed with.

It was expected that honesty be respected as the best policy in every situation. Integrity and honesty were basic to every endeavor and you were trusted to do the right thing.

Being honest in all your dealings with your fellowman was understood. No exceptions were made, nor expected

Chapter 6

> ***"The average man who wins what we call success is no genius. He is a man who has merely the ordinary qualities that he shares with his fellows, but who has developed these ordinary qualities to more than an ordinary degree."***
>
> ***Theodore Roosevelt***

Classes for the new school year started in the afternoon at 1:00 p.m. because of the split sessions. The two schools (Idaho Falls High School and Skyline High School) were using the same facility until the new Skyline building was completed on the West side of town. I.F. attended classes in the morning from 7 a.m. until 12 p.m. We then went in the afternoon until 6:00 p.m.

School that first Monday was the typical first day of school. We all went to our classes to see who our teacher was and the different kids in our classes. Who were the cute girls in the class upon whom you could maybe make a good impression? Who were the ones you could count on for good notes in case you lapsed in that department? Who were the kids you had to watch out for for a variety of reasons? Who were the brains in the class that could give you some help with the subject matter if required, and who were sure to skew the bell curve as the course progressed?

It was the usual drill at the first of the term. It was a fun day with a lot of excitement in the halls, generally goofing off and checking out the new sophomore girls that had come up from junior high. Some of them were pretty cute, too. Academics and all that went with it were the necessary evils that had to be taken care of so that we could participate in our first love-athletics.

Coach taught a psychology class and was a very popular

teacher. Everyone wanted to get into his class. He was working on his doctorate before he got sick and had three hours of classroom work left before he could start on his doctoral dissertation. He used this knowledge both in the classroom and on the football field to the benefit of student and athlete alike.

We knew that Coach was struggling with the burden he bore with his condition but I didn't realize to what extent until one day he asked me to stop by his "resting room." I didn't even know he had a resting room so he had to explain to me where it was. Kids are pretty oblivious to much of what is going on around them, especially when it involved a situation like we were facing, with one we honored and respected like we did Coach. I would guess that this may be true to a great extent with all such situations in life where people have to face circumstances where one has no control over the condition and have to do what you could and hope for the best. Many times the only option was to ignore, as best you could, the trappings of the specific situation since there was nothing you could do anyway. This was my situation in this instance.

When I found the room, it was nothing more than a large converted storage room just in front of the gym and across from the wrestling room, actually under the stairs that ascended to the upper level seating of the gym. I walked in that afternoon looking for him and found him lying on a cot. If he ever felt sick or really tired he would go to this room and lie down. Later in the year he did this quite often and the kids in his scheduled class for that respective period would stay in the classroom even though there was no teaching going on. They would not wander around the halls because they knew this would cause trouble for Coach, another sign of the feelings that all the kids in school had for him whether they were involved in athletics or not. These feelings were in the hearts of all, not just us lucky enough to spend those special times with him on the practice field and on the sidelines.

Classes got to be a real drag in a real hurry, especially chemistry and trig.. Football and the guys I played with made school fun and exciting. The other was necessary and tolerated. But without sports, I don't know how I could have stood all the homework and hassels some of the teachers put you through.

The Grizzlies had football practice from 9:00 a.m. to 11:00 a.m. every morning and that really worked out well. You didn't have to get up too early and had plenty of time between practice and classes to take care of things hanging in the wind. The day was complete at a reasonable hour for after school employment at the local grocery store or wherever, or for other demands on your time. Many of the teachers at school expected you do homework after school from the amount of material they assigned!

At practice we began working on our I.F. gameplan. The Tigers would be our first opponent of the year. It was going to be a really weird game, with our J.V. squad playing their J.V. squad the first half, and then the varsity squads playing the second half. I suppose you could say it was an exhibition game of sorts.

The defensive unit started working against I.F.'s offensive style of play. We learned what we should expect and how to react to different movements in their backfield.

Monday, Tuesday and Wednesday were very intense workouts and we had a lot of good contact drills along with some good mental preparation. We continually went over plays to make sure everyone knew what his assignment was. A lot of mistakes were made, but by Thursday we felt we were coming along quite well, as did the coaching staff. This gave us a good deal of confidence, but we were still a little bit apprehensive about how good we really were and how we would do in a real game. That apprehension extended to our concern for our head coach and there was quiet talk among the players wondering if Coach was going to make it because some days that first week of school he really looked bad.

Wednesday after practice we always picked up our game uniforms and took our practice uniforms home to be washed. There was no valet service except for the stellar service our mothers provided to keep us looking presentable for practice-at least for the first day of practice for the week. By Wednesday, those practice uniforms really needed the touch of a mother's hand! To designate different squads, (offensive, defensive, kick-off, etc.) the trainers supplied solid-colored green, yellow, red, black, blue, gold or orange vests to be worn over your individual jersey. Practice pants were grass stained and dirty and didn't look very good. We were really a pretty rag-tag-looking outfit during the week as we practiced.

On Thursdays we dressed in our game uniforms for practice and went over our plays time and time again without any real physical exertion or contact. It was all a mental practice. Our game uniforms always felt so good because everything fit just right and they looked very sharp, white pants, light blue socks and a short sleeve, light blue jersey. It was interesting the way you felt when you put on the game uniform. It brought on a feeling of confidence in a special sort of way. They say that clothes make the man and these threads had a definite effect on the way we thought of ourselves and even the way we acted.

After all this mental preparation, Coach called us all together and said, "Okay boys, two laps around the field."

So away we went. We all came back huffing and puffing and Coach had us sit down on the ground. There were only rare occasions when we were allowed to sit on the ground. During scrimmages or when you were waiting your time to participate in the current goings on, it was often a temptation to sit down. This was strictly forbidden. If you were seen to be resting in such a fashion, you would be castigated by the standard refrain, "Don't **let the angle worms crawl up your butt! GET UP OFF YOUR DUFF!"** That little exchange only occurred once or twice at the first of the season. NO ONE required the same invitation more than once.

We all sat down on this occasion surrounding coach on his milk stool. The grass on the playing field was lush and green in this season of the year. We were lucky enough to have real grass on our field. I say that not only in reference to the phony "AstroTurf" some poor athletes have to compete on, but also to the stuff that people in many other locations around the U.S. call grass. I have seen bermuda, St. Augustine and other such material that they try to pass of as grass, but that wiry, thick-bladed green stuff is a poor substitute for the Blue Grass that grew so well in Idaho, far from the white-railed pastures of Kentucky from whence it supposedly came.

The mysterious groundsman had already chalked the lines on the field in preparation for the game the next day. They were the regulation four inches in width and straight and bright. I say "mysterious" because I never did see anyone actually working on the field but it always looked great for game day. He did a masterful job.

Coach talked to us about what we were going to do in the game against I.F. and asked only that we do our best and give our all. If we gave our best and lost, that was fine. But he also said that if we did do our best, there was no way we would lose. We talked and joked for a few minutes and really felt good about each other and the relationship we had as a team with Coach. These were moments which would never be forgotten, watching a man give more than anyone would expect, or even imagine, to a bunch of boys who would do anything they could for him in return. The only thing we could do for Coach would be to win the games we would play that season. The opportunity would come in every game to return that dedication and love in the only way we knew how.

Coach stood up and yelled, **"Who do we play tomorrow night?"**

"Halloween High!" came the response.

Coach yelled back, **"Who are we going to beat tomorrow night?"**

We all shouted back, **"The pumpkin pushers!"**

We then started to push each other around and yell. The emotion was very high; we were ready for Friday night. After all the yelling was done Coach asked us to stay after school (remember, we practiced in the morning before school) and listen to a special tape by Bob Richards.

We showered and went to school, but it was tougher than usual for me to pay attention in class because I was so preoccupied with the up-coming game. After school we all went over to the field house and assembled in one of the classrooms that was next door to the dressing room.

"Field house" was really a stretch. It was the refurbished auto shop building that was at the far side of the practice field. It was a tin building that now housed our locker room and some classrooms to accommodate the two separate high schools attending one facility. The Tigers kept the locker rooms in the actual high school building and they remodeled the old auto repair shop building to provide a couple of needed classrooms and the dressing rooms required for our team sports. The auto shop courses were moved to an area under the grandstand for the football stadium.

Coach was there with a large, old, reel-to-reel tape recorder. A tape was mounted on the machine that would shortly be played to us. As I later thought about the content of the tape we heard that afternoon, I remembered an incident my brother Rob had told me about. He had heard that same tape played in his high school experience with Coach.

To confirm the real message of the tape, he told me of an afternoon during the Christmas vacation immediately following Rob's graduation in 1963. He had come home from college and was visiting Coach at the high school during a wrestling practice for the Tiger wrestlers.

The three-week Christmas vacation was too long for a wrestler to maintain top form in both condition and technique without continued practice while school was academically in recess for the holiday period. Coach was conducting the session and when Rob walked in and after some initial conversation, a thoughtful look came across Coach's face.

"Get some togs and shoes from the equipment manager and get dressed. There's no one who can give Mike a workout since the other guys in his weight class all went away for the holidays. I need you to get out there on the mat with him and give him a good bout."

Rob heard the words fall from Coach's lips but couldn't believe what he was hearing. Rob had played college football and was in good physical condition, but had not wrestled since the State Wrestling competition in Boise nearly a year ago. You'd have to be crazy to get on the mat with anyone after that length of time, let alone someone like Mike who was in good wrestling condition-well into the season.

There was another reason.

"Coach! You must be joking. I'm not getting on the mat with him. There's no way. He'll kill me like he did last year," said an incredulous Rob.

Mike was now a senior, a junior member of the wrestling team when Rob was a senior the previous year. Mike was in a lower weight class the previous year but over the summer had grown and put on some extra weight provided by the conditioning and weight lifting he had done. Even without these improvements, Mike had always beaten Rob due to his skill on the mat.

Coach replied, "No, you'll beat him. You won't let him beat you. You're a college stud now and would never let a mere high schooler whip you. Now get dressed and get back in here! It's merely a matter of attitude and mindset.. Don't worry, you'll not get embarrassed."

As usual, Coach knew the real fear, being embarrassed, and the strength of will and mental commitment that would carry the day.

True to Coach's prediction, Rob came back and gave Mike a good work out, never letting him get the upper hand and coming away victor. As Rob would be the first to tell you, not a sweet victory, but a victory, nonetheless. He paid for those 5-6 minutes on the mat for days to come being nowhere near physically prepared to do battle but being victorious due to mental toughness and determination.

That's what this message by Bob Richards was all about. Coach believed it and demonstrated quite effectively that it worked and operated in the lives of the young men and women he worked with. He gave them the opportunity to prove the principle for themselves in countless incidents like Rob had just experienced.

The objective that winter day during the Christmas vacation was not to give Mike a work out. It was to prove to Rob the value of attitude, mental toughness and determination. It worked.

Coach said a few words about the upcoming game and then turned the tape recorder on. Bob Richards began to speak:

"Thank you very much for such a warm response, I am delighted to be with you this afternoon. I suppose all of you are wondering just what in the world a pole-vaulting preacher is going to say to you. Everywhere I go throughout America they often kid me about the fact that I am both a preacher and an athlete. I am sometimes called a high-flying parson; they sometimes refer to me as a decathlon deacon. I made a trip to India not too long ago and everywhere I went they referred to me as the ricocheting reverend. It is really humorous to get some of the remarks they make about a preacher in sports. I think the funniest one of all is the one coined by a writer in Cleveland when he said I was the only preacher he knew that was trying to get to heaven on his own strength. Be that as it may, I have had some wonderful experiences in this world of sports and I would like to share some of them with you here this afternoon.

"Now I had better warn you in the very beginning, friends, that I am a decathlon man and you all know that decathlon men can go on and on. They never get tired. Secondly, I am a Church of the Brethren preacher and if you know anything about these folks, they are long-winded. I can't think of anyone worse to invite to an occasion of this kind than a preacher who is in shape. I think that is about the worst thing that could happen to anyone. Thirdly, I had the privilege of teaching philosophy for three years and if any of you know anything about philosophy teachers, you know they can go down deeper, stay longer and come up with less than anyone else. So you are really in for it and I hope you will get as comfortable as possible.

"It is out of three worlds primarily that I would like to speak to you this afternoon. A little bit of religion, a little bit about the philosophy of life and a great deal in this wonderful world of sports. Now I am going to speak out of a world that I know best, friends, because in this world of grime and grit, muscle and bone, you can see life. I maintain that this is one of the most beautiful symbolical representations of life there is. This thrilling world of athletics, men struggling for goals, men hurting, men in pain, but going on for victory. I maintain that what happens on the gridiron is exactly what happens in living and what takes place on the ball diamond or on the track, these are struggles of life. So I want to communicate to you out of the world I know best. I believe every person here wants to be a champion in one endeavor or another. Everyone is playing the grand game, the game of life, and I believe the world of sports can speak to each and every person in this audience. I also believe this sports world can speak to our culture. This may seem I am over stretching the sports category, but we live in an age of mediocrity, friends, when people are so prone to throw things together in a slip shod way. I love the sports world, because you can't be mediocre. You've got to go beyond the ordinary, you've got to reach out and try to excel. I love the sports world also because in the age of the passive, you've got to get active.

"Now, we live in a time when people are so prone to just let life move them, they are so passive. A full-page ad illustrated this for me not too long ago. Now, you don't have to exercise yourself. All you do is lay on this machine and it exercises you. I couldn't help but think this symbolizes the philosophy of our time where we just let life mold us.

"Well, in the sports world, friends, you've got to become active. You've got to take life, so to speak, by the horns. You've got to get out there and run, do chin-ups and sit-ups. You can't just sit around and daydream in the locker room; you can't sit in the stands and criticize. Pretty soon you've got to go out there and hurt and take that thing in your own hands. You take a quarterback catching a long punt. Two big ends and two big tackles are coming down on him. He doesn't call a committee meeting. He has to take that ball and he has got to move. And may I dare to suggest this is one of the greatest needs of our time, for thinking people to act.

"Well, in the sports world you have got to put your ideas into muscle, you've got to act on that which you know. I love the sports world because in the age of socialized man, or bureaucratic man, or as the book calls it, organizational man, you still get to the individual. In the sports world the guard can't rely on the tackle to do his job for him, the tackle can't rely on the end; the quarterback can't rely on the fullback. Each and every person must do his assigned task and the team only functions when each individual makes his block or everyone does what he is supposed to do. That is why in sports they keep track of earned run averages or batting averages or the number of blocks or tackles, because underneath the team there is a person and an individual functioning. This is a great lesson for us to learn today. Underneath society there are individuals and you only change society when individuals live up to their responsibilities. I love this sports world because in an age of something for nothing, the sports world says you only get out of it what you put into it. We live in a time when people are so prone to gamble, to rely on luck, to expect some circumstance in life to change their fortune. In sports you only get out of it what you put into it. Look at the number of hours spent in running. You can only run as long as those lungs are trained to go. You can only jump as high as those muscles will lift you.. In other words you must rely on work, discipline and faith. You just don't get something for nothing.

"I am reminded of the story of the lady who walked in to get a life insurance policy. She went in and said she would like $100,000 worth and the salesman said that it would be so much for the first premium and the lady said, 'Oh, I don't want to pay for it, just charge it and deduct it from the first claim.'

"Well, people have this philosophy of life. But if you could be in this sports world you would see that a man only breaks records as he trains, as he works, as he gives his all. I love sports, too, because it is a simple world.. It talks about a guy hitting the tape at a certain time, it talks about a guy crossing the mark and not making any excuses. It is a simple world where the drama of life is being portrayed. Maybe I am wrong, but I believe this. The greatest teacher who ever lived spoke in a language so simple that the smallest child could understand him and yet when you trace out the implications of his thoughts they go beyond the deepest comprehension of man. This is wisdom, when you can say something simply, and the sports world does.

"In these simple stories I maintain you can get something about life. Also it is a world of struggle and I personally don't believe a man or woman is prepared for life until they are prepared for knocks and bumps and bruises. Life is not easy; it isn't a bed of roses. A person will accomplish in life when he learns that you have to hurt, you've got to go through the sweat, blood and tears, so to speak. Well the sport world will teach you this.

"Anyone who has ever gone through a line in football and knows what it is to hit a 250-pound lineman, you know what it is to go through 11 men before you reach a goal. You are prepared to face obstacles. Anyone, who has ever run a race and really gone out for a record, knows what it is when those lungs are pounding and there is lactic acid in your muscles and you're tired.

"Well, that is life, friends. You only understand life when you see it as a struggle. This is why I love the statement of Plato, the great philosopher who said, 'A boy or girl is not ready for the higher reaches of mathematical inquiry or philosophical speculation until they are first of all toughened in the spirit by athletics.' I maintain the sports world can prepare a boy or girl for the bumps and bruises of life. That is why the statement on the gridiron at West Point is so significant for me, 'On these friendly fields of strife are sown the seeds that on other fields and other days are born the fruits of victory.' It is a world of struggle. Well, I would like to lift out of this world of struggle some simple stories and my theme is the struggle for life's higher goals, believing that out of this sports world you can see life emerge.

"The first thing I want to say to you is this: If you want to accomplish in the world of sport or any realm of life, you have got to get a goal, a high one. You have got to keep your eye on that goal and you've got to follow through with all you've got. Now this is simple, isn't it? Any of you that have ever participated in sports know the axiom of keep your eye on the ball and follow through. Duke Snyder tells me the secret of hitting: You have got to keep your eye on that ball, hit the thing squarely and follow through straight toward those stands. Any phenomenon in sports can be summarized by these words. Keep your eye on the goal and follow through. Aristotle, the great philosopher, said this, 'Man is a goal seeking animal and his life only has meaning as he is striving for goals.' Jesus put it in a profound way when he said this, 'If your eye be single, your whole body is full of light.. But if your eye be evil, your whole body is full of darkness.' I think what he meant is this: If your eye is in focus, if you know where you are going, if you can clearly see life, then your whole body works with you. It's integrated. But if your eye is out of focus, if there is nothing but a blur, a fog, then your whole body is disintegrated, out of harmony and you are working against yourself. You have to have something to strive for. You have to have a goal.

"I think of one of the greatest football games I have ever seen. The Rose Bowl game. Michigan State is playing against UCLA; the score is 14-14, less than one minute to play. UCLA took over on their own 48-yard line and they could have won the ball game, but five guys started to call signals in the huddle. The captain and the quarterback were arguing. There were offsides penalties and everyone coaching from the sidelines. They found themselves on their one-yard line forced to punt with 13 seconds left. With seven seconds left, Michigan State took over on the UCLA 41-yard line. Duffy Dority called off the bench a young sophomore, put his arm around this kid and said, 'Now Dave, there are seven seconds left. This is what you have to do. Clearly determine where those goal posts are and when you know exactly where they are, keep your eye on that ball, move forward and drive the ball straight through those uprights.'

"This sophomore boy, the greatest challenge in his life, went into the game. The whole crowd was electric with anticipation. The snap of the ball and the kid moved forward hit the ball dead center and moved straight toward those goal posts. I've never seen a kick like it in my life. The ball turned over exactly once, split the uprights and 10,000 Michigan State rooters landed on top of me. I'll never forget it as long as I live.

"Do you get the simple dramatic story? No boy ever kicked a field goal but what those goal posts are clearly silhouetted in the sea of faces in the background. Moving forward with all he has, keeping his eye on the ball and following through, straight toward those goal posts.

"Forgive this personal reference, but when I was a boy of thirteen, a coach sent me in to pole vault. Well, I tied for first at 6 feet 9 inches. Now that isn't even a good high jump today and I was using a pole. But a friend gave me a picture of a guy going over the bar at 15 feet, 8 1/2 inches. Well, I put this picture on my bedroom wall and consciously or unconsciously every time I moved into that bedroom the picture had an impact on my life. It became an image in the back of my mind. This is what I wanted to be.

"Now, I never made my goal, friends. I came within 2 1/2 inches of it, but I never quite made it. But do you see what that goal meant to my life? It pulled out every ability I had; it gave every step down the runway meaning, it gave every chin-up and every bit of weight training purpose.

"You have got to have a goal, and you have got to have something to pull you out. In this regard I think of the greatest story in track and field. The story of a young boy who wanted to become a champion. He asked his coach how he could and his coach said, 'Well son, you have got to train hard and get your knees high.' The boy, Charlie Pattock, went on to win an Olympic Gold Medal. Here is where the story begins. He came home to America and was giving speeches all over. In one of his audiences a skinny little Negro boy came up and said, 'Gee, Mr. Pattock, I would give anything if I could be like you.' Charlie said, 'You can.'

"That boy won four Olympic Gold Medals. It was none other than Jesse Owens. Jesse came back to Cleveland, Ohio. Walking down the street a young nine year old came up to him and asked him for his autograph and said, 'Gee, Mr. Owens, I'd give anything if I could be like you.' Jesse said, 'Well son, you can if you will work and keep the dream in your heart.' That boy, so skinny that they all called him bones, grew up to tie Jesse Owens' Olympic record in the 100-meter dash.

"You watch things like this and you realize that dreams can come true. Goals can pull people out. You have got to have a goal regardless of how tremendous it is and you've got to let that goal pull you out. Now, of course, the hard thing is the follow through.

"I saw this dramatically in Helsinki, Finland during the 1952 Olympics. Bob Mathias was on his way to a gold medal in the Decathlon, but in his javelin throw he just wasn't following through. He was going through the motions, but he wasn't hitting it with everything he had. Well, his coach and I were up in the stands and his coach couldn't make him understand he had to follow through. Well, he wasn't allowed on the field and his shouts couldn't be heard, so he got an idea. Maybe the crowd would help him.

"Now I don't know if you folks realize it, but in Scandinavia whenever a fellow runs, the whole crowd runs with him. They vicariously identify themselves with the runner and I've listened to Swedes coming off the curve and the crowd yelling a chant in Swedish, **'Hail Sweden, land of our birth, we'll ever be true to thee, hail, hail, hail.'** The crowd would stand up and yell this over and over and that runner would just give his utmost. Believe me if you'll run, you'll run in a moment like that. I watched this as the whole crowd of 70,000, stomping their feet in unison, clapping their hands going zak tu pek, zak tu peck and that guy down there on the track is keeping pace to the chant in the stands. Halfway through they are chanting faster, the guy is perspiring, but he picks up the pace and holds the chant. The last lap or so they are chanting faster and faster. Here is that guy worn out, knees high, his face a mask of torture driving down into the tape. You know, they have driven him to 20 world records.

"Well, Stan Jackson got the idea, maybe he could get the stands to help him let Mathias know. So a bunch of us got **together and started yelling, 'Follow - through - Bob. Follow - through - Bob.'** Now some of these Fins, Norwegians and

Swedes who couldn't speak English were going, **'Follow - through - Bum. Follow - through - Bum.'**

"Well, to make the story short the whole stands began to roar. Bob looked up and got the message. On his next throw he gave it everything he had and let the javelin go. He threw it 30 feet further and went on to break the record in the decathlon. You see, you can't just go through the motions. You have got to follow through with everything that you've got.

"Here again, forgive this personal reference, but in 20 years of pole vaulting since I started as a 13 year old boy, I spent 10,000 hours training. You want to be good at something in life; you put 10,000 hours of work into it. You want to be a scholar, you want to be great in the athletic world, you want to be a great statesman, a doctor, a lawyer, anything in life. If you want to be great in business, in selling, put 10,000 hours of work into it and see what happens to your life. Here is one of the great axioms of sports.. You have got to get a goal and you have got to keep your eye on that goal and you must follow through with work and with all you've got.

"Secondly, the sports world says you will be frustrated. Now I know this is a hard one. We only like to talk about the champion, the fella who wins the gold medal. But the sports world is bigger than newspaper write-ups, friends. It talks about frustration, it talks about boys giving all they have, but they lose by a point. It talks about men running down to the end and they still fail. It talks about a baseball pitcher pitching a no-hit game and he is in the eleventh inning as a home run goes over his head. There are many frustrating moments like this.

"I think of a guy, Jim Peters, running the greatest race of his life, 20 minutes ahead of everyone else. He broke into the stadium in Vancouver, Canada.. He had run 26 miles on his way to a world record in the marathon, but in 95-degree heat, lactic acid built up in his muscles. Just as he made the turn he heard the roar of the crowd. With just 385 yards left he collapsed on the track. He struggled to his feet again trying to go on, but he couldn't, falling down 16 times. When he couldn't get up anymore he crawled on his hands and knees to a white line that he thought was the finish line and collapsed over it unconscious. He was 200 yards short of his goal.

"Now, you can't go up to a kid like that and say, 'Ya got to put out a little bit more.' **There are times when a guy puts out everything he's got and he still fails, he still doesn't win. But may I dare to suggest this, that in the striving, in the development of a will, a man is learning a great lesson about life. Somehow there is more victory in a striving like that than there is in victory itself.**

"And even beyond that, there can be defeat in victory if the person does not learn this. Now this may sound strange, but let me illustrate it. Which one of these fellows would you rather be? A six-foot, four-inch guy who weighs 190 pounds and can high jump six feet, 8 inches, broad jump 25 feet and run the 100-meter dash in 10.2. The guy was enormous, he could do anything. Would you rather be a boy like that who experts claimed would break every record, or the kid with a cut foot? Cut so bad that every time he ran a race it hurt him.

"Or which one of these kids would you rather be? An All-American his junior year at the University of Illinois who broke every one of the records there.. Or would you rather be a kid 132 pounds, denied a uniform because he was too small and he had a clubfoot?

"Or which one of these? An Olympic champion with a gold medal in his hand, waving at 100,000 people in victory. Or would you rather be a boy who was supposed to win, but wound up fourth and they lowered the British Flag to half-mast?

"Before you make up your mind let me tell you about these six boys. The guy with all the ability in the world never made the Olympic team; he lost his temper repeatedly, walked off the track and wouldn't even finish the race. He was fighting coaches, officials, everyone. The other boy was Rayford Johnson who went on to set a world record in the Decathlon. Today he is one of the outstanding athletes in the world.

"The All-American halfback didn't even finish school. He took himself so seriously, thought he couldn't play with his buddies. He dropped out of school and they haven't seen him since. The other boy at 132 pounds with the clubfoot went on to make All-State Pennsylvania. He was second string All-American and is now down at the University of Florida molding men as a coach.

"The guy with the gold medal committed suicide six months later. The other boy was Roger Banister, who, the following year, became the first man to run the mile in less than four minutes. **You can't tell me, friends, that there can't be victory in defeat and defeat in victory.**

"It depends upon the attitude a man has. It isn't where you are that counts.. It's the direction you are heading. One of the great things about the sports world is that it can teach you to take frustration and to come back out of it and go on to victory. Moses never entered the Promised Land. David never saw the kingdom united. Jesus hung on a cross and there is no greater symbol of frustration in the world than this one. And yet out of these frustrations have come the dreams of men. It is a great lesson you must learn about life.

"Thirdly, you have got to hang on. You will be frustrated, but you have got to stay in there and battle, you must keep right on going. The sports world is filled with so many beautiful stories of this.

"I think of a boy on his way to become an All-American. There was a terrific game one afternoon and he had his right leg practically ruined. He had operation after operation on his knee and his All-American hopes were dashed. He would never play football again, he was told by his doctors. So this guy took up shot putting. I can't understand how anyone could fall in love with shot putting, but anyway. Pole-vaulting is a different thing. This guy began to throw that shot put through the summer and the knee doctors claimed would never bend, began to bend a little. Pretty soon he could bend it even more and just a month ago that guy put the shot 65 feet, seven inches.

"Now do you get my point? If you hang on even by a shred of desire it is amazing what can happen in your life. I think of two guys I met in New York not too long ago, both football players, Andy Robesteli and Johnny Unitas. You should hear the stories. Andy was dropped from the Rams because he wasn't good enough. He decided he was going to work harder than ever before. Seven consecutive years later he made all pro end with the Giants.

"Johnny Unitas was turned down by several schools. They didn't want him and he ended up at the University of Louisville. He was about a fifth-round draft choice for the Pittsburgh Steelers and ended up as fifth string quarterback and was dropped from the team. They didn't want him. He kept himself in shape when no one knew he even existed. The Colts were building a championship team and told a newspaper all they needed was a quarterback. On a two-cent post card, Johnny sent in his reply and said, 'Give me a chance, Coach.. I know I can do it if you will just give me a chance.' A 65-cent phone call back and Johnny Unitas was signed. Two years later he was named the outstanding football player in the world. You talk about hanging on.

"With less than a minute left in the greatest football game ever played Unitas went into the huddle and said, 'Men, we are three points behind, but we are going to move down the field. I'll hit Berry for so many and we will tie this game, and then in overtime we will win it.' This is exactly what happened.

"Now this is what I mean by hanging on. You have got to stay in there and battle. If you can get beneath the statistics of victory and defeat you will discover this. It is hanging on that does it. There can be victory if you will just stay in there and battle and keep pressing on towards your goal.

"Lastly, and I close with this, make sure you are reaching out for the greatest there is, and I mean by that, more than just world records. I mean more than just profits in business or just education, although you need to go for these. But I am talking about something infinitely greater. Reach out for the highest goals there are, God, character, morality. Now this may seem strange for you to talk about the spiritual world of God in sports. But I wish you could be with me and see how, in the sports world, we do pray. I've seen guys in ultimate concern kneel down and pray, 'Oh God, help me do my best.' I see guys get off their knees and go out and triumph. I put my hand on the shoulder of Bobby Morrow and said, 'Bobby, you ever pray when you run?'

"This guy who won three gold medals said, 'Bob, I never run a race in my life but what I pray.' You watch guys like this hit the tape and say, 'God did it.' You watch two guys racing down the track neck and neck, one just barely edges out the other at the tape, you hear the roar of 102,000 people and then, suddenly, the hush as he kneels down to thank God.

"I've seen this in the sports world and I've come to believe it is more than just muscle and bone. There is a spiritual something that throbs through many of these great athletes. They are what they are on the track because of what they are in their spirits. Think of Peter Dawkins, polio as a boy, he overcomes it through football. He goes to West Point Military Academy and is one of the top seven students. He wins the Heisman Trophy, the Maxwell Trophy and every Sunday morning he leads his buddies into that church to worship and pray. A spiritual something. Bud Wilkinson put it this way, 'You show me a boy with a spiritual commitment and I'll show you a better football player. The discipline of his life will be greater and he'll work harder.' Somehow when a divine dimension touches your life it makes a difference.

"I close with this one last story. Lou Little tells it about his greatest football team. They were on their way to the conference championship, just one more game. He had a boy on his squad who couldn't quite make the team for four straight years. Three days before the game Lou was given a telegram to give to this boy telling him his only living relative had just died. Well, the boy looked at that telegram and said, 'Coach, I will be back for Saturday's game.'

"The morning of the game this boy walked up to Lou and told him he wanted to be put into the game. 'I know I haven't made this team yet, but put me in on this kick-off and I'll prove to you that I am worthy of it,' he said. Well, Lou could see he was emotionally disturbed and Lou made all kinds of excuses, but finally he thought the boy couldn't do too much harm on the kick-off and put him in.

"The roar of the crowd at the kick-off, the opposing team took the ball on the goal line and started to move up field. Suddenly on the seven yard line there is a tremendous tackle. The boy had dropped him in his tracks. On the next play Lou left him in, he made the next tackle, he was in on the next, you couldn't move him out of there. He made practically every tackle. He was doing terrific down field blocking. He was the reason the team won the championship that day.

"After the game all the guys were pounding him on the back. When they were all done the coach went up and said, 'Son, I don't understand. Today you were an All-American. I've never seen you play like that before in four straight years. What happened?' The boy looked up at the coach and said, 'Well Coach, you knew my Dad died, you handed me the telegram. You knew he was blind didn't you?' Coach said, 'Yes, I've seen you lead him around campus many times.' The boy looked up and said, 'Coach, today is the first football game my Dad ever saw me play.' It makes a difference, friends, when those unseeing eyes are watching."

The tape ended, Coach Ravsten stood up and turned the tape

recorder off. He stood there for a few seconds not saying a word and then said; "Last year was a very long year for me as I am sure it was for you. I know this year will be different, but how much different all depends on each of you. We as coaches can help teach the skills, but when you are out there on the field there is nothing we can do. To win this year and go undefeated, as you have all been saying, will take all you have to give and more. Remember this, if you give your best in a game, that is all we or anyone can ask. If you will do that, we will go undefeated. If you don't, we will lose one or two games. Now go home and get a good night's rest and we'll see you in the morning.."

As we stood up and walked out the door there were very few words spoken, for this meeting had an impact on us like none I had ever attended before. Craig Hickman and I got into the car and drove home without much conversation. We were both thinking of what was ahead of us tomorrow and for the succeeding nine weeks. We longed for success!

Lessons Learned:

Trustworthiness and loyalty to your team members was expected and learned as we all experienced the importance of these values in our activity on the playing field.

You had to rely on your teammates to do the job they were responsible to do. One man could not cover two jobs; each one had to do his own. You trusted you were being backed up by the performance of others and they in turn relied on your loyalty to perform your duties so the ultimate objective could be achieved.

Defense of another's character and the building up of individual worth by being loyal to them as they trusted you to do was an axiom that resulted in the formation of bonds that continue to last through time.

Chapter 7

> ***"Treat people as if they were what they ought to be and you help them to become what they are capable of."***
>
> ***Goethe***

Friday morning I got up, had some breakfast and then went over to the school for a very brief practice which consisted of running through some plays and going over the mental aspects of the game. Afterward, I went home with the other guys in the neighborhood, showered and got ready for school. We had "uniforms" for game days that were much different from those we wore on the field at game time. Each team member purchased, at his own expense, a navy blue blazer and tie along with a pair of gray slacks. We wore this outfit on game day to ready our minds to the coming encounter with the opposition as much as to "advertise" for the game that night, as if that were necessary.

There wasn't much to do in the city of Idaho Falls as a teenager on a Friday night other than go to the football game or basketball game. The outdoor theater had closed for the season so you couldn't get a group together and try to sneak into the Motor Vu by backing in the "OUT" gate or putting the guys in the trunk.

One night during the summer I had loaded three buddies into the trunk of our white '57 Chevy Belair and drove up to the ticket window to purchase one ticket for me to get into the movie. Once inside the gate and parked, you would open the trunk and the guys would take their place inside the car to enjoy the movie. Well, imagine my surprise to see my Sunday school teacher who was the manager of the Rio Theater on Broadway in town along with the Motor Vu at the outskirts of town. He was standing there in the kiosk selling tickets! I suppose that someone, usually some kid from school, had come up sick and he had to fill in. There was no place to go since there were cars behind me in line and I couldn't get out of line. I just handed him the money through my rolled-down window hoping he was too busy or aggravated at being thrust into this lowly position to notice who was sitting there in the car purchasing just one ticket. No one ever went to the Motor Vu alone.

Well, he did notice and said, " Hi, Bruce! All by yourself tonight?" You can't lie to your Sunday school teacher so I replied, "No, I got three other guys in the trunk." He laughed and gave me my one ticket and told me to enjoy the movie. To this day I don't know if he figured I was just joking, or if he knew and just let us in anyway, or if he were just nice enough to think that would never occur. We enjoyed the movie, regardless.

It was after the outdoor theater season now and even if there was something else to do, the place to be on football night was at the football game. Besides, going to the game resulted in your being right there when the Victory Dance (whether the team won or lost) started immediately following the game. It was always held in the school gym and provided one of the few organized activities for our age group during our high school careers. Some would go down by the Snake River to watch the submarine races with their girlfriends (assuming you were "lucky" enough to have a set of wheels to get there and a girl to sit beside you). It was that or go to the game, so nearly everyone was at the game.

By and large the stands were full of students whether we "advertised" or not.. In any case, we all looked sharp individually as well as collectively when we all got together as a team. It's intriguing how what you wear affects your attitude and demeanor. The guys all looked sharp, were sharp and hopefully would stay sharp through the game tonight.

I was quite nervous as I went to school. I could feel those

pre-game butterflies coming on again. When I got to school and walked down the hall, I at first felt somewhat conspicuous wearing my blazer and tie, but Coach always said we would go first class and this is how we would dress.

It was good to see the other guys in the hall with their blazers on and groups of us would get together for a minute and talk as time permitted between classes as we moved from room to room through the day. I went over to my Algebra class that was taught in the classroom next to our dressing room and did not pay any attention at all to the current subject matter. I was going over my football assignments in my mind during the entire class. What will I do if the back lines up on my left side, and what will I do if he lines up on the other side, what would be the best set to call in different situations? On and on with a variety of possibilities.

After Algebra I went to Mechanical Drawing, which would finish the day scholastically for me. At 3:00 p.m. all of the football players got to go home and have an early dinner. After a delicious meal prepared by my mother, I went to my room to lie down and rest a bit. Mom always made sure I had something good to eat even though this required her to interrupt a busy schedule of caring for her responsibilities in the home for my dad and seven brothers and sisters, to say nothing of her involvement in the community and church.

Rest was just about impossible because I was so nervous. In fact the butterflies were getting so bad I began to feel nauseated. I got up, called my neighbor and friend, Craig, and asked him if he was ready to go. Mom wished me good luck and said she and Dad would be there for the game that night. I picked up Craig and we drove over to the school. The closer we got, the more nervous I got. We parked the car and walked into the dressing room. We were two of the first ones there, and that same old feeling came back. The last time I had experienced this feeling had been last November when we played our final game of the season. A feeling of excitement, fear and fun all wrapped up into one package was foisted upon me in force.

I dressed slowly, making sure everything was just right, I wanted to be as comfortable as possible, walked over to wrap my ankles and put on a second pair of socks. I was sitting against the wall putting my shoes on, at the same time watching other guys getting dressed. I realized once more how much I loved this. It was great to be part of such a team. You could pick out most of the guys on first string because they knew they would be playing and they seemed to be a bit more quiet, serious and methodical in their actions.

I enjoyed the relationship I had with most of the guys and the support they were. I considered nearly everyone a friend, not just a member of the same team. I thought about this being my first game as a team captain and wondered exactly what would happen. In a few minutes I would be leading the team out onto the field to warm up. I wanted to be a good captain and wondered if I would be able to do the job and get everything done that was asked of me..

As I sat there I noticed Coach come out of his office. He stepped up on a bench and everyone began to quiet down. Coach yelled out, **"Okay guys, let's finish getting dressed. I want the lights off now and you to just sit or lie down and go over your assignment in your head. Think about what you will need to do to get the job done."** The lights went off and it got very quiet. I could see a few still finishing their dressing and whispering as they moved around slowly. I saw Coach standing there looking at all of us. He was silhouetted against the light coming from the coaches' office.

"Couch," Coach called, "come over here." I got up and walked over to Coach. "Get someone to pray," he said. So I walked over to Hickman and asked him if he would be so kind to offer a prayer just before we took the field that evening.

After about five minutes all of the coaches came out of the office. The lights came back on and Coach was standing in the middle of the room and said, "I want you to go out tonight and really take it to them. We are going to show them, the town and the entire state just what kind of a team we have here. I want you to remember the tape we listened to last night. Be honest with yourself, give your all and you will feel good about the way you play. If you will all do this, I promise we will win."

Coach turned to Kenny Barnes, our quarterback, and said, "Kenny, if we win the toss and get the ball first, we'll run a down-and-out deep to Goddard. Let's go for six on the first play. Now let's have prayer and go on out to warm up. The junior varsity is still on the field so go to the back of the stadium and do your warm ups there. Okay, everyone kneel down and let's have prayer."

Coach looked over at me and I looked at Hickman. Craig prayed, asking that we would all do our best and that no one would be hurt. We all got to our feet and slowly began to unleash the emotion and nervous energy we all had. We started to yell and pound each other on the back.

Coach yelled, **"Captains, take them out."**

We both moved to the door and out we went. I noticed a lot of people watching us as we burst from the door and ran out to the back of the stadium to do our warm ups. Kenny and I got everyone lined up and started the side-straddle hop.

There must be some unwritten rule in athletic heaven that says every warm-up session must begin with this exercise. I was amazed at the amount of noise coming out of the team as we chanted, **"Beat I.F. Beat I.F."** I was not sure how the rest of the team felt, but this was as high as I could ever remember being; and from the noise the other guys were making, I thought they felt the same way.

I noticed all the kids at the top of the stadium standing up and looking over the back wall at us warming up. We got the calisthenics done and the J.V.'s were still playing. There was a lot of noise coming from the stadium but it was impossible to tell who was winning. I was afraid if they didn't hurry and finish that first half, we might go flat. I had been yelling so much my voice was about gone already and my throat was getting sore. Just then I saw the J.V.'s coming off the field and heard someone say they had been defeated. As they made their way to the dressing room they looked as dejected as they looked hot and tired.

As we ran onto the field a roar went up from the crowd. The stadium was full. We went through our pre-game drills and even though it was night in Idaho and early fall, it was still warm. Even with evidence to the contrary, I was worried we were not high enough emotionally, so I tried to get everyone even more "fired up."

We finished our drills down near the end zone at the south end of the field and all got together without any coaches and talked for a minute. If one of the team had something to say, we gave him our attention. Don Johnson asked to be heard and said, "Okay guys, this is it. Our goal is 10-0 and this is the first one. Remember this is for Coach. Don't give up. We can do it. We are a team and we support each other. No excuses just make good."

It was the same thing you may hear from a coach at the beginning of such a game, and indeed we had heard the same message, if not words, from our mentor in earlier times. It was different coming from a team member, not that we respected a peer more than a member of the coaching staff, but it showed that individual team members shared the drive that would enable us to meet our goal. We listened to both sources and felt the power of the message.

We all ran to the sideline and gathered around Coach who was standing there with his milk stool in one hand and a soda pop in the other. He looked a bit tired, but we could tell he was really looking forward to this. His outward appearance was not the greatest, far from it, but if you looked into his eyes you could see the same fire and enthusiasm that was there in years past when health was not a concern.

The ref came to the sideline and invited Kenny and me to the center of the field for the coin toss. I could hear our school band and the student body behind me yelling and cheering for us. There was just as much noise coming from the I.F. section. There was lots of energy in the air, and with the immediate result of the J.V. portion of the game hanging there, I could feel the pressure.

I looked up into the crowd and tried to spot my parents, but I knew it would be next to impossible to see them. As we walked to the middle of the field and I again scanned the crowd for my parents, I was a little surprised at the number of people in the stands. There was not a seat to be had on either side of the field and people were standing along the fences surrounding the stadium.

We shook hands with the captains of I.F., which was kind of odd because we knew them so well. We had been teammates a couple of years previous and now we were standing as opponents on the field of battle. We were all ready to play our hearts out to come off victors after 24 minutes of game time-remember, this first "game" of the season was to be for only two quarters, not the full four quarters of 12 minutes each.

The ref said, "Okay I.F., you call the coin in the air when I toss it. As you can see, it is a quarter, one side heads, the other tails." As he tossed it into the air he said, "Okay captain, call it." "Heads," he said as the quarter landed in the grass. The ref bent down, picked up the coin and announced that it was tails. "Okay Skyline, you have won the toss. What would you like to do?"

"We will receive," Kenny said with emphasis on the "will." I almost burst out laughing, probably as a result of the tension rather than despite it. He sounded like Bill Cosby describing the same occasion on one of his tapes that was so popular around that time frame.

"What goal would you like to defend?" the ref asked I.F. They chose to defend the north goal so the ref moved us around indicating which goals were to be defended and gave the signal that we would receive. At that note, a roar went up from our side of the field. We shook hands and ran to the sideline.. Coach had all of us together and called a return left kick-off formation.

The receiving team ran out on the field and got ready. Coach grabbed Kenny's arm and said, "First play, just like we discussed in the locker room." Kenny nodded his head and looked out to the field as the I.F. kicking team got into position. The National Anthem was played as we all stood there with our helmets off and hands over our hearts. The song came to an end, our helmets went back on and we were ready to go.

As I stood there, I could hear the opposing fight songs coming from the bands and the breeze whistling through the ear holes in my helmet if I turned just the right way. The return team huddled for a few seconds and broke, taking their positions just in front of the 40-yard line from sideline to sideline. Our team began to chant, "Go! Go! Go!" As it got louder the adrenaline began to flow even more. I heard the whistle from the ref and watched the I.F. kicker approach the ball. There was an audible "thump" as his right, high-top black football shoe contacted the ball beginning the 1967 football season for us.

The ball soared into the air and 22 boys began running to their designated places on the field. The ball drifted a bit to the left and Rios took it. The return was set up for that side. He began to run right, sucking the defense with him. Our other receiver, Lords, was now running toward him. Rios handed the ball to Lords who was now going full steam as he turned the corner. The line of blockers was in place as he came around the corner. The defense saw what was happening and reacted to it. Suddenly, I saw one of the big I.F. linemen flip high into the air. A roar went up from our side of the field. The poor guy just hadn't seen Struss, one of our offensive linemen. Struss had caught him just right and had really sent him flying.

Lords was still on his feet and it looked like he might go all the way. I.F.. players were lying all over the field. But at the 40-yard line he was forced out of bounds. Darn, he was so close to going all the way! But what a start. We were all excited on the sideline; especially knowing what the first play from scrimmage was going to be. Players switched position as necessary to complete the first string offensive unit and huddled for the first time that season in a real game. They all broke from the huddle in unison and took their positions at the line of scrimmage.

"HUT, HUT, HUT." (There were no audibles and other such theatrics in southern Idaho football in those days. The ball was hiked on the count the quarterback had indicated in the huddle and the count was invariably determined by the guttural, "HUT," spoken by the quarterback just after, **"READY - SET."** Nothing fancy in the least, but it worked great for us.)

Barnes grabbed the ball as it was expertly hiked through the legs of the center on the second **"HUT"** and rolled to his right. Jack Goddard, our super split end, was running down the field through the middle. He hesitated for just a split second after covering about 10 yards from the line of scrimmage and veered to the right sideline and down the field. Jack turned and looked back over his left shoulder just as Kenny threw the ball. Jack was on the Idaho Falls 30-yard line as the ball came down into his outstretched hands. He stumbled and almost fell, but managed to regain his balance just as the defender caught up with him, jumping on his back, forcing him to the ground.

We all went crazy on the sideline! What a fantastic first play! The ref spotted the ball just outside the 20-yard line. The offense huddled quickly; Kenny took the hike and handed off to Revello who plunged forward over right tackle. I was pleased to see him pick up a quick seven yards. Next play we picked up five more and two running plays later we were in for our first score of the year. Lords came in and kicked the extra point for a score of 7-0.

The offense came to the sideline and we all mobbed them,

slapping them on their backs and helmets. We were all very happy and Coach looked pleased. He was having as much fun as we were. The kicking team went out on the field and we all lined up. It was my job to set the kicking team and tell them when to go, so I lined up with my back to the opposing team and set our team behind the 40 yard line. We kicked off and they returned the ball to the 25. I never got to go down on the kick-off because I was to act as a safety valve and make sure no one returned a kick-off. I would have much rather been running downfield, banging bodies and going for the tackle.

We called a quick huddle and I called regular defense. Again, football in those days, especially in the Eastern Idaho Conference was pretty plain-Jane-just down-and-out, in-your-face football with all the finesse of a bunch of kids who loved to play the game as it was meant to be played-as far as we were concerned. We didn't have any high falutin' defensive sets or offensive plays. Coach probably felt we were doing well to run a standard 5-4, 6-3, or goal line defense. And rightly so.

There was a real tension in the huddle on the first play of each game, but today there was some extra concern about I.F.'s fullback. He was big, strong and very fast. He weighed about 220, bench pressed over 300 pounds and ran the 100-yard dash in about 11.4 seconds. We had talked a lot about him and even though he was intimidating, we all knew how to bring him down. We'd found the year before that if you hit him below the knees he came down real easy. But if you hit him above the knees he would break your shoulder. So we put in the shortest guys we could find on defense! Just kidding.

I.F. brought their team up to the line. We were ready and we all looked into each other's eyes. I noticed how wide and active everyone's eyes were and imagined mine were just the same waiting for the first play from scrimmage for the defensive team. The butterflies suddenly disappeared as the ball was hiked. Their quarterback took the ball and turned to his left, the ball was pitched to the fullback and he came to our right side.

I looked over and saw Mike Kyle, who was more worried about the fullback than anyone. Perhaps he had good reason, being five feet, eight inches tall and weighing 150 pounds, going against six feet, two inches and 220 pounds. I began to slide to my right, ready to hit him low and bring him down. All of a sudden, I was on the ground. One of their tailbacks had come across the line from my blind side and knocked me flat. I quickly jumped up just in time to see Mike hit the fullback just below the knees and he came down right at the line of scrimmage.

I ran over to Mike and slapped him on the back. He'd really done a great job. His eyes were as big as apples and he was breathing really hard. He was feeling really good about that tackle as everyone congratulated him in the huddle. He gave a little smile and said, "I'll take him on any day." We all laughed and the tension was banished completely as we broke the huddle to line up on the ball.

I.F. tried two more running plays and managed to pick up a total of four yards. Craig Lords came onto the field for fourth down to receive the punt. We called return right and Lords caught the ball on our 25. We had the blocking wall set up and he got around the corner all the way up to the 50-yard line where he was knocked out of bounds.

Our offense moved out onto the field again and Barnes started right where he left off. He hit Hurley on a down and out to the left for 10 yards. He was mixing running plays perfectly with the passing plays and we were moving at will down the field. The gun went off and the quarter ended. The time was going so fast because we were having so much fun.

We were about to score again when Barnes rolled to his right, looking down field for someone to open up. He was hit really hard from his blind side and went down as he twisted to his left. He wasn't getting up. Coach and the trainers ran out onto the field, but Barnes was just lying there. He was groaning and rolling around a bit and told Coach his knee hurt really badly. As they turned him over he yelled out in pain. Coach knew immediately he was out for the season and yelled to the sideline for some help.

I ran out on the field. Barnes was standing up when I got there and I could see tears in his eyes and the pain on his face. He put one arm around my shoulder and one around Coach Jacoby's and we headed off the field. I knew I might have to go back in the game in just a few minutes so I asked another player to come over and help Barnes into the locker room.

Kim Hall, our second-string quarterback, was on the field now and I knew how he must have been feeling. Just one year earlier I had had the same experience. He was a junior and had practiced hard, but he didn't have the polish or the experience Barnes had. On the first play from scrimmage we got smothered on a running play. On the second, we fumbled and I.F. recovered. It was an inauspicious start for Hall even though it was by no means his fault. Sometimes when something like what had just happened to Barnes occurs, it takes the wind out of your sails and causes some relapse and doubt to creep in. That's what had just happened to us and we now had to shake it off and play like we knew we could. We had to demonstrate what we were capable of.

The defense went onto the field and we did the job by stopping them after just two series of downs. They punted to Craig Lords and we set the fence again and gave the ball back to the offense with good field position. On the first play we fumbled. However, this time we managed to recover. But two plays later we fumbled once more and lost the ball. Suddenly this game had turned from a possible rout into a very exciting game-for the fans and the I.F.. squad!

On the second defensive play of the series, Leonard, our all-state defensive end, came up to me limping and asked me to call time out. The I.F. fullback had hit him hard with a crack back block right at the knees. The rule at that time was that an offensive player could block an opposing player below the waist if you were within a certain distance from the line of scrimmage. You had to keep an eye out for these kind of blocks, called "crack back" blocks because they were so dangerous. In today's game they are strictly forbidden for the damage they can cause to the one being blocked. Now all blocks must be from the front and above the waist.

Leonard limped tenderly off the field. His replacement, Crockett, came out on the field and after a few plays we forced them to punt again. When I got to the sideline I found they had taken Leonard to the hospital with Barnes.

The game went on with our offense unable to move the ball without the confidence of their leader, Barnes. I.F.'s offense was likewise unable to move the ball against our defense, thankfully. The game ended 7-0. Not much of an offensive showing. We had expected to continue the success of the first few offensive series, but that evaporated with the injury to Kenny Barnes. As we walked off the field after the game, we all felt rather discouraged despite the win. Kenny was through for the year, we were all sure of that. How could we ever go undefeated with the offensive showing we had displayed tonight? But we felt good about the defense.

I walked into the dressing room and began to strip the battle togs from my body. The coaches were in the office talking and there was a real feeling of concern among all of us. What would happen in the next few weeks? Coach stood up on a bench and said, "All right guys, everyone quiet. Barnes and Leonard have been taken to the hospital and will both be operated on tomorrow. They both suffered severe trauma to a knee and we have lost something, but it is going to make us stronger. It's very interesting. You guys know, as I do, they were the only two guys who didn't work out hard this last summer in the conditioning program. They felt weight training was not important. As you can see, skill is not all that is required to be successful. You have to be totally prepared.

"Now we have those who are 100% dedicated. I know you are all concerned about them, as am I, but they're okay. We have some rebuilding to do because they were very good talent-wise, if not strength-wise. But believe me, we are going to work hard with Kim this week. He has the ability to do the job and can step in and do every bit as good a job as Kenny. He just needs some more experience. The main reason Kenny started over Kim was because Kenny was a senior. I have been impressed with Kim and his abilities and we will fine-tune those abilities this next week. We had a good game and I am especially pleased with the defense. We shut them down completely; they couldn't do a thing. The offense looked good at times until Kenny got hurt, then our timing was thrown off and we couldn't hand off the ball or anything else without dropping it. We can easily correct that with practice---it's not a problem.

"I am proud of you boys. You looked good tonight. You look better than any team I have ever coached and we can do what you have all been talking about.. That 10-0 goal is obtainable, but you will have to continue working and playing hard. Now get dressed and I'll see all of you Monday morning one half hour early, because we have a lot of work to do."

I turned in my game uniform and took a long, hot shower. That was another benefit of being a football player. You could luxuriate in the shower as long as you bloody-well liked. In my family of eight kids, you got wet in the shower, turned it off, soaped up, then turned the water back on and rinsed off. You might get a total of two minutes of water on your body, max. Otherwise, there would be no hot water for the later washees in the family. And believe me, if one of those later washees didn't get some warm water at least, you were in for it. There was no sneaking any "hour showers" at our house!

I washed off the dried blood on my hand. Someone had stepped on my hand and torn a chunk of flesh from my knuckle.

It hadn't hurt until the water cleaned it out, but I could really tell it was there now. I dressed and walked out the door with Mike Sheffer, one of our defensive tackles.

A few of us got together and went over to the Westbank Restaurant to get something to eat. It was the place to go after a game if you didn't go to the Victory Dance because that was where all the unattached girls went. Tonight we ignored those sweet young things because we had more important matters on our minds. We were all talking about what had happened and wondering if Kim could step in and take Kenny's place. Was it still possible to go undefeated? Could we really do it?

As we sat there eating our hamburgers and talking, Hickman said, "Hey guys, look what Coach has done. He is supposed to be dead and sometimes, watching him, I think he may drop over at any moment. He scares the bejeebies out of me when he gets up on the bench in the dressing room and teeters so precariously there giving us our pep talks and instructions. But he's there every day. He's not giving up and neither can we. We have to keep going. It just means we'll have to do a better job, that's all."

I crawled into bed that night concerned about what would happen in the next few weeks but confident that we could meet our goal.

Lessons Learned:

Knowing that what people think of themselves, and if that thought process is positive in nature and the person really believes what is being attempted can really be achieved, there are no limits to what can be accomplished.

A good self-image is paramount to success. To drag around an anchor of self doubt or worth will impede progress more than any other influence, real or imagined.

By recognizing the value, abilities and talents that individuals have within and then treating them as the invaluable assets they are to themselves and others, will build a better world for all.

Potential is a terrible word. It belies the fact that everyone has the ability to rise above whatever supposed barrier there is out there defined as "potential." There are no limits to the greatness that an individual can rise to if treated like the offspring of a superior being, which we all are.

Chapter 8

"I always turn to the sports pages first, which record people's accomplishments, the front page is nothing but man's failures."
Chief Justice Earl Warren

On Monday morning I got up and ate breakfast with my family. Breakfast and dinner were always a time for family and we always ate together. With 10 around the table at meal times it was often a circus of sorts. Just getting everyone at the table for family prayer and the blessing of the food was especially challenging in the mornings. Mom was always up early and had a great meal on the table to start the day off right, but we kids were not what you'd describe as "morning people."

I had it down as to exactly how much time it would take (minimum) to get up, get ready for the day in the bathroom and get to the table, eat and get out the door to meet the obligations of the day. Today they talk of "just-in-time deliveries" to minimize inventory costs in the manufacturing process. Well, I had the same concept down as it related to minimizing the time I had to spend in any one day with my eyes open and out of bed. My brothers and sisters had the same basic plan in one form or another although we didn't know that we were years ahead of our time in regard to this economic principle we had developed for our everyday lives.

It all worked great if it worked, this min-time plan of mine. But if one of the siblings got out of sync in the morning, it was chaos. Most of the kids shared one bathroom while my parents had the one on the upper floor to themselves. They could never understand what all the travail was about when one unthinking son or daughter would stay more than the allotted time in the "ready room" in the morning or got in there out of turn, locking the door and throwing the rest of the schedule out the window. When Dad came down for breakfast and we were called, it was expected that we be in our places in short order. Most times we had it down, but there were those times when things went awry.

The actual eating process was another thing. My dad would sit at one end of the table and Mom at the other with four kids on either side between them. Everyone had an assigned seat and no one even thought about sitting anywhere but where you had sat for your short history in this world. I never knew the reason for this arrangement---was it because my Dad (along with my older brother, Rob) could not tell my twin sisters apart and had to have them in specific seats to properly address them? Or was it just for orderliness and efficiency? In any case, it worked well and everyone got fed properly.

In partial answer to the first postulation above and its possible debunking for the reason for the seating arrangement, the twins soon learned to respond to whichever name they were addressed by-Julie or Joanne. They were like all identical twins in the 7th sense (someone already took the 6th sense) they shared. They could always feel what the other was feeling (even when separated later in life by 100's of miles!), or know the thoughts that were being conjured up in the other twin's mind. I guess that they would receive the audible signal of the name being spoken by Dad or Rob and would instantly process this input and decide that even if they were being addressed inaccurately, they would respond appropriately. This worked even if the both of them were close together and could both hear the person speaking. It was uncanny. I'm certain that there are those behavioral scientists out there scoffing at this little bit of psychological phenomenon and shaking their heads in abject horror. Go ahead. I saw it and know it happened.

At meal times we did learn the meaning of, "He/She who hesitates is lost." If you did not dive in and get your share of the food when presented after the blessing on the food, you may go a little hungry-at least until the popcorn was popped that night, every night.

My dad learned early on how to insure he did not miss out on his fair share. He would always be asking you some question, distracting your attention or asking you to get something from the cupboard for him. This only affected me after my brother moved on to college and I took his place next to Dad. Only then did I realize where the look of consternation on Rob's face came from so often as he would return his attention to the meal before him and find the roll that he had just finished slathering with raspberry jam previous to the interruption had disappeared, or the perfect piece of chicken he had just selected from the platter had somehow ended up on Dad's plate. Dad was also always trying to slip some nasty thing like sauerkraut on your plate or put some foul sauce on your meat. Meal times were a lot of fun at our house.

This particular morning went without a hitch and we all ate breakfast and went our separate ways to work or school or in my case, to practice. I dressed and went out to the practice field. A few minutes later Coach came out with his milk stool and yelled, **"Okay, let's get going."** We all lined up for warm-up drills. Because of the injury to Kenny Barnes, I was the only captain now, so I led everyone through the warm-ups, beginning with, you got it, side straddle hops.

After stretching and getting the blood flowing, we all gathered together for award time. Gale Struss got a star to put on his helmet for the fantastic block on the opening kick-off. A few other stars were given out and Coach talked about Kenny and Craig being out for the year and how adjustments would be made for us to get the job done.

Coach was standing in front of us and said, "I told all of you Friday night Kenny is a great quarterback, one of the best I have seen. But the main reason he started ahead of Kim was because he was a senior and Kim was a junior.. Now Kim lacks the experience, but he will get a lot of that this week in practice."

Coach then went on to build up Larry Crockett who had taken Craig Leonard's place. Coach always made sure he built you up in front of other people as well as one-on-one. On the other hand, he also tried to keep it private if he had to discipline you, except when you messed up on the football field. Then he would yell and the entire world would know. But that was part of the game. There was never an instance where you were subjected to disrespect, however. Coach was always a gentleman and rarely, if ever, used profanity or crass behavior. We learned great principles of discipline and respect from these sessions.

Practice started for the week with a great deal of time being given to prepare Kim and Larry for their new found positions. Since I had been through the same experience the year before, I knew the pressure they had on them as the entire team watched and wondered if they could measure up. Coach was constantly building them up as they made mistakes, giving them the self-confidence they needed to face different situations. They would need to react and think quickly to do the job they each had to do.

We were preparing for the Pocatello game coming up on Friday night. The defense went over what Pocatello would be running at us and the offense went over their game plan. By the end of the week, we all felt comfortable about the upcoming game as a result of the week's practice sessions but recognized that practice is one thing and the actual game can be much different. We were "confident" but there was still a twinge of doubt as to whether Kim and Larry would be able to do the job.

On Friday, we all wore our blazers to school and then went home to eat about 3:00 p.m. This would be our first real test since we would be playing a full four quarters instead of the two quarters we played against Idaho Falls. Last year Pocatello kicked our collective tails in the first game of the year. Would they do it again? Were we ready?

We went out on the field and did some preliminary warming up and then went back in to finish getting ready, both mentally and in regard to equipment. After we were all dressed, the school principal came into the locker room through the back door and talked to us about Coach and what a great person he was. The principal kept looking over his shoulder to where Coach was in his office, along with the other coaches. As it appeared they were about to come out, the principal left without them seeing him.

While we appreciated what was being said about our mentor, we probably knew better than most what kind of man he was and how much we relied on him to motivate and help us to become the kind of young men he knew we could be. But it was great to see and hear others recognize the excellent job he was doing in the effort in which Coach was engaged. It brought to mind the question, would these things be happening if Coach were not in the physical condition he was? He treated us no differently this season than last or the one before. He was consistent.

These plaudits were probably coming due to the health situation in which Coach found himself. He taught us to be consistent in our approach to all we did. It would be well if all of us could learn this lesson and not wait to build up or pat someone on the back when it is obvious they are in need of it, but do some "preventative maintenance" on people long before the need is evident and obvious. There is no criticism in this observation, only a reinforcement of the need for us to be the kind of individual that we should be in all things, at all times and in all places-as Coach taught us on the field, in the classroom and in our other associations with him.

Coach came out, talked to us and gave us the final tone-up speech. He told us we were all ready and would be able to win this game if we would just perform to our capabilities and not let mental mistakes occur. He reinforced once again the fact that Kim was ready to guide the offense to victory. With a roar of determination we all went out onto the field.

I led everyone out and we met in the south end zone and we talked to each other as a team. "No excuses." "Just do the job and make good." "Face up to responsibilities and give 100 percent." There was never a script or order for these brief gatherings. Whoever had something on his mind would voice it in whatever terms he wanted. We all understood and appreciated the emotion and commitment that was voiced under the goal posts at those times and it helped us to be even more determined to do the job right and accept whatever may come-as long as it was victory!

We lined up on the field to kick-off because we lost the toss. The National Anthem was played as we all stood there. As the song ended our helmets went on and we could hear the rumble from the crowd. I faced my team and set them for the kick-off. As I heard the whistle, I put my arms out to the side and yelled, **"Set."** Craig Lords, our kicker, came to the ball and I dropped my arms and shouted, **"Go!"** It was a good kick and I turned to my left to watch when, **SMACK**, everything went black.

One of the Pocatello guys had zeroed in on me, hit me from the blind side and I went down, out cold. I woke up with an ammonia capsule under my nose. Boy, that stuff was terrible! I thought it would take the top of my head right off! Coach Ravsten, Jacoby and Rasmussen were standing over me. Coach Ravsten knelt down and looked right into my eyes. I really felt funny, a bit sick to my stomach and my head hurt.

Coach was laughing as he said, "You're okay, but boy did you ever take a good shot."

I was standing now and zigzagged my way to the sideline with Coach holding on to my arm. I was not really sure where I was for a few minutes. But it wasn't long before I wanted to get back into the game, so I convinced Coach I was fine and he let me into the game.

Pocatello was moving the ball and had already made two first downs. Even though I'd convinced Coach I was okay, it took six plays before I really remembered what I was supposed to be doing and who I was to key off. That, in part, resulted in another first down. We stopped them on the next series and they punted.

It was a good first quarter with us scoring three times and stopping their offense completely. In the second quarter our offense slowed down and only scored once. Pocatello just couldn't seem to move the ball against us at all and we were having a great time on defense. We went into the locker room elated at half time. Kim had really done a fantastic job leading the offense and the guys on the offensive squad had supported his efforts in superb fashion; in fact, we all had done a super job so far.

We received the second half kick-off and scored the first time down the field. The score was now 30-0, but we had not made an extra point yet. We had missed the kick after each touchdown. I think I mentioned before that being a kicker was not a high priority for a young man going out for football. Who wanted to kick a dang ball when you could race through a hole in the defensive line and wend your way to the goal line, fending off tacklers and demonstrating your speed and dexterity? We had a kicker but it was obvious we were going to have to work on the kicking game next week.

Poky continued to try to move the ball, but just couldn't get it on track. Our defense was just too good and fast. We shut them right down. At the beginning of the fourth quarter we scored again, finally got the extra point and the score moved to 37-0. Second string now moved into the game to give them some experience and the Indians a chance to save some face-what was left! The subs played a good part of the fourth quarter.

With about two minutes left in the game Coach let first string defense go back in. Pocatello had a little running back that was fast and strong. He seemed like a really nice kid and was very quick at changing directions. They handed off to him and he ran right at Jamie Bauchman, our defensive left tackle. Jamie smacked him good, right at the line of scrimmage and I could hear the running back moaning and yelling. He was rolling around on the ground saying, **"Oh Ref, it hurts! Oh Ref, it hurts!"**

Time out was called. Fred Finlayson was standing there gawking at him with his helmet pushed up on his head, only half on, while the rest of us were in the huddle. The look on Fred's face was enough to make you laugh. Jamie reached back from the huddle and grabbed Fred's jersey, jerking him into the huddle.

"Get back here Fred," Jamie said. We all got a really good laugh out of it.

Then Fred looked up and saw 18 seconds left on the clock, threw his arms around me and said, "We're going to win, Couch."

We all cracked up. Sometimes it takes more time for some things to sink in for some guys. After last season, who could blame that slow recognition time? Usually, we were on the other side of this kind score.

"Brilliant," Sheffer said, "Real brilliant." The gun went off and we all headed for the locker room.

In the dressing room Coach walked around, shook everyone's hand and told us what a good job we had done. It felt good, really good. We now had the confidence to press on. He told us to get some good rest over the weekend and to be at practice early on Monday.

We were all very happy as we walked to the gym for the Victory Dance. My head still hurt and I still felt a little sick to my stomach. That hit on the kick-off was the worst I had ever taken. I would keep my eyes open from then on and not be so lacksidasical during the kick-off thinking that I would not need to worry for a few seconds, anyway-hey, I was the safety valve! You shouldn't get hit that fast, and I could guarantee you I would not get caught unawares like that again. I still couldn't remember the first few minutes of the game. As I sat there watching the dance with Jamie Bauchman and talking about the game, I wondered how Coach was feeling and what he was doing right then.

On Monday morning we met out on the practice field for a short team meeting. Coach was sitting on his three-legged stool and was very happy after our very decisive win Friday night. Everyone was joking and having a good time. There was a good feeling being shared by all. This was a real team. We were all acting together, so different from last year. Coach handed out the awards, stickers to put on our helmets. We got them for touchdowns, good blocks, super tackles, an interception or special effort of some kind.

Then Coach stood up to give us a preview of our next game, Minico. "Minico beat us last year," Coach began. "They beat us 20-13 and we need to even the score this Friday night. And from what I saw last Friday night, we have a great shot at doing just that and having a good time doing it! But remember, we have a lot of work to do this week to get ready. I'm very proud of you boys.

"You all showed me some real character and dedication the past two games. Above all, I want you to learn and know the meaning of the word character, make it a part of you and use it all of your life. I don't want you to ever forget the lessons you learn while we are together. Every athletic contest is a large section of life packed into a few hours of struggle and adversity.

"In a game you must, if you're to be successful, conquer all the strong emotions such as fear, anger, self love, jealousy and frustration. Athletics is life condensed. All we are not, is stripped away. Self-conquest is the greatest victory.

"Remember this all of your life. Remember this the next time you are in a game. No person has, or ever will be, consistently successful until he has conquered himself. Give 100 percent of what you have and you will feel good, win or lose. Cheat and you will feel bad."

Coach looked tired all of a sudden and sat down on his stool. No one said a word. We all sat there for a few seconds thinking about what we had just heard. I looked around at the other players and saw the effect Coach had on all of us.

Coach stood up again and said, "Okay, let's get started on drills."

We started off with the defense learning what Minico would throw at us and what we should look for. We did this on Monday, Tuesday and Wednesday without much practice on fundamentals.

Wednesday was always a fun day because it was "Challenge Box" day. Number three man could challenge number two, and number two could challenge number one. And it usually worked out that number two would challenge number one every week. The two guys involved would face each other. Each had a little box laid out on the grass that he had to stay in.

The box was made by putting lime from the yardage and sideline marker supply in lines to make a rectangular box that measured about five feet deep and four feet wide. The two boxes met at the line of scrimmage. Each player would then get down in their stance facing the other with the respective coaches and the rest of the team watching. The feeling that was generated around the challenge boxes is impossible to describe, there was so much intensity and excitement as the team began to clap and yell. The noise from players watching and players in the arena, punishing each other, would at times become almost deafening. Each team, defense and offense as well as special teams, would have their members and responsible coaches gathered to see which player would start the next game. Coach would blow the whistle and the object was to run right through your opponent and throw him out of his box. The best three out of five won. It was always mean and emotions ran very high with the cheering and encouragement from everyone.

Bob Nelson, one of the outside linebackers, and I were standing there cheering everyone on when he said to me, "That really looks like fun Couch. Come on, let's get in there." Up until that time (which I was perfectly comfortable with) there had been few challenges to the first string defensive squad members so we hadn't had the "opportunity" to get in the box yet this year. We were both on first string in different positions and only decided to get into it for the fun of it.

I looked at him and said, "Yeah, why not?" There were already three groups going at it so the two of us got down into a box that was empty. I got down into a three-point stance and waited for the whistle as a bunch of the defensive players gathered around us and began to cheer us on. I looked across the line at Bob and thought, "I need to get lower than he is. We are about the same size and if I can get my shoulder into his chest it will all be over."

The whistle blew! My facemask was about two inches off the ground, but so was his---we had read each other's mind. There was a loud crash as our helmets collided. Our feet were churning with grass and dirt flying from behind both of us. Coach looked over to see what all the commotion and noise was. The first one was a stalemate and we both got back into our stances ready for the next whistle.

Suddenly, I felt a sharp kick in the rear end. "You two dumb farts-get out of there! That's just what we need now is to get one or both of you hurt." Coach Ravsten was standing there with a look of disdain on his face. Our challenge box experience came to an abrupt and ignominious end.

However, the drill "Bull in the Ring" was played about once each week and I thought it was tougher than the challenge boxes anyway.

On Friday morning we got ready to play Minico and all came dressed in our blue blazers ready to travel. Along the way we stopped at a restaurant to eat.. Jamie Bauchman was Catholic and got off the bus in front of me. As we walked into the restaurant, he got Coach off to the side and said, "Coach, today is Friday and as a Catholic I'm not supposed to eat any meat." After a moment of contemplation he continued, "But I know that is what you have ordered for everyone so I'll just go ahead and have the meat with the rest of the guys."

Coach stopped for a minute, looked at Jamie sternly and said, "Jamie, it's your religious belief that you don't eat meat on Friday and you should eat fish, right? So stand up for what you believe. You will eat fish. Always stand up for what you believe. Have the guts to show your convictions. You eat fish and the rest of us will eat beef."

I knew there were some other Catholic guys on the team, but they didn't have the fortitude that Jamie had. I sat down by Jamie and looked at him and said, "Boy, looked like Coach kind of got on you there."

"Yeah, but he taught me a lesson, a lesson I guess I will never forget," Jamie replied.

After finishing our lunch, we got back on the bus and continued to Minico. We walked in, found our dressing room and then walked around the halls of the school for a while. It was fun to see the signs hanging in the halls about how they were going to grind us into the dirt. Some of the kids were still walking around in the halls and they gave us a few wisecrack comments as we walked by. Soon we went back to the visiting team's dressing room to begin our preparations for the evening's game.

This was always a special time, as everyone would become very serious and contemplative. We dressed, taped our ankles, knees, shoulder or whatever happened to be a weak spot on our bodies. We then laid down on the floor and it was always a very quiet time while everyone thought of his assignment. The lights would go out and for a few minutes we would just sit or lay all over the locker room with hardly a word being spoken. If anything was said, it was in a whisper.

It was another good game for us and after returning home, I picked up the paper on Sunday to read the account of the game.

"The Skyline Grizzlies started the game by kicking off to the Spartans. Dennis Hobbes returned the ball to the 24-yard line, but they failed to move the ball any great length the first three downs so they were forced to punt to the Grizzlies. Skyline took over on the Minico 45-yard line. A long pass moved the ball to the seven-yard line where Gary Revello took the ball in. Craig Lords kicked the extra point.

"After a couple of unsuccessful offensive series by Minico and resultant punts, Skyline took over on the Minico 20-yard line to start the second quarter and didn't waste any time pushing it up to the one-yard line where they then carried it in for another six points. The extra point was made and the score moved to 14-0.

"Minico then took the ball on their 20-yard line, but the Grizzlies pushed the Spartans back to their own eight-yard line where they were forced to punt on fourth down. Revello returned the punt 45 yards to put the Grizzlies on the Minico four-yard line. Minico stopped the powerful Grizzly offense and took over on the two-yard line, but again were forced to punt. The Grizzlies moved the ball to the 24-yard line of Minico and on the next play moved to the nine-yard line for a first down. On the next play they moved into the end zone for another six points. The conversion was blocked, making the score at the end of the first half 20-0.

"Skyline kicked to Minico to start the second half having won the toss at the beginning of the game but choosing to defend the upwind goal due to the velocity of the wind at game time. [Did I tell you the wind blew in Idaho?] The Spartans took the ball on their own 24-yard line but were forced to punt on fourth down giving Skyline the ball on the Minico 36-yard line. Minico turned strong defensively and regained possession on their own 35. Bruce Couch intercepted a Spartan pass and pushed his way through to the Minico 31-yard line. A 22-yard pass to Jack Goddard placed the Grizzlies on the nine-yard line where Kim Hall passed to Bill Thomas for the touchdown. The conversion attempt failed.

"The only score in the fourth quarter took place when Lords

returned a Minico punt for 40 yards and a touchdown. The game ended with Minico having possession on the Skyline 20-yard line."

As I sat there on the couch (which, by the way we called a "divan" in our house, another form of divine which I'm sure is the root for our surname. It reminds me of the times we would go to my Uncle John and Aunt Grace's house. Should you have to use "the facilities" it was the better part of valor not to refer to them as the "John." You could call them the "Grace," but never the "John" as ordered by Uncle John-who else?) after reading the account of the game in the paper, I thought it was really quite an easy game.

We were not challenged at any point and did pretty much whatever we wanted to. The second and third string players got to play a great deal and we all gained some confidence, hopefully not too much confidence! There was always the danger of becoming over confidant.

Lessons Learned:

To accept responsibility for one's actions rather than blame others or expect someone else to come along and save you from the situation you find yourself in is too often a principle that is lost today.

It seems that too many individuals have not the courage to accept the position they find themselves in by their own design or not. They run to find an excuse or reason why, rather than expend that same energy on solving the crisis or extricating themselves from the situation.

Individual responsibility is an all too rare commodity these days and one that needs to be learned and fostered again. Change and progress will only happen on an individual basis.

The acceptance of responsibility is also an elevating process. There is always one standing by to help, if we but do all that we can to move to a higher plane and work hard to change our own circumstances.

Chapter 9

"A hero is one who knows how to hang on one minute longer."

Norwegian Proverb

On Monday we had our usual awards ceremony for excellent play in the Minico game. We were all feeling very good about ourselves and the team. So far in three games, no one had scored a point on us, yet we had scored 82 points against our opponents. Kim had done a great job of stepping in to take Kenny's place. We had long since stopped worrying about his ability to lead the offense and score points.

After the awards were presented, Coach grabbed Craig Lords and told him to practice kicking extra points an extra half-hour each day this week. Even though an extra point had not even come close to making a difference in a game, we had missed too many and you never knew, someday it could make the difference in a game.

Our next opponent would be Highland High School, another high school 50 miles down I-15 in Pocatello. Coach told us they were big, with a fullback who weighed 220 pounds and was quite nimble on his feet to add to the threat of his bulk. That size in the backfield was an anomaly in the Eastern Idaho Conference. Most running backs we faced did not tip the scale at anything over 200 pounds, so someone of that description was a bit intimidating. We had faced the same basic uniform size with the I.F. fullback, but the big difference was that this Highland Ram ran close to the ground and was very hard to bring down by all accounts.

We spent the week learning what they did, how they did it, and how we should react to the different play sets we would most probably see from both the offensive and defensive perspective.

We felt the game would be very much the same as the Pocatello game. However, this game would be a bit different in one aspect because it would be held during the afternoon rather than at night. Junior Varsity games were generally played during the daylight hours, usually on a Thursday afternoon after school, but varsity contests were nearly always played on Friday nights.

We worked hard during the week and felt quite confident we would be able to perform competently, do the job and we'd have no problem with Highland as had been the case with the our first three opponents.

Friday morning I got up and ate a good breakfast, put on my blue blazer and tie, and asked my mother to take Craig, Bob, Kim and me over to the dressing room where we would catch the bus for Pocatello and the conflict of the afternoon. As we got out of the car at school, Mom told me she and Dad would be down for the game. She told us she was proud of all of us and the job we were doing for Coach.

As we rounded the corner of the field house, we saw a big Greyhound bus waiting so we ran into the dressing room and got our gear. (No yellow fellow for this trip even though it was only 50 miles down the road---someone was watching out for us!). We walked out to the bus as the cheerleaders were putting a sign on the fence next to the bus and a lot of people were mingling around talking. We put our equipment in the luggage compartment under the bus and got on with the rest of the team.

None of the coaches were on the bus yet, but all of the players were. A man stepped onto the bus and closed the door. It was a nice, sunny, warm day and we had the windows open, talking to some of the girls from the Pep Club who had come to wish us luck. This stranger stood at the front of the bus and said, "Boys, my name is Doctor Smith. I would like you to close the windows so you won't be distracted and listen to what I have to say for a moment."

There was a seriousness and sense of foreboding that

permeated the entire bus and caused us all to sit up and take notice.

"I am Coach Ravsten's doctor and I would like to talk to you for a minute about what Coach is going through. Sometimes you think you are putting out a lot to play football; that you sacrifice, you give your all. You lift weights and hurt, you run, you get cut and bruised, you hurt your shins, ankles and hands. Sometimes you get hit in the head and it hurts, and once in awhile you get knocked out. It's not easy. Football is a difficult sport. It's a demanding sport, but a very good sport.

"Well, I would just like to tell you about your coach and what he faces each and every day. Coach Ravsten has to take drugs to keep the cancer from growing and I know you all know about that. This drug will not allow his body to heal itself if he gets a cut. He has very little saliva in his mouth, that is why you always see him with a cup of ice or a bottle of pop in his hands.

"He is in a great deal of pain most of the time, but we try to eliminate as much of that pain as we can. You boys need to know the courage and dedication this man is showing for you, because this is what keeps him alive. He has a goal, a goal he has had for many years, the dream of coaching a team to an undefeated season.

"He loves you boys; he worries about you, not only on the football field, but also off. He wonders what kind of men you will become and is very concerned about his impact upon your lives. He talks about teaching correct principles that will help you on the football field, yes, but is more concerned about those principles that will help you all through your life.

"This is his goal in coaching, to help you grow and be a benefit to society. He doesn't want any of you to be freeloaders. He teaches you to carry your own weight and make sure you always put more back in than you take out. If you will put forth one-tenth the effort he has to give every day, you will easily win this game today, and any other for that matter. I won't be able to be to the game. But believe me, boys, I will be listening on the radio and I'll be pulling for you. I'll be pulling for Coach because I know how much this means to him. Work hard and give him a great victory. Good luck!!!"

He stood there for a few seconds looking at us. It was very quiet and very solemn. Not a word was spoken. I looked out the window and saw the cheerleaders chattering and laughing. They didn't realize what was taking place inside the bus. There were deep feelings being passed from boy to boy along with a deep concern and dedication to a man we all called "Coach."

The doctor turned and got off the bus just as the coaches came around the corner of the building. Not a word was spoken as the coaches got on the bus. It was still very quiet and Coach Ravsten was standing at the front looking at us, wondering what had brought on this solemnity rather than the raccuousness that usually accompanied such a gathering of young men.

He didn't waste much time on this contemplation, but said, "Okay boys, let's get this buggy on the road and have some fun!" He turned and gingerly sat in his seat at the front of the bus. The bus started and the girls began to shout and cheer (they were cheerleaders and members of the Pep Club, after all) jumping up and down and giving us all the encouragement they could as we drove out of the parking lot and on down the street.

Members of each team, offense and defense, naturally gravitated to sitting together and we talked about our assignments on the way down and how we could help each other. The day was just beautiful, in fact, a little too warm for us. It felt more like summer than the middle of autumn with winter fast approaching. As we drove down I-15 you could scc that the harvesting was complete and the fields were bare. The foothills to the east were now covered in the reds, yellows and oranges mingled amongst the emerald green backdrop provided by the lodgepole pines, spruce trees and other evergreens signaling that fall was in full swing and winter was about to descend upon us-but not this day.

It was a beautiful fall day in the neighborhood!

We arrived and unloaded our gear. I walked into the dressing room with Hickman and we found a couple of lockers in which to put our clothes. I kept thinking about the doctor and what he had told us. I felt so sorry for Coach, more so now than ever before, because I hadn't realized what he was really going through. I felt so sorry for his wife and children because I now felt for sure that he wouldn't live much longer. The question was how long would he live? It just wasn't fair that such a good man, who did so much good for the young people he worked with, should have to die so young and when he was doing so much for so many.

And it just wasn't for the young people and the effect he had on them. You could see the love and respect that adults had for him, too. He wasn't just "Coach" or "Mr. Ravsten" on the playing fields, in the hallways or classrooms of school. Coach was "Vernon" to many a friend and associate.

There was many an evening when the doorbell would ring "late" at night at a friend's house and there would be Vernon, standing at the door, with and invitation to go out and get an ice cream. "Late" because it was invariably after 9-9:30 p.m. after he had completed his "homework" of grading papers and preparing for the new day tomorrow. "Late," too, because the sidewalks were rolled up in Idaho Falls beginning about 10 p.m., so it was normally an adventure to go out on the town to find an ice cream at that "late" hour for Vernon and his friends.

Coach was also actively engaged in service to those of his local church congregation. During the time my brother Rob was in school, he was the youth leader of boys ages 16-19 on Sunday mornings and provided them with religious instruction. With his secular position and the normal instincts of the young men he was responsible for during that hour on Sabbath mornings, it would have been easy for the discussion to revolve around football, wrestling or sports in general. But "Brother" Ravsten would have none of that and made sure the boys received the moral teachings they were so in need of, especially at that time of life.

He also later served as the president of the group of men (Elders Quorum) in his church and was responsible to the congregational leader (Bishop) for their lives and the lives of their families. As such, he was intimately involved with the challenges and trials that many in the church experienced and they would come to him for assistance and advice. Many an hour would be spent in service to others leading his group in volunteer labor at the church farm, assisting a young, single mother in need, counseling a quorum member in time of trial or adversity or enjoying a social event with the men of his group and their families.

He was a very giving and loving man and was always showing the proper example to anyone who had the privilege of associating with him. Why was it? Why did such a good man have to suffer and see his family go through the terrible times they were facing?

I couldn't answer that.

I unpacked my football gear and spread it out on the floor, as much for a distraction as for the fact that we would soon have to be dressed and ready for the game.

The dressing room again became very quiet with just a few guys talking in low voices. I knew the doctor's comments had had a great impact upon all of us. I noticed how cold my feet and hands were even with the warmth of the day as I finished dressing and lay down on the floor. I looked over and saw Coach Jacoby joking with a couple of guys as he taped their ankles. Coach Ravsten was talking with Hall and Goddard as they were being taped. He was reminding them of the game plans we had gone over time and time again during practice.

Later, Coach came out of the visiting coaches' room and said, "Okay boys, sit down and think about your assignment today. Let's get ourselves mentally prepared for the game."

It's amazing what your environment, expectations or habit patterns have on you. I found it difficult, lying there, to think about the game because most of our games were at night and it was dark in the locker room at this point of our immediate preparation before a game. Now the sun was coming through the windows and it was nowhere near dark at all. It just didn't feel like game time.

After a few minutes Coach called me over and told me to pick someone for prayer. The room was very quiet now with guys lying all over the floor and sitting in corners or on benches with various expressions on their faces, as they were lost in thought. As I looked around the room, I wondered how many were thinking about what we would normally be thinking about at this point-the upcoming game-and how many were thinking about Dr. Smith's comments from earlier that pleasant autumn afternoon.

Coach stepped out of the coaches' room again and said, "Get up guys, and gather 'round here." Once everyone had surrounded him, he continued. "We have a few minutes and I would like to tell you a story about a small college team in Illinois that was playing a larger Minnesota team. The Minnesota team was favored by 35 points that day. In the Illinois locker room, the team attitude showed they were the underdogs. But there was one guy in there who started walking around grabbing guys by the jersey, pulling them up to him, looking them right in the eyes and saying with a snarl, 'We can beat them! We can beat them! You've got to believe we can beat them!'

"Well, they went out on that field and beat Minnesota by 21 points. Now, today we are not the underdogs and we should win, but sometimes that can be more dangerous than anything else. You've got to believe in yourself. Continue to believe that you can do it, even if things get tough! Now let's kneel down and have prayer."

Those were the days when the good, old American values

that underpinned the foundation of the United States were not under attack by the foolish rabble rousers that have nothing better to do today than take away the freedoms that America was founded to protect. You could have a prayer in those days that no one even gave a second thought to as abridging our rights or offending anyone.

We all appreciated the fact that from whatever background or creed the boy selected to give the pre-game prayer was from, the thoughts he expressed from his heart were appreciated and accepted as something we all needed. There was a respect and honor for a being greater than any of us and the awareness that we needed his help and valued the blessings so far granted.

After the prayer we all stood up and began to yell, shout and hit each other on the shoulder pads to get the adrenaline flowing as we ran outside to get on a school bus that would take us the short two block ride to the stadium. It was the same stadium that Idaho State University used and was very nice, with a well-groomed field. We all climbed out of the bus, grateful to be there in the immediate sense because that many boys in football uniforms made the bus uncomfortable. There just wasn't nearly as much room on the bus with the guys all fitted out in the armor of the day as there was just a couple of hours earlier on the way down from Idaho Falls.

We got our warm-up drills finished, but didn't have a chance to meet as players and talk as we usually do. The ref called Struss and me together and we walked out to the middle of the field to meet the captains of Highland. The coin was flipped and Highland won the toss. They chose to receive so we would be kicking off to them, defending the south goal. Rarely did it matter which goal you defended and I never came to an understanding of why they even gave you the choice. I suppose it was the bone they threw you to salve the loss of the coin toss. We shook hands with the Highland captains again and came back to the sidelines. The defensive unit went out for the kick-off..

Coach had told us they were big, but I didn't realize until then, just how big!

Lords teed the ball up for the kick and away we went. Highland ran the ball out to the 25-yard line and had it there, first and ten. They only got one first down and had to punt to us. We took the ball, but couldn't move it and punted. They were running their big fullback a lot and this guy was very difficult to bring down. He wasn't as fast as advertised; not as fast as the I.F. fullback, but he was much harder to stop once he got up a head of steam.

Our left defensive end was having a good time with their tight end. They were both knocking each other all over the place and complimenting one another on it. On one play I saw their fullback coming up the middle with the ball so I slipped over and hit him head on. Moving into him hard, I heard him moan as I hit his thigh. But we just bounced off each other, and he kept on moving. I was sprawled out there, my helmet and knees on the ground and my rear end sticking up in the air. My shoulder went numb and began to burn. It hurt badly, but I jumped up because I knew I'd get pulled out of the game if Coach saw me. My shoulder burned, but I had experienced that pain before and it was not as bad as it could be. I was okay.

Highland was actually moving the ball on us! No one had done that before. Early in the second quarter they got a first and goal at the nine-yard line. They came wide around the right side and gained one yard. On the next play they gained four yards. On third down they went wide again to the right and Bob Nelson took their tailback out of bounds on the right side of the field at the four-yard line, the line of scrimmage.

Fourth and four, and they decided to go for it! The quarterback handed off to the fullback and we stacked him up at the two-yard line. As I hit the mass of humanity and pushed along with the other members of the defense, I was hit from behind by our two safeties, Hickman and Johnson, one after the other in rapid succession. Johnson slid off to my right and stuck his helmet right in the back of Nelson, one of our linebackers, as we began to push the fullback over on his back.

As I lay on the bottom of the pile of humanity, I heard Nelson screaming, "Johnson, you S.O.B. The next time you stick me in the back like that, I am going to kill you."

Everyone in the pile began to laugh, on both sides. Even with that bit of levity, this was a tough game and I had the feeling that it wouldn't be getting any easier. We had stopped this drive for a score just two yards short of pay dirt. How many more would there be in the rest of the game? I really didn't want to think about it.

As we went to the sideline, we yelled at the offense and told them to get us some points. Coach told us what a good job we had done and patted us on the back as we came off the field. Coach Rasmussen came over to me with a look of concern on his face. He had seen me favoring the shoulder I had hurt when I tackled the fullback earlier. I guess I had been unconsciously lifting it between downs or rubbing it with my hand.

"Couch, what's the matter with your shoulder?"

I told him I was okay but I would like to wrap it at half time. He got mad because I hadn't wrapped it before the game. The shoulder wasn't a big problem, but it had gotten hurt a couple of times and it's always better to be safe than sorry-and now I was sorry; probably as much that Coach Rasmussen was concerned as that it was hurting a bit. It didn't hurt much now, but Coach told me we would definitely wrap it at the half break.

Our offense went out but they couldn't move the ball and had to punt after only one series on offense. Our defense was spending a great deal of time on the field which was great since I loved the time playing, but it would not be good if this continued. For one thing it would mean we were not scoring and being out on the field all that time would inevitably wear us down and they may score on us, whereas before now, no one had accomplished that feat in the short season behind us. The latter was beginning to be a point of pride with us. No one had scored a point on our team so far this season and while that is really unreasonable to think you could go through a season not only undefeated but also unscored on was really stretching it.

But we could dream anyway.

Highland had really surprised us. In the second quarter our defense was able to shut Highland off, but their defense was equally tough and shut down our offense in like manner.

We went in at the half and Coach really didn't say much. He was very weak physically and I could see how he was struggling. We made some defensive adjustments to what they were doing offensively, but most of the half time was spent figuring out how to get our offense going. Highland was well coached and prepared for this game and seemed to know exactly what we were going to do on every play. Our offense had been completely stumped. The score was 0-0, but we had been a second-half team all along so none of us were overly concerned about it, but at the same time, concerned.

I got my shoulder wrapped and rubbed down. It felt much better with a little liniment on it and I could feel more mobility and less pain as I put my jersey back on. I could hear Nelson still riding Johnson for sticking him in the middle of the back on the goal line stand. I looked over and noticed Coach wasn't feeling well at all. He seemed to be in real pain.

After resting we went out on the field for the second half warm-up exercises.. Then, for about 30 seconds, we all met as a team in the end zone and just talked to each other. The basic message was, "Come on guys, we can't let down. We have to win this for Coach. Don't forget what the doctor told us. Don't let up. Give everything you can and then some more."

Struss (who had been selected to replace Kenny in the role of offensive captain) and I met in the middle of the field with the captains from Highland. The ref said it had been a good first half with few penalties and he wanted to see the same in the second half. We ran back to our sideline and the offense positioned themselves on the field to receive the kick-off. The ball came down to Lords who took it on the five-yard line and ran it out to the 30.. The offense got one first down, then another, and suddenly we had the ball on Highland's 31-yard line.

It was fourth and one for a first down. If we could get this first down we felt confident we would be able to move on in for a score. Kim turned with the ball and handed off to Bill, our fullback. He was big; big enough to make it through the Highland line for at least one yard and the inch or two that would award us a first down that we so desperately wanted. He slanted off to left tackle, but instead of running low, he was standing straight up. As he approached the line, he was met by churning Highland players. We could all see from the sideline that if he would lower his head and shoulders and drive hard, he would pick up the first down. But he didn't, and lost a yard. We couldn't believe it and were really upset on the sideline. We felt demoralized and discouraged.

Out the corner of my eye, I noticed Coach Ravsten sitting on the bench with a couple of the other coaches standing and kneeling beside him. They had an ammonia pill under his nose. He had passed out and they were bringing him around. I looked back over my shoulder as I ran onto the field with the rest of the defensive unit. We were all looking back to see how Coach was doing. He didn't look good at all and I wondered if he was going to die right there on the sideline. I can tell you, it's not the best thought with which to begin a defensive series!

Highland took the ball and began to move down the field. They were throwing the ball a bit in the second half, which was out of character for them, and had picked up a number of first downs. They were now on our 20-yard line where it was third and three. We had to stop them there. Highland's quarterback hurried back for what looked like a quick look-in pass then suddenly handed off to the fullback on a draw play. The fullback angled to his left, running toward the left flag marking the goal line.

I wasn't faked out at all and began to pursue him. I saw Mike, our outside linebacker, get his legs knocked out from under him and go down pretty hard. The fullback was getting close to me and I threw my shoulder into his right knee and he came down hard with his hip in my back. We both collapsed out of bounds on the seven-yard line. I had the wind knocked out of me and couldn't breathe, but after about thirty seconds I was okay. But Highland had the ball first and goal on the seven and we were about halfway through the third quarter. The score was still 0-0.

On first down they tried a rollout pass that Johnson almost picked off for us. On second down they tried their tailback on a cross buck that picked up two yards. On third down their fullback came right at Jamie and me. We both hit him at the same moment and he only got two yards. It was fourth and three. Highland called time out and I ran over to the sideline to confer with the coaches.

Coach had passed out again. It was amazing that he was still on the sidelines. I couldn't understand why they hadn't taken him into the locker room, if not to the hospital. Since Coach was unavailable, I talked to Coach Rasmussen who said they wouldn't kick a field goal because they simply didn't have a kicker. He told me to key off the fullback because he would most likely get the ball. I looked over and saw that Coach was standing up now, but he was holding an ammonia pill under his nose to keep him awake.

I looked up into our section of the stands and saw everyone standing and yelling, **"Defense, Defense!"** As I turned and ran back onto the field I saw the Highland quarterback running from his side of the field back to his huddle.

I told Jamie to watch the fullback closely. As they came up on the ball, I looked down and saw my feet were just inside the goal line. I hoped that that's as far as the ball carrier would get in the worst case as I saw the ball hiked into the quarterback's hands. He turned toward the fullback and I moved toward the hole where I thought he would likely come. Jamie was right in front of me going for the fullback, too, as the quarterback handed off to him. The 220-pound intimidator suddenly dropped the ball and then just as quickly fell on it at the six-yard line. We were all jumping and yelling and slapping each other on the back. We had stopped them again (with a little help from some slippery hands-but we accepted it)!

Our offense took the ball but couldn't move it again and we had to punt out of the end zone which is about as scary a position to be in as we wanted to be in. The punt was short, probably due to the pressure of standing in one's own end zone to kick the ball and knowing that you <u>had</u> to get a good one off. After one offensive series, Highland was on our 20-yard line just as the gun went off, ending the third quarter. On the first play of the fourth quarter, Highland ran a tailback sweep and picked up 12 yards. We suddenly had our backs to the wall again. This was getting serious and scary. It seemed like the whole second half had been played right in front of our goal line. They had the ball first and goal from the eight yard line. I was feeling exhausted because the defense had been on the field for most of the second half.

Tempers began to flare in the huddle as much from anxiety as anything, and some muttered words were exchanged. Jamie yelled at a couple of guys and told them to shut up.

"We've stopped them twice now and we can do it again," he said. As we broke from the huddle we were together again, of one mind and purpose.

On first down, their fullback came at our right defensive tackle. Nick shoved off his blocker, wrapped his arms around the big fullback and toppled him backward to the ground. A one-yard gain. On second down they tried the left tackle and Jamie stuck him good for no gain. On third, they went around our left end and picked up a few yards before the halfback was forced out of bounds at the five-yard line with Nelson pushing him out.

It was now fourth and five and I heard some of the Highland players say, "Maybe we should try a field goal." I figured there might be a chance that they would try a kick since they had surprised us in nearly everything else about this game so far. Then I heard the quarterback say, "He can't even kick an extra point. There is no way he will ever make it."

On fourth and goal, with five yards separating the current position of the ball with the white, four inch demarcation line between what we considered life and the alternative at the moment, they lined up for a running play. The quarterback handed off to the tailback and he danced and darted up to the two-yard line, but that was it. We'd done it again. Three goal line stands and we'd stopped them every time. As we ran to the sideline we felt great. The crowd on our side was standing, shouting and cheering. It was a very good feeling, indeed, as we left the field on the exchange of possession.

Our offense seemed a bit more motivated now and they were moving the ball. We got out to the twenty-yard line on our first play from scrimmage and continued to move the ball on each play. We got across midfield and down to the Highland 38-yard line where we fumbled with Highland recovering the ball. We felt very discouraged because we had been moving so well and felt it was our time to put the ball across the goal line.

Highland quickly picked up a first down to our 40-yard line. On second down they tried a pass and sent their left tight end on a slant across the middle. We didn't pick him up until it was too late. Once I saw where the play was going and looked back, I could see him all alone waving his arms as he was running slowly down the field. He was as wide open as a bear's mouth along the side of the road up in Yellowstone, looking for a cookie from passing motorists. The Highland quarterback saw him and lofted the ball into his hands at the 25-yard line. He continued unmolested into the end zone with Hickman right behind him.

The Highland side of the field went crazy, screaming, yelling and their band playing. We were shocked and sick. They'd done it; they'd scored. No one had done that to us so far this season and it was a real bell ringer for us.. As they lined up for the extra point, we knew they couldn't kick and they would go after the extra point by running it in from the two-yard line. We could stop them because we had done it so many times before. That would leave us the opportunity to still win by getting a touchdown and an extra point. They had scored; it was now our turn after stopping this extra point try..

The ball was hiked to the quarterback and he handed off to the tailback going to his right. We all reacted very quickly and had the play well in hand when the tailback handed off to the right split end on a reverse. We had over-reacted and all yelled, **"Reverse, reverse!"** But it was too late, and he slipped into the end zone just barely making it with five defensive men in very hot pursuit.

Shucky darn (or words to that effect). With just over five minutes left in the game the score was now 7-0 for the Highland Rams. We felt like we had had an oversize potato rammed right down our throats. The defense walked dejectedly to the sideline as the receiving team came out on the field. Things didn't look too good as far as our immediate future as a team was concerned, but Coach was looking better now, with a Pepsi in one hand and an ammonia capsule in the other.

Highland kicked the ball high and straight down the middle of the field. Lords fielded the kick at the six-yard line and took off straight back up the field where it had come from. He was upended at the 18-yard line-an inauspicious start to our last five minutes of life in this game.

Highland was as high as a kite and they really had the momentum going for them. Our offense ran around the right end for three and a cross buck for an 11-yard gain. It was a good run and it helped put some life back into us, but time was running out quickly and we had to score now!

In the next series, we ended up with fourth and five to go for a first down. We decided to punt and try to keep them in a hole. On the snap, Highland's linebacker ran through the line untouched and blocked the punt. Another Highland player picked up the ball and began to run down field. He was headed for the flag on his left side of the field and it looked like he was going to go all the way when Johnson caught him and drove him out of bounds at the five-yard line.

We were all sick as the defense walked slowly onto the field. What were our chances of stopping them again? We had had three goal line stands so far and I didn't know if we could do it again. There were just over three minutes left in the game and they had the ball first down and goal from the five-yard line-four tries to make only five yards and a score. We were all very discouraged as we huddled in the end zone.

There was a great deal of tension and anger among all of us. **"Goal line,"** I barked out (it didn't take a rocket scientist to figure what defense was called for in this instance!).

Jamie looked at all of us and I could see tears in his eyes, tears of anger and frustration. "Come on you guys, let's not let them score again. If they beat us, let it be by seven, not 14!" I tried looking into the eyes of everyone in the huddle and noticed how they were darting all over the field and looking at each other. Discouraged or not, there was a fierceness there, emotion like I had never seen in my life.

As we broke the huddle, Jamie grabbed me by the shoulders and said, "Couch, I'm going to slip into the gap instead of playing my man head to head. They're going to run that fullback at us four times and I want to meet him in the backfield." I told him to go for it and I would cover for him as best I could.

Highland came up on the ball and the tension was unbelievable. Eyes were wide, hearts were big and desire was overflowing with every player set to give his all. There was very little noise coming from the stands. The bands were quiet and there was no yelling.

I slipped up and patted Jamie on the rear end to encourage him. I saw his legs quivering and felt the intensity in the air. Then I slid over and did the same with Nick on the right side of the ball. Their center was over the ball, ready to hike it to the quarterback and looking right at me. I could tell he was going to be coming my way.

"Down! Set!" the quarterback barked.

I yelled to Jamie, **"Coming at you, Jamie."**

The ball was hiked and I saw the center coming right at me as I had supposed.. I could see from his angle of attack which hole the fullback would try to hit. I hit the center on the right side of his helmet and threw him to the ground as I saw Jamie set himself to tackle the fullback, who was moving like a bull straight toward him. There was a big smack of pads and grunts of effort as Jamie wrapped his arms around the fullback. I hit him just as they were starting to fall to the ground along with about four other guys with blue and white jerseys on. No gain at all.

Back in the huddle everyone gave Jamie a smack on the helmet. "Watch a reverse," Johnson said.

"Watch everything!" Fred said. The feelings were extremely intense as we supported and encouraged each other. The discouragement was gone and we were acting as one body. And were all as high as you could get. How long could this go on?

Highland came up to the line again. I looked at the center and could see he was coming at me once more since he was not very good at hiding his intentions. From his stance it looked like the flow of the play would be coming from the opposite side this time. So I yelled at Nick, **"Coming your way, Nick.. Get ready."**

Right or wrong, and whether or not the quarterback could discern who Nick even was and that we supposedly knew what was coming or where the play was going, there was no such thing as changing the play at the line of scrimmage as so often occurs in the football of today. What you called in the huddle was the play you ran, come hell or high water, or in the case of football season in Idaho, ice or high snow drifts.

On the snap, the center lunged out at me and I hit him on the right side of his helmet, pushing him to my left. He fell flat on his face and I looked up to see Nick holding onto the fullback with one arm and trying to drag him down. He was sliding to our right but inching forward toward the goal line. I shot in and hit him at the knees while Mike hit him from the other side. He came down and I knew he wasn't in, but he had picked up some yardage.

As we unpiled I saw the ref spot the ball at the two-yard line. In the huddle I yelled, **"Come on guys, he picked up three yards on that play. One more like that and we can all go home. Don't let him in!"**

It was now third down. We stopped them before and we could stop them again. That was all that we could think. Just two more times. Jamie grabbed Nick, the other defensive tackle, and told him to slip into the gap and go for the fullback. I told them I'd cover for them. Overconfidence, but what the heck, we had to get the fullback.

Highland came up on the ball and I could hear people screaming from both sides. The stands were now going crazy.

"Down! Set!"

Suddenly the stands became very quiet; there was no noise at all again.

The ball was hiked and I could see they were coming at Nick again, so I yelled, **"Nick!"**

I moved over to help plug up the hole. The center had slipped as he tried to get off the ball quickly and didn't get to me so I hit the fullback at the same instant Nick did, followed by three other guys. I couldn't tell how close he was, but as we unpiled the ref placed the ball with the laces on the one-yard line. It was now fourth down with less than a yard to go.

We all huddled up as the ref blew his whistle, indicating the ball was ready for play and time was counting to the next snap of the ball. "How much time?" someone asked in the huddle.

"Good hell, don't worry about the time. Just don't let him in," Jamie yelled.

I could see the tears in his eyes along with the emotion coming from every player in the huddle.

Jamie said, "He's coming at me this time, guys, I know it. Help me and we can stop him."

We all went up to the line and I watched Jamie getting set in his four-point stance, adjusting and readjusting his footing. Highland came up on the ball and the quarterback looked up and down the line. It was very quiet again. It seemed like we were playing in the middle of an abandoned cow pasture-there was no noise at all in the entire stadium. You could hear the labored breathing of the players and the shuffle and bite of spikes being sunk into the turf on the field. The center looked up at me from his stance and I could see the sweat rolling down both sides of his face.

He gave himself away again by the way he got into his stance. If he was going to pull down the line, he would be a little higher in his stance and would sneak a look toward his destination as he came up to the ball before the rest of the line arrived and then again just before the quarterback would set the team. If he was going to come straight out at me, he would not look left or right and never at me and be lower in his crouch over the ball.

I had learned to watch this indicator and when I saw him staring at the ground just in front of the ball, I yelled, **"Coming at you, Jamie."**

The center was coming out to get me meaning that the play was up the middle by the fullback-who else! The ball was hiked and the quarterback handed off to the fullback who was bulling his way right at Jamie.

I moved quickly up into the proposed hole. But the center dove at me; knocking my feet out from under me and I went down but quickly launched myself at the mass of bodies piling up at the goal line. If he fell forward he would be into the end zone, so we had to push him back.

We all hesitated for a moment in a quivering pile reminiscent of a tight English rugby scrum and then the pile slowly toppled backwards as we all fell to the ground. I lay there on the pile and I could hear the Highland players yelling and cheering that they had scored and I felt sick. We had let Coach down. I unscrambled from the pile and saw the ref shaking his head. He didn't have his hands in the air and he was spotting the ball on the one-inch line. The Highland players were yelling at him and jumping up and down throwing their arms all over the place.

"No," the ref said, "You didn't get in."

I looked up at the clock and it said one minute and thirty-eight seconds. Things didn't look good for scoring, let alone winning. We were exhausted both emotionally and physically as we walked off the field.

The offense was coming onto the field and I yelled, to no one **in particular and everyone in general, "Would you guys get off your dead butts, and do what you're supposed to do?"** But they were so intent on the task at hand; they didn't hear a word I said.

I walked the last 15 yards off the field and looked up to see Coach standing about ten yards onto the field. He was standing there with his arms open, tears streaming down his cheeks and hugging the defensive players as we came off the field. I heard him say, "Thank you, boys, thank you. I asked and you gave your all." He grabbed me and as he wrapped his arms around me, I could feel his body shake as he sobbed in my arms. I, too, began to cry.

After a few seconds we broke and I walked onto the sideline as Coach grabbed another guy coming off the field. I tried to keep my head down, embarrassed at my display of emotion, but when I glanced up I noticed almost everyone on the sideline was now crying. I looked up to the clock and through blurry, tear-filled eyes, saw that same one minute and 38 seconds. It was impossible. We had lost the game. I felt so bad and continued to cry because I thought we had let Coach down. We had not kept our promise.

The offense huddled at the back of the end zone while Kim was on the sideline with Coach. Kim looked at Coach and asked, "What play do you want me to call?"

Coach looked up at the clock, almost absentmindedly took another whiff of the ammonia capsule and simply said, "Just get it out, you haven't got much time. Use a lot of down and out patterns so the receiver can get out of bounds."

Kim ran out to the huddle where there was a lot of initial confusion with everyone talking. Kim yelled, **"All right, shut up"** and called the play---strong right with tight end and a split back. He would roll right and hit someone in the flat. As Kim came up on the ball he noticed the middle linebacker had slipped over and was playing to blitz far to the right. Kim saw a beautiful opportunity for a quarterback sneak. He hit the center on the rear end and yelled, "**Hut**." The center knew what a slap on the rear meant (that was the extent of changing the play at the line of scrimmage-the QB and center knew, but everyone else was still doing what they had decided to do in the huddle). The center moved out sharply to block the safety. Kim took the ball, followed the center and was finally brought down at the 15-yard line. First down and a good move on Kim's part. It gave the offense some maneuvering room outside of our end zone. Everyone was yelling and slapping Kim on the helmet.

"Come on you guys," Kim said, "We don't have much time."

Kim called the same pass play, rolled to his right and saw

Thomas wide open. He threw the ball on the run and hit Thomas on the 25-yard line. He quickly moved another five yards before stepping out of bounds as he was hit at the 30-yard line.

We all went crazy on the sideline, but then we saw a yellow flag. I prayed the penalty would be against Highland. The ref stepped up and gave the holding signal and pointed toward one of our players.

Kim was sick and told me later that he thought, "These refs are going to 'home town' us. They aren't even going to give us a chance. They will keep us down inside the 10 and give the ball back to Highland."

The ref moved the ball back to the seven-yard line, one-half the distance to the goal line. Everyone in the huddle was very dejected and upset but Kim pulled them together.

"Come on guys, don't quit. This game isn't over yet!"

I was standing on the sideline looking at the clock. Exactly one minute on the clock. Ninety-three yards and one inch for a touchdown. "No way," I thought to myself.

Kim called the same pass play to the left this time and it opened up exactly the way it had done to the right. Goddard was open this time and went to the 22. The play took seven seconds. So there were now 53 seconds on the clock as it was stopped with Goddard going out of bounds.

Suddenly there was a lot of excitement in the huddle as Val Carpenter, our 145-pound guard, who was trying to pass block a 190-pound defensive lineman, called out, "We can do it guys, we can score. We can't give up, we owe that much at least to Coach."

Kim called the next play, which was a draw, thinking the linebackers would have dropped off, expecting another pass. The play was executed perfectly as Fluke waited until the last second to take the ball and rambled up field for six yards. I thought to myself, "If he were only faster he could have picked up 20 yards. But we'll take what we can get."

That play took six seconds and Kim called a time out. He ran to the sideline and I walked up and stood next to Coach. He really looked a lot better now and was very excited, yet at the same time, very calm. The peaks and valleys that man went through in so short an amount of time was incredible.

We were now out to the 28 and had some working room, but there were only 47 seconds left in the game. We had two time outs remaining. Kim was standing there with Coach's arm around his shoulder.

"You are doing a great job, Kim," Coach said. "But no more runs. We've got to pass the ball if we ever expect to get it into the end zone before the final gun sounds. Use two different passes with a double set one way, hook the outside receiver and run the inside receiver down and out. Pick one of the two, but make sure you hit them in the numbers. Don't overthrow or they will intercept. Now the other pass will be a fly pass over on Hurley's side, the weak side."

Coach quickly took another sniff of the ammonia pill.

"You can do it, Kim. I have all the faith in the world in you. If you can't do it, then no one can. Now go do it!"

Kim ran to the huddle and called the next play, a fly to Hurley. He was wide open and was knocked out of bounds at the 35. I looked at the clock again.. Forty-three seconds, and 65 yards to pay dirt. We just didn't have enough time.

Kim was up on the ball again. At the snap of the ball he dropped straight back from the center. I saw Thomas and Goddard run past me on the double set.. "How long could we do this before they caught on to what was happening?" I wondered. Goddard turned in short this time and Thomas went deep and stopped. As Thomas turned, the ball was right there for him to gather in. He struggled to get out of bounds but didn't make it. So we called time out with the ball on their 48-yard line.

"Well, maybe we can make it," I thought.

Kim was on the sideline talking to Coach.

"You're doing an outstanding job, Kim. Just keep it up. We

have 35 seconds now, we can do it."

Kim ran back onto the field and called strong right. At the snap, he rolled right, but nothing was open. Kim saw a linebacker coming at him hard and fast. He set and threw the ball out of bounds just as he was hit. His eyes watered and his face hurt as blood began to flow from his nose. He called time out and came to the sideline. I could see the blood on his hands and all over his face. Coach was cleaning him up and stopping the bleeding.

"We are now out of time outs," Coach said. "We only have 31 seconds left so use the sidelines and get that ball down field."

On the next play Kim called a slant over the middle to Thomas who was on the right side. Kim dropped back and saw the linebacker trailing Thomas by about three yards and looped the ball to him at the 36-yard line.

As Thomas grabbed the ball he thought, "I have got to get out of bounds or score. The safety is coming right at me and that linebacker is not far behind."

I saw Thomas do a great spin just as the safety tried to hit him and he was off and running to the goal line. That linebacker was quickly coming up on him and Thomas decided the better part of valor was to go for the sideline. The linebacker dove and caught him, but Thomas stayed on his feet and fought for the sideline, going out of bounds at the 29-yard line.

The clock now said 18 seconds. That last play could be the death knell because it took so much time. Kim was up on the ball again. Hurley ran down to the 20 and curled out just as the ball hit him in the numbers and he stepped out of bounds just inside the 20. We had 13 seconds now. Two more plays were all we had time for, or just one, if we couldn't get out of bounds.

Kim faced the huddle, which really resembled the back of the stage at the Los Angeles Amphitheater from what I had seen in the movies. The five down linemen were in a little semi-circle with their hands on their knees. The ends were standing at each side with the backs standing behind the linemen. The quarterback would step into this little cove of players with his back to the line of scrimmage and this time called a roll out to the right.

As they came up on the ball there was almost total silence as everyone watched intently from the stands and both sidelines.

"Ready, set," Kim called out and put his hands down ready to receive the ball.

"Hut, hut."

The ball came up into his hands and the clock started down. Thomas cut over to the right from the left side toward the end zone. Goddard went down the right side and slanted left into the middle. He suddenly reversed and slanted out to the right again. Kim was rolling right and saw both Thomas and Goddard in the open. Two linebackers were coming at Kim full speed as he cocked his arm and let the ball fly. One linebacker put his shoulder pad right into his ribs while the other jumped on top of him. Thomas and Goddard were both in the same vicinity, with Goddard right at the goal line and Thomas five yards deep in the end zone. Both were running toward the right sideline as the ball sailed just over Goddard's head and he knew instantly that Thomas had the best shot at it. Another of those rocket science deductions! The ball landed lightly in Thomas' hands.

Kim heard a roar go up from the crowd as he lay there on the ground. He wasn't sure if it was the roar of the Highland side of the field or our side since he was a bit confused after the tremendous hit he had taken from the two linebackers coming on the blitz.

I couldn't believe it. We were all screaming and jumping up and down on the sideline. I looked at the clock that showed just seven seconds left in the game. I looked at Coach who was sitting on his milk stool with his head bent down, an ammonia capsule under his nose, tears streaming down his cheeks and off his chin.

Coach stood up, grabbed Lords and said, "Get in there and

kick that extra point!"

Craig very calmly walked out on the field toward the goal line. Everyone was tense and nervous because Lords had missed about the last five or six attempts. If he missed this one, it was all over-we lose. Craig's mother (we called her Momma Lords-they lived just one house down from us when our family lived on 24th Street) was at home listening to the game on the radio and as we learned later, was praying we would run the ball in for the extra point.

The huddle was quick and offense and defense came up on the ball for this all-important play. Finlayson was the center and was over the ball ready to hike it when he got blasted. Flags went all over the place. Remember the discussion earlier about rattling the center? It can really make a difference.. And the forty-two inches the offending team incurred as penalty for the offside was normally nothing in a kicking situation like this one.

In any case, offsides on Highland-half the distance to the goal line. Another quick huddle, up on the ball, the ball was hiked and the Skyline and Highland interior linemen fired into one another. The ball came back to Kim who was the holder. He grabbed it and placed it on the ground. Lords took one step and kicked the ball hard, dead center, with his head down. He kept his head down until he heard a roar from the crowd. Then he looked to see the ball split the uprights. We had tied the game. (Remember, this was before the change of rules that allowed two points if you ran the ball over the goal line on an extra point try-whether you ran it over or kicked the ball through the uprights, you got one point.)

The offense ran to the sideline ecstatic about the touchdown and extra point.. The kicking team was going out on the field very aware there were still seven seconds left in the game and we couldn't let anything happen. We would try an onside kick and try to get the ball. We lined up, everyone was set and I was going after that ball.

When the whistle blew, I signaled everyone to go down and I turned just as Lords kicked the ball right at the top white stripe, which circled the ball at each of its pointy ends. The ball bounded across the ground as I ran behind it. Nelson was in the best position to get the ball, but he didn't get to it before one of the Highland players quickly fell on it and called time out.

Highland had a quick huddle and came up on the ball. The quarterback faded back and I dropped back and picked up the tailback coming out of the backfield. The ball sailed just over my head and I turned to see Hickman intercept the ball and step out of bounds. There were only three seconds left in the game. Everyone was jumping on Hickman and yelling as we ran over to the sideline and the offense came onto the field.

Kim called the same play we had scored on and everyone moved into his position. This was it and we all knew it. Kim took the ball and rolled right just as before and looked down field to see Thomas and Goddard open. He quickly set and cocked his arm and began to come forward with his throw. "We are going to win," he thought to himself.

Suddenly the defensive tackle from Highland hit Kim and knocked him to the ground. Kim didn't get a complete follow through and the ball sailed through the air and dropped five yards short of Goddard who had nothing but green grass in front of him. The game was over.

Kim lay there on the grass and tears came to his eyes. We hadn't won. We had let Coach down. The offense walked slowly to the sideline.

I was just standing there feeling the same way Kim did. We had blown it, bad. I started to walk over to the bus as the stands began to empty. I hurt, it was hot and I had scratches and bruises all over. I had never hurt like this before. A couple of the girls from the marching team ran up and I could see the concern on their faces. They asked a few questions, but I really didn't pay much attention to what they were saying. I didn't want to talk; I felt more like crying. I wished they would go away and leave me alone.

"Good game, Bruce," they said.

But all I could mumble was, "Not good enough."

I just wanted to get on the bus and go back to the school for a hot shower. I saw my parents on the track that surrounded the field and they came up and talked to me for a few minutes. My Dad asked what the problem was with my shoulder, but I told him it was nothing, I was okay. I walked over to the bus and was one of the last ones to get on.

As I stepped up into the bus I looked at everyone sitting there. Some of the best friends I had ever had. Friends who had been through a great deal together. Everyone had their head down and all were crying, every one of them.. I saw a vacant seat almost to the back on the driver's side. Hickman was sitting there by himself. As I slowly walked to the back, a lot of guys put out their hand and mumbled, "Good game, Couch." I couldn't say anything because now I was crying, too.

I sat down next to Hickman who was really having a rough time. He was crying like a baby, just sobbing. His hand was covering his eyes and his head was down.

He put his hand on my shoulder and sobbed, "I'm sorry, Couch. I lost the game for us."

I whimpered back, "You didn't lose the game for us, we all did. And besides that, we tied. We didn't lose."

What a scene this was, a busload of the "toughest" guys on campus, weeping like a bunch of babies-no, not weeping, bawling like a bunch of babies.

I heard some commotion up front and saw Coach struggle up the stairs of the bus. He told the driver to close the door and wait just a minute. Coach turned and faced us with a hand on a rail on each side of the aisle. I could see the tears streaming down his face as he stood there. He was having a tough time composing himself and hung his head for a few moments. He looked up and the tears were still streaming down his face. He wasn't helping any of us with our composure, that was for sure.

"What are you guys crying about?" Coach said as he wiped the tears away with the back of his hand and choked back another sob.

After a few seconds of calming himself, he continued, "As long as I have been a coach, I have always tried to develop character in the boys I've coached.."

He stopped for a minute, wiped away more tears and composed himself again. "I have never seen such character and dedication," he went on. "I would like to thank you young men from the bottom of my heart. Not boys, but men. You have learned principles and exercised character today that most men will never learn or exhibit in their entire lives. I thank you for what you did today and I know it was done for me. I want you to know how much I love you guys. You are all winners today and will be for the rest of your lives. I want you all to look in the mirror and know that. We didn't plan to lose; we didn't practice to lose. We used every ounce of energy and every spark of our spirit all the way and we, sure as heck, didn't lose. The score **board says we didn't win, but I have never seen a bigger or better victory in my life.** We are still undefeated on paper and in our hearts, are we not?"

We all yelled back, "Yes!"

Coach sat down and told the bus driver to take us back to the dressing room. I sat there and wiped the tears away with the back of my grass-stained bloody hand and looked up to see Craig. I could tell he was feeling better, but not much.

I suddenly didn't feel so bad because I recognized what Coach had been teaching us for the past three years. It really doesn't matter if you win, even though Coach and all of us hated to lose. It was a lot more fun to win. But the important thing was that you played your best, you gave your all, to do the best job that you could do.

I realized that was what I had just done. I knew that was what we all had done. We had given 100 percent of what we had to give. Even though we had made some stupid mistakes, we still had given our all. There were no excuses.. We couldn't blame the refs or anyone else. And we were still undefeated in our hearts as well as in actuality.

We quickly showered and got back on the bus dressed in our navy blue blazers and headed for home. I was sitting next to Hickman who still felt bad about letting them score on him. As we were driving down the freeway, Coach stood up in the front and said, "Hickman, come on up here." Everyone stopped talking and watched as Hickman walked up to the front and sat down next to Coach.

I wondered what Coach was saying as he sat there and put his arm around Hickman. He was there for about five minutes, came back and sat down next to me again. I could see tears in his eyes and I asked him what Coach wanted. "He just told me not to feel badly about the Highland game and that there is no one on the team that could have done a better job." Craig stopped for a minute and then said, "He also said the coaches have as much confidence in me as they would in Larry Wilson who plays safety for St. Louis." I could see Craig was feeling much better now. A tremendous weight had been lifted from his shoulders and I felt good inside for all of us.

At home there was a great deal of praise from family and friends about what an exciting game it was. But no one knew the feelings we had experienced on the sideline, in the locker room, on the field and especially on the bus after the game.

Lessons Learned:

We learned patience and perseverance from our experience with Coach in obvious ways. He was an outstanding example of these two values in regard to the great difficulties he was facing on a daily basis.

He also taught us on the playing field, or on the mat or in the classroom, the value of being patient with the learning and growing process. It sometimes-no, most times-takes time to effect change, incorporate principles, learn new material, see growth.

Patience is required to see the goal achieved. Perseverance is required to insure it happens the way perceived. To give up when just one more moment would have made the difference between the agony of defeat and the joy of victory is the saddest story that can be told.

It was once said, "Hell begins on the day when God grants a clear vision of all that we might have achieved, of all the gifts which we might have wasted, of all that we might have done which we did not do." (Gian-Carlo Menotti)

Patience and perseverance will bring us home to where we desire to be, having achieved all we were sent forth to do

Chapter 10

"The difference between a successful person and others is not a lack of strength, not a lack of knowledge, but rather a lack of will."
Vince Lombardi

There was a dance going on Saturday night and since we didn't have to worry about a curfew, five of us got together and decided to crash the Sophomore Hop. We didn't want to be destructive or anything so we planned out what we thought would be fun for everyone.

About 6:00 p.m., I asked Dad if I could use his car that night and he said that would be fine. My folks weren't the go-out-on-the-town type of people. If there was to be a night out, it would usually involve going over to the church for a social or down the street to a neighbor's for a get together. I suppose their "stick close to home" syndrome was born with my brother and reinforced with the succeeding births of each of my siblings. They kind of wanted to be close to home to insure that we all would survive to be possible candidates for adulthood. I'm sure that our nearly burning down the house while they were over at the Lords' house attending a neighborhood adult party or our encounter with grandpa's power saw with near missing fingers or the 10,000 other encounters with a strange circumstance involving their children had a little to do with their desires to "stick close to home."

With his approval and the keys in my hand, I backed out of the driveway and went over and picked up one of my friends in the neighborhood. We picked up three other guys and headed for a potato cellar on another friend's farm. We walked down into the cool cellar with some flashlights and a gunnysack. Idaho is replete with gunnysacks---there's never a dearth of them for whatever you need one for, and they have many uses. This particular night we were going to utilize them for their "holding capability." Normally a gunnysack held nothing but potatoes, about 80-90 pounds of them, but tonight we had a little lighter fare in mind. There were always sparrows in the cellars and if you put the light in their eyes at night they would freeze on the spot. So we walked around and picked a dozen birds off their roosts for the night and put them in the sack.

We then headed for Tautphaus Park to catch a Canadian goose. It was dark now and we pulled off the road and down into the barrow pit so if the police showed up they wouldn't immediately find our car. Craig Leonard jumped over the fence where about 50 geese were penned and began to chase them. I had never heard such noise in my entire life. I learned later from my brother that the USAF uses geese as "guard dogs" at their air bases in Germany because of the raucous noise they raise when disturbed. I was sure the police would be there at any moment.

The cacophony of flapping wings and honking geese moved down the fence line and then away from the road as Leonard chased the geese in an attempt to grab one. After a few minutes the noise subsided and as I peered through the night air, I saw Leonard walking down the road with a big Canadian honker, one hand around its neck and the other cradling its body and thrashing legs as close to his body as he could. You'd have thought that we would have brought another gunnysack for this critter, but no, we hadn't planned that far in advance.

Leonard got into the car and sat in the back seat right behind me. That stupid goose was all over the place and Craig was having a rough time controlling him. At one point the goose leaned forward and bit me on the right ear. I cussed Leonard and told him to control the dumb bird or I would stop and put them both out on the side of the road.

We were driving along First Street and decided to pull into the Frost Top Drive-In, the local hang out for teenagers, for a root beer. The Frost Top was at the northeastern end of the loop that teenagers made while "Dragging Main." Out of the parking lot you would go down First Street to the Yellowstone Highway and turn south to E Street, turning right at the Arctic Circle Drive-In. At Park Avenue you would turn back south and then east on Broadway to Shoup Avenue and back north to D Street. You would then turn right on D Street to US 91, North on US 91 (Yellowstone Highway) to First Street and east to the point of origin. You could see nearly everyone in town who were not already out watching the submarine races or some other undercover activity if you made the loop a couple of times in a row with momentary stops along the way to adjust the flow of traffic and reposition yourself in it.

Those were the days when carhops were still in vogue. You could even go to a service station and get SERVICE, imagine that! Well anyway, this poor girl came up and attempted to take our order. It seemed to be an unwritten rule that you gave the carhops a devil of a time as they attempted to just do their job and satisfy your hunger or thirst as the case may be. The cuter the carhop, the worse time you would give her. We were giving her a really tough time; embarrassing and teasing her to the extent that I guess she didn't even notice the goose.

The sparrows had gone back to sleep in the bag, I suppose, because they were not causing us any grief whatever---not even a peep. This Canuk, however, was a different story all together. After a few minutes, the carhop came back with our orders. As she bent down to put the tray on the window, the goose lurched forward, trying to get out the window. It attacked the nearest thing that presented itself to the beak attached to that long neck and bit her on her upper torso, on the pointy side.

Now my five sisters have quite emphatically made it known that this area of the female human body is the tenderest of all.

My brothers and I argued the point (no pun intended), but were out voted 5 to 3. Regardless, she screamed and everyone in the parking lot looked over to see what was going on. I wasn't sure if she was more hurt, or mad, or embarrassed, but whatever it was, she really was now. We didn't help matters any by our uncontrollable laughter, but between it all we got our order and paid the bill.

With all the attention that had been aroused with the car hop screaming and the honking of the goose, we decided it would be best if we got out of there, so off we went for our last stop before getting to the dance. We crossed the Snake River to the west side of town where we knew a pig farm was located. I pulled up alongside the fence separating the dirt road and the pigsty.

We all jumped out. There was a huge pen with about 50 pigs inside. We all walked around the edge of the fence trying to lean over and grab a pig. But we soon saw the pigs weren't too excited about staying close to the fence so we could grab them (perhaps one of the goose's friends had called ahead with a warning). I don't know if the USAF uses pigs as "guard dogs," but if not, they're missing a sure bet! They were making as much, if not more, noise than the stupid geese. We were sure the police would be pulling up at any moment.

I just said to heck with this, and jumped over the fence, quickly sinking in pig manure up to my calves. Now to be sure, a pig establishment has an aroma all its own and we could smell it quite well on the other side of the fence, but it took on a whole new dimension when I realized that I was really IN IT! And it was on me. Boy, did it ever stink! Well, to heck with it, I was committed. So I started chasing pigs all over the pen. Two more guys jumped in and began to chase pigs, too. I grabbed a medium-sized pig and started to head for the car when it started kicking so hard I was afraid it would break one of my ribs. So I dropped it. Suddenly, we heard some noise coming from the farmer's house. I yelled for everyone to get in the car and we jumped inside still covered with pig manure. We didn't get a pig, but we sure did smell like it.

We drove over to the high school and pulled up to the curb. The dance was being held in the cafeteria where all but the most formal dances were held at Idaho Falls/Skyline High School. The cafeteria was in the basement of the high school building, right below the library. It had big windows set in deep window wells to let in the light and make it more airy and nice. We had unlocked one of the windows during the day and left it ajar. There was also a door leading directly to the outside to be used in time of emergency to escape in case of fire or some other such disaster. We had left it unlocked, too, so we could get the goose and the pig in without hurting them by dropping them into the cafeteria from a window.

We pushed the window open and emptied the contents of the gunnysack (12 sparrows) into the room. The birds began to fly through the crepe paper decorations hanging from the ceiling creating quite a stir among the dancers. At the same time, we turned the goose loose through the door and he was chasing and snapping at a girl who was unfortunate enough to be the closest living thing to the door as we opened it. After a few minutes the goose saw a light sitting on the floor and walked over to pick a fight. He pecked at the light a few times and it broke with a loud pop. This scared the goose and he took off after someone else. With all the commotion, yelling, honking, pecking, screaming, fluttering of wings and general pandemonium, we figured we had better be getting on down the road so we took off running to the car and drove home.

Jim Hales and I decided to go back to the dance and see what mayhem had resulted. We showered and Jim came over to pick me up in his car because my dad's car stunk so badly. We got to the dance and walked in.

The assistant principal saw us come in immediately started to laugh, and said, "Okay you guys, where in the world did you get all of those critters?"

"What are you talking about?" I said.

"You know darn well what I am talking about." he replied.

We talked for a few minutes and asked him what happened to the goose. He told us they had caught him and just put him outside. We hung around a little longer, talked to some friends and then left. As we headed for the car we saw the goose walking through an intersection in front of the school. We took off after him, thinking we would take him back to the zoo. After a short chase we had him in the car and were headed to Tautphaus Park and the zoo.

"But what if the police catch us there?" Jim said. "What will we do then?"

We thought about it for a minute and decided the best thing to do was to take the goose to the police station. We needed to have a little more fun before the night was over.

At the police station we walked in with the goose and told the officer on duty we had found the goose over by the high school and was afraid for its safety.

He asked us some questions and then said, "Someone must have been playing around. We heard there was a possible goose at some dance at the school, but later heard there wasn't one after all. I'll just throw this goose in the drunk tank with a few of the boys until an officer comes in and we can get it back to the park."

We were shocked as he walked over and dropped the goose into the cell. We could hear the goose and someone swearing as the goose chased the current occupant(s) behind the bars of the city lock-up. We drove home and got to bed about midnight.

Early the next morning my Dad came thundering down the stairs and just as he opened the bedroom door, I suddenly realized that I had forgotten to clean up his car.

"What in the Sam Hell (that was his favorite colloquialism- I guess it was "Hell". Maybe it was "Hill" and I just never knew. When it was put into use, the occasion usually called for a "Hell" so I just assumed all these years....) **did you do with that car last night?" he yelled.**

"It smells worse than a pig pen!"

I didn't say anything other than I would clean it up and bring the car to him at work, so he took the station wagon to work and I got up and got busy on the clean up. You could still get a whiff of pig when we got rid of that car three years later.

On Monday we gave out performance awards for the Highland game and began another week of practice. We would be playing a small school called Marsh Valley on the up-coming Friday night. We really shouldn't have been playing them because they were such a small school, but you never knew about the strength of their athletes and their ability.

I remember going down to Marsh Valley when my brother was wrestling and watched him in a match with a guy we all figured was finishing high school on the GI Bill. Those farmers (and that's all there were in Marsh Valley-farmers) were big and strong and usually had big hearts, too. So we worked hard as we prepared for them and the Friday night tilt.

The week went by fast and on Friday we got out of school early again and went home to eat and take a short nap before going back to the school to dress.

The game began and we immediately dominated the other team in every way. After the first half concluded, we had the second string go in and play most of the second half. The score ended up 34 to nothing and after the game we had a victory dance. I didn't see any evidence of any feathered friends so I figured they had long since escaped back to freedom. I hoped so, anyway. I had a good time dancing with a number of girls and went home.

On Monday we had numerous awards to pass out. The Marsh Valley game was too easy and lots of guys shined. But it was a lot of fun for all of us, especially after the intensity of the Highland game.

On Friday we would play Blackfoot, a school 30 miles south of Idaho Falls. Last year they had upset us and we had revenge in our hearts as we prepared for the game. Blackfoot was another smaller school and should never have beaten us last year. The town was the home of the Eastern Idaho Mental Hospital and even though that fact had absolutely nothing to do with anything, when you said "Blackfoot," everyone conjured up the thought of the "nut house" and its associated connotations. They had beaten us badly last year and we wanted a very lopsided victory this year so we practiced hard all week in preparation.

The week was suddenly gone and we were on the bus headed for Blackfoot. We dressed, had our pep talk from Coach and went out to the field to do our warm ups. We all met as players in the end zone as had become our tradition, for a moment out of earshot of any adult. We talked about our commitment to Coach and the immediate challenge.

Someone said, "Hey, let's remember last year and kick their butt for us, as well as for Coach. Let's let them have it."

The game began and I couldn't believe how easy it was to do whatever we wanted. We stopped their every drive and scored at will. At half time the score was 21 to 0. But this wasn't enough; we wanted another 21 points. But Coach was having none of that and told us to take it a little easy on them.

We began the third quarter and moved at will. I intercepted a pass and ran it back to about their 20. Coach sent in the second string and they failed to score. For the balance of the game, very few first stringers were playing on defense. I was still in the game, I suppose because I was the captain and had to call the defensive alignment for each down. I had to work a little harder when I didn't have the first string team support. Second-string players were making mistakes the first string wouldn't have made, but we were having a good time anyway.

Early in the fourth quarter, their quarterback took the ball and began to roll to his left, our right. I moved along the line watching for blockers coming off the line and anticipating a good angle to shoot in and hit him behind the line of scrimmage. I could see him turning up field between two blockers. I lowered my head and shot in to make the stop. I hit him just over the line of scrimmage and heard a big crack. My shoulder quickly went numb and then began to burn like it was on fire. The pain was terrible and I was rolling around on top of the quarterback, who was moaning terribly in pain also. One of the refs came over and half-kicked me to get me to move off the other guy.

The ref said to me, "Get off him! Can't you see he's hurt?"

Johnson was standing there and started yelling at the ref and pushed him away from me saying, **"Can't you see he's hurt, too?"**

I was lying there on the ground saying nothing because it hurt too much. I was afraid my shoulder was broken. All of a sudden, I looked up and saw Coach kneeling over me with a look of concern. He asked where it hurt and put his hand down my jersey to feel for anything out of place.

He said, "I don't think you have broken anything, but you sure should have, the way you hit that kid."

I said, "Coach, I heard something crack and I'm afraid I broke it."

Coach replied, "I think the crack you heard was you breaking that kid's leg. They're getting an ambulance and a stretcher to carry him off the field."

Coach Jacoby was there and we looked over to see the Blackfoot coaches huddled over their quarterback. I heard Coach Jacoby affirming that the crack we had all heard was the opposing QB's leg.

"I'm okay now," I told the coaches and stood up and walked to the sideline with Coach Ravsten's arm around my shoulder, which was hurting badly despite the fact that I was "all right."

"You really hit that kid," Coach said again.

I looked up into his yellow eyes and could see the pain he

lived with constantly.

Coach looked at me and said, "Go on, run off the field and be a hero."

It's not that it was a "hero" to break someone's leg or even put him out of the game. That was not Coach's game or mine. But it was a great hit and it deserved a bit of indulgence, so I ran off as everyone clapped. Over my shoulder I could see the Blackfoot coaches carrying their quarterback off the field on a stretcher. They put him in an ambulance and drove off to the hospital.

I felt bad because I'd hurt him that seriously. I hadn't meant to, I just wanted to stop him behind the line for a loss. The game went on and I knew I was out for the rest of it. The entire second string was now in the game and Blackfoot moved down the field to score six points. But when they tried to run it in for the extra point, they didn't make it. I wished the game would hurry and end because I just wanted to get into a nice, hot shower. The game finally ended at 31-6 and we all ran to the locker room. After a long, hot shower I felt a lot better, but my shoulder still hurt.

I was sitting on the bench pulling up a sock when Coach sat down next to me. "I knew you hit that kid hard, but I didn't know you hit him that hard. We asked how the kid is doing and the Blackfoot coaches tell us his thighbone is broken in three places. They may need to put a pin in his leg."

I really felt bad now and looked up at Coach and said, "I wish I could tell him I'm sorry."

"Well," Coach said, "We will send him a card next week."

We all got on the bus and headed for home getting there quite late, no dancing or running around tonight. I went right to bed.

On Monday we got our awards as we sat around Coach on his milk stool and then began practice for Bonneville. They were the third school in town and were composed of nearly all "farmers" while Skyline and Idaho Falls were considered the "city slickers." There were ample students from each category in each school but that was the characterization and it stuck. This was a big game for us. They had beaten us pretty badly last year. Practice went well and we were all healthy for the game on Friday afternoon to be played at Bonneville.

We kicked off to Bonneville after our meeting as a team. Bonneville couldn't move the ball and they were forced to punt. Our punt returns had been very successful so far this year. We always looked forward to a return with excitement, knowing we had a good chance to break one loose for a touchdown. Lords came in to run the ball back and I called return right in the huddle. This meant we would set up a blocking fence along the right side and Lords would run between it and the right sideline.

We lined up and Bonneville snapped the ball. We all held our man there on the line of scrimmage for a count of three and then pulled off to the right to set up the "fence." That meant that we would run to the sideline (right in this situation) and about eight yards from the sideline, turn back toward the center of the field forming a "fence" for the return man to run behind, knocking down any potential tackler who would try to stop him.

It set up quite nicely and I saw Lords catch the ball in the middle of the field on our 36-yard line and start up field. I saw Crockett get a good block on the first Bonneville player downfield. The Bonneville players were running down the field intent on the ball carrier. I saw a player running for Lords, but he didn't see me, and I hit him hard on his blind side. What a great feeling that was as he flew through the air not knowing what had hit him. Lords scampered on by and down field where another very similar block took place. He was moving full speed now and I looked up in time to see Bauchman cream another unsuspecting Bonneville player. Lords sidestepped another tackler and was all by himself as he slipped into the end zone. We were all jumping up and down as we ran into the end zone and smothered Lords. This was so much fun!

We kicked off to Bonneville and they were again unable to

move the ball. The rest of the first half turned into a punting contest between the two teams with neither team being able to move the ball offensively at all. But just before half-time they got down close to the goal line with a long pass play and snuck one in on a double reverse, but they failed to make the extra point.

We headed into the locker room leading by 1 point.

Coach came in and I could see the fatigue on his face. He was also very upset and did a good deal of yelling at the offense telling them they were not playing up to potential.

"You guys aren't losers or quitters," he yelled at them. "You are winners, so act like it out there."

Coach had always had an ability to arouse deep feeling in his players and I could see the effect this was having on the offense as we all sat there in silence.

We went back out onto the field but it was pretty much a repeat of the first half in the third quarter. Both teams went scoreless. We were close to scoring as the quarter ended and on the first play of the fourth quarter, we pushed the ball over the goal line for six points. Lords actually kicked another extra point and the score was 14-6 in our favor.

Fourth quarter-this was always our quarter. The defense was solid, as usual, and the offense finally got on-track. We scored two more times quite easily, one of them being the most beautiful open field runs I had ever seen. The play was a double reverse with Bill Thomas running back and forth across the field directing traffic and picking up blockers as he moved down the field. The play took up almost a full minute as he was all over the field. The ball was snapped at our 46-yard line but he must have run 146 yards on his way to score.

The game ended and we were all very happy with the results. I would have felt much better if we could have scored two or three more touchdowns, but we'd won, and no one could really ask for more.

That night we had a good victory dance at the school and

afterward a bunch of us headed over to the Westbank Restaurant for some food. The Westbank was just where you'd think it would be-on the west bank of the Snake River overlooking the waterfalls that gave the city its name. It wasn't the Ritz Carlton but it was probably one of the nicest places for a good meal in I.F. We always had a good time there but things sometimes tended to get a bit on the rowdy side.

The hostess was a big woman who had the personality of a gorilla. We were standing at her station waiting to be seated and she was complaining about the way we always came there and caused trouble.

She asked, "Don't you kids have anywhere to go at night?"

"Sure," said Hickman.

"Where," she asked.

I was as interested in the up-coming reply as she appeared to be.

"Right here," Hickman shot back. The guys all got a good laugh out of it, but she wasn't amused at all.

We sat down, ordered a hamburger and were talking about girls and whatever came up, when I heard someone yell, **"Couch, grab this."**

I looked up to see a salt shaker come flying across the restaurant, but I couldn't get to it and it crashed into the wall next to our table. I looked up to see the gorilla storming across the room to our table.

"You football players are all the same," she yelled out, "Now hurry and finish your food, get out of here and don't come back."

We tried in vain to tell her we had nothing to do with it, but she didn't believe a word we said. We finished our meal and headed home.

Monday was award time again. Some of the guys were getting so many stars on their helmets that you could hardly see the headgear for the stars. It was great to see everyone feeling good about themselves and the team as a whole.. We were proud to be Skyline Grizzlies and the record we had so far this season.

We began practice for the Madison game, our next opponent. They were the only team we had beaten the year before, besides the big win over Idaho Falls High. Madison was in Rexburg, a little town north of Idaho Falls wedged between Sugar City and Rigby and just east of the Menan Butte.

The latter was an ancient volcanic remnant where thousands of jackrabbits could be seen running between the rims of the crater. We would often go up there with our .22 rifles and shoot those pesky critters that could raise such havoc with the local farmers' crops. The rabbit population was often out of control resulting in rabbit drives to lower the numbers to manageable levels. Those events would surely raise the ire and sensibilities of the animal lovers of today! They never would have been held, I'm sure, had the environmentalists and other such rabble-rousers been organized at the time. But that was when intelligence and common sense was more in vogue rather than the heretical notions of the "hare" brains of today.

Anyway, we thought this game would be much the same as a rabbit drive or Saturday afternoon at Menan Butte picking off rabbits at will. Practice was quite relaxed all week, but this was Homecoming, our first as a school, and we wanted to make sure it was a good one.

We all went to bed early the night before this game. Probably because we all remembered last year when half the team had stayed out late the night before a game and had gone to Idaho Falls' Homecoming since we didn't have one that year (pretty tough having a Homecoming when there was no one yet to come home!).

Homecoming at Idaho Falls High School had its traditions. One that was the most interesting and unique was the competition between classes to see which group could amass the biggest woodpile. The pile would be set afire the night before the big game at a Pep Rally. The contest had started years ago and had grown every year to the current state of affairs.

The usual site for the contest was in the parking lot next to the school but with its being improved and paved due to the amount of cars that were being driven to school as time went on, it was moved to a large vacant lot the city owned east of the high school. In fact the lot was a full city block in size. This was appropriate since the size of the piles had grown perceptibly as each year came and went.

This particular year the piles were HUGE. Some would say that the annual event was a good thing because it resulted in the gathering up of all the flammable material that had been lying around as junk for the past year. As the size of the contest and the appetite of the individual class members increased each year, the supply of the "legal" wood was soon overcome by the demand to have a larger pile than the class next door.

The piles were indeed "next door" to each other and they grew each day-actually each night as the scroungers would scour the surrounding environs for any piece of wood that was not nailed down. And even that did not in every case insure that the wood "nailed down" would not end up in the pile anyway. The scavengers would just bring it and whatever it was nailed to!

You could see outhouses in the pile, signs, 2x4's, limbs, doors, trees, derrick poles, railroad ties, mailbox posts, scrub brush, bales of straw-you name it, it was there if it could burn. The respective classes would have 24-hour guards on their piles to prevent competing students from pilfering from their already "hot" tinder pile.

The piles grew and grew and everyone looked with anticipation to the night of the Pep Rally. The initial position of the piles was centered in the vacant lot-the first stick thrown down was within feet of the exact center of the area. Easiest access to the piles was off 12th Street and as the piles grew, it wasn't noticed that the piles were getting closer and closer to that side of the lot.

The night of the rally saw three of the biggest piles one had ever seen. The "creativity and ingenuity" of the collectors was only exceeded by the height and breadth of the HUGE piles that were about to be lit. Once the cheers and calls for victory had run their course, the selected honorees from each class ran to their pile and torched it off. There was soon a fire of enormous size and heat.

Now, I know you are going to say that the following is a bit exaggerated, but I can promise you it's not. You could roast your weenie from a 110 yards away. Marshmellows would melt before you could get them on your straightened-out coat hanger. And worse, the paint on the houses across 12th Street blistered because of the heat! That was the last year for that contest. But it was a great one. The sophomore class won that year. Probably due to the fact that they were the most populous class at school that year.

Coach was hot then, too. He was so mad when we lost that game last year; he put us through a series of running drills the next Monday that liked to kill us all. That was something none of us would ever forget and something we didn't want to experience again.

As we dressed in our uniform for the evening, I noticed a very somber mood in the locker room. It was very quiet, more so than on other occasions so far this year. We were all lying there on the floor, sitting against the walls or on the benches with the lights off as usual. We were waiting to go out when Coach opened the door to the coach's office and came out. The lights went on and Coach was standing there.

I noticed how thin his face was getting and the greenish cast his skin had taken on of late. I wondered how much pain he endured every day. He talked about this being our first Homecoming and how we would be setting the example and the traditions that would be part of this school for years to come. He drove home again the principle of giving our all.

"Give your all and you will feel good. Don't, and you will feel it-cheated in the end. This applies to everything you do in life, not just in a football game," he said.

Coach finished and looked around the locker room for a few seconds. I could see how he loved this, teaching young boys how to be men. "Couch, where are you?" he called out.

"Right here, Coach," I answered.

"Let's have prayer and then I have a letter for the captain of the team to read to the players."

We quickly had prayer and all the coaches left the room. I opened the sealed envelope Coach had handed to me as he left which was addressed to "Captain, Skyline Grizzlies." I stood up on one of the benches to read it. It was from Ray Groth, who had played football for Coach a few years before at Idaho Falls High School and had been a super quarterback. He went on to play for the University of Utah and was very successful there, too.

I looked down at the single hand written page and began to read:

Dear Skyline Football Team:

I wanted to write this letter to you before your Homecoming game and tell you how lucky you are to have a coach like Coach Ravsten. He is one in a million and has taught me more about myself and life than any other person I have ever known. The impact he has had on me will go with me forever. For you see, he has built the foundation of my character, which he so often talked to all of us about.

I remember so many times when I was tired, discouraged and lacked the confidence in myself and the ability to do the job. Coach always had a way of building not only me, but also the entire team. He has an ability to get 100% effort out of those he works with. He knows what life is all about and helps us all to face life and the challenges that come to us daily.

When you go out on the field today, I hope you will all have the love for Coach that I have. I love him as I love my own father. The best way to show your love is to play up to your ability and beyond. Give 100 percent because he is giving 110 percent for each and every one of you.

Good luck today. You will never know how much each of you means to Coach. I am sure he means the same to each of you. Show him your love now because it won't be long and you won't be able to.

Ray Groth

I paused for a minute and continued to stare at the last sentence. I knew it was true. My vision went blurry from the tears coming into my eyes and I had a huge lump in my throat. I looked up to see all of the team with their heads down, looking at the floor. I could see a number of them wiping tears from their eyes as I stepped down from the bench.

A moment later, the door opened to the coach's office and the coaches all walked out. Coach Ravsten looked at all of us and saw the determination in our eyes.

Then he looked at me and simply said, "Take them out, Couch."

I stepped to the door and looked back. It was an awesome, even beautiful sight in a funny sort of way, to see a bunch of boys that a coach had turned into men, men with tears in their eyes and a deep love in their hearts.

I looked at them and yelled, "**Ready**?"

A roar came back, "**Ready**!"

I opened the door and out onto the field we ran.

The following newspaper article recapped the game in Sunday's paper. (It was actually printed and delivered on Saturday but it was the "Sunday" paper with the color comics and all.) The story was there in black and white and it was a fair representation of what had happened on the surface, but no one knew the true story of the game, except for those of us who worked so hard for a man we truly loved.

**HALL, GODDARD, REVELLO
HELP PACE GRIZZLIES**

Kim Hall, Skyline High School's quarterback, helped to insure the success of the school's first Homecoming celebration Friday as he ran for one touchdown and passed for three more to lead the Grizzlies to a 46-6 Eastern Idaho Conference win over Madison's Bobcats. The Grizzlies, currently ranked fifth in the Idaho State Associated Press football poll, started out with an explosion that gave them three touchdowns in the first four minutes of the first quarter, but didn't score again until the third period.

For the most part, the game centered on the running of Gary Revello, Craig Lords and Leonard Rios, the passing of Hall and the magic hands of rangy end Jack Goddard who caught two touchdown passes. Rios also caught two touchdown tosses to add to his ground churning laurels.

The Grizzlies gained more than 500 yards against the Bobcat defense that couldn't find the combination to hold Skyline until late in the first period, but by that time the score was 19-0 for the Idaho Falls school.

Madison received the opening kick-off, but was forced to punt. On the first play from scrimmage, Hall passed to Goddard who carried to the opponent's 15-yard line and Revello ran it to the six on the next play. On the third play from scrimmage Hall kept the ball and finding no receivers open, ran it across for the first score of the game. Lords booted the extra point.

Skyline kicked off and held Madison who was again forced to punt. Lords took the punt on the 50 and ran it all the way back to the two-yard line before being knocked out of bounds. On the first play from scrimmage, halfback Bill Thomas pounded into the end zone. Lords' extra point try failed and it was 13-0.

Skyline again kicked off and held Madison. When Madison

punted on fourth down, Rios took the ball all the way back to the 19 from his own 30. Hall connected with Goddard to the nine and hit Rios on the next play on the two. Rios stepped in for the six points. Lords passed to Hurley for the extra point, but the pass was incomplete and the Grizzlies led 19-0 while having run only seven plays from the line of scrimmage.

It was shortly after this that the Madison defense finally began to click against the powerful Skyline Grizzlies for the remainder of the first quarter and through the second period.

Skyline threatened just before the first quarter ended, but a series of penalties slowed their progress before they could get the ball into scoring territory. Fullback Richard Farnsworth ran the ball from the seven to the two-yard line and plunged over on the next play, but the referees ruled that he dropped the ball and Madison took over on the 20.

The school marching band presented a somewhat rain-spattered half time salute and prize-winning homecoming floats were paraded around the field.

Back on the field to start the third period, the Grizzlies appeared about ready to repeat their earlier first period performance. They received the opening kick-off and within two plays from scrimmage, had put the ball across the goal line for another touchdown. This was done by Revello rambling to the 38 of Madison on an off-tackle trot. Sliding around right end from the 18, he went into the end zone untouched. Lords kicked the extra point.

After Madison failed to move the ball on the first two plays after they had received the kick-off, Arden Bird quick kicked and the surprised Grizzlies had to take over on their own 25-yard line. Revello, Rios and Terry Evans did the lion's share of the ground gaining to the Madison 30 and then Hall took to the air, hitting Goddard for a first down on the 19 and then zeroing in on Rios in the end zone for another touchdown pass. Lords failed to make the extra point and it was 32-0 for the Grizzlies.

The Bobcats had their turn and launched an offensive attack that took them deep into enemy territory via the penalty route against Skyline. Gordon Genta, a halfback, passed to end Jack Smith who caught the ball in the end zone for Madison's only score of the game. The pass play attempt for the extra point failed.

In the fourth period the Grizzlies picked up the ball again and Hall unleashed a bomb to the Madison 46. Goddard made a sensational catch with a Madison defender all over him and made his way into the end zone to make it 38-6. Lords kicked the extra point and it was 39-6.

The Grizzlies wrapped up the scoring when the second string quarterback passed to Goddard from the Madison 40 for another touchdown. The point try was good by Lords and the scoring was over for the night.

The Grizzlies drew 110 yards in penalties for the night, most of them 15 yarder's, while Madison managed to lose but 40 by way of the red handkerchief.

"It was such an easy game for us," Coach Ravsten said. "Our defense simply overwhelmed them. We blitzed and stacked them like crazy. Everything seemed to work. Second and third string got a chance to play a lot."

After the game Coach came around and shook all of our hands and said thanks. He wasn't looking good and he went right home. We all finished dressing and went over to the Victory dance. It was a really good dance and we all had a very good time. Afterward we all went over to the Westbank to get something to eat. I wondered if they would let us in after our last little episode there. But nothing happened and we all enjoyed our hamburgers and went home to bed.

Lessons Learned:

To be dedicated to a cause is an admirable trait. Dedication to proper principles will bring happiness and joy.

Dedication will give the strength necessary to battle through when the night seems the darkest or the challenge the most intimidating. It will provide the power to defeat the challengers and overcome the obstacles that stand in the way.

Encompassed in dedication is a realization that the sought for goal or objective is worthy of being attained and the effort required in achieving it worth the expenditure, no matter what that expenditure might entail.

A thought process must precede this dedicatory exercise and within that process, the overall situation be examined. With an understanding of the goal and the reasons for achieving it, one can go forward, confident that the effort required will be rewarded in the end.

To seek after that which is virtuous, lovely or can be praised or said well of is a goal that can be dedicated to with assurance that once the journey is complete, the reward will be worth the effort.

Chapter 11

"When we do the best that we can, we never know what miracle is wrought in our life, or in the life of another."
Helen Keller

When I got up on Monday and drove over to the school for practice, I realized the season was almost over. Fall was my favorite time of the year. Besides being the season of the year that football was played, I loved the crisp clear air and the different smells that autumn brought, carried on the breezes through the falling leaves. The hills were ablaze with the reds, greens, golds and yellows that resulted from the trees turning with the approaching winter. It wasn't hot during the days and not too cool in the evenings. It was just a great time of the year and I loved it. Despite this reveling in the glories of fall, all of a sudden I got this sick, lonely feeling in the pit of my stomach. I didn't want the football season to end.

As usual, just before the real grind of Monday morning practice, we had the normal awards for outstanding play in the previous Friday night's game. This little session lasted a bit longer than customary because of the number of team members getting in the game and doing such an admirable job. Monday practices were a grind because you usually had some bumps and bruises or tender ankles, shoulders or thighs that hadn't quite rested up from the previous game. These extremities were hollering out for more of the rest and recuperation they had enjoyed on Saturday and Sunday.

Never mind the pain and discomfort. One of Coach's favorite statements, especially when you went down hard and came up bleeding was, "Rub a little dirt in it and it'll be okay!" So you didn't mope around with your head hung down or let on that you were hurting in any way, unless, of course it was serious.

The one who really had the serious hurt was showing us the way beyond pain and suffering and we began to practice under his tutelage for Burley, who we would play there on Friday afternoon. Coach Ravsten had a very strong personal rivalry with the coach over there. In fact, we had heard that it was a strong dislike. I don't know where that came from-Coach certainly didn't make any mention of personalities involved in the matter but we had the same instant dislike, imagined or not.

Last year Burley had run us into the ground. Burley is another small farming community in Southern Idaho that just for the sake of size we should beat, but last year we just couldn't stop them. This year would be different. We would get them good-we just wanted to make up for the past year's humiliation.

Their offense involved the shotgun play-set and it had really given us fits last year. We practiced really hard during the week and felt very confident we would be able to stop them this year.

On Wednesday after practice, I was messing around with Terry Evans and Bob Nelson "fighting" over a can of pop. The can flew out of someone's hand and hit me in the forehead, splitting my head open. Ten stitches later the wound was all closed up, but how was I going to wear my helmet? Coach saw me at school and asked what had happened. He just shook his head and said disgustedly, "No sympathy from me. You shouldn't have been screwing around."

On Friday we all dressed in our blazers and went over to the school early. As my mother dropped us off, she told me she and Dad would drive over for the game and see us there. That was the same "bon voyage" I always got when being dropped off for an away game. I really appreciated the support my parents gave the team and me. There were a lot of other parents that likewise drove to every away game to cheer the team on and lend their support. I think it was as much for Coach Ravsten as for their sons that they made those trips. If this man could make the sacrifice for their sons, they surely could.. And they all respected Coach as a person, too.

We ran into the locker room, got our gear, put it in the luggage compartment under the bus and climbed on. This was another Teton Stage Lines Coach that was much more comfortable than those hard-seated yellow fellows. Comfortable or not in the seating area, I was still concerned about the stitches in my head. All week I had not participated in any contact drills or scrimmages. I just ran through the plays without my helmet on because of the bandaged area covering the stitches on my head. I hadn't tackled anyone nor had any contact since I'd gotten them. It was a welcome respite from the rigors of weekly practice, but I would have given back the stitches in trade for the head banging of practice, if the truth were known.

It was a long trip over to Burley but we had a good time on the bus talking and telling jokes. The game was set for 1:00 p.m. It was another beautiful, warm and sunny fall day-a perfect day for football, not too hot, not too cold. In fact, it was a perfect day for anything!

We arrived and quickly dressed, after which Coach gave a pep talk and we went out to warm up. I noticed that Coach was having a downer of a day and looked very weak. Most of the time I just accepted the way things were and didn't really notice any drastic changes. You know, if it's incremental on a daily basis, sometimes it's not so easy to discern. Especially if you were in denial which was the case with most, if not all of us on the team. No one wanted to think that this could end one day; that Coach would not always be there to cheer us on, show us a new block, teach us the way, encourage us in our failings or kick us in the butt when we needed it, which was often. But if you really were up to a reality check and looked, you could see a change taking place in his body. He was losing a lot of weight in his face and chest, yet his stomach was protruding quite noticeably. Back to denial. It was easier.

Out on the field we got all warmed up and I noticed my folks and a number of other parents from our neighborhood sitting on the bleachers right behind our bench on the visitors side of the field.

We won the toss and elected to receive. Rios took the ball at about the goal line and got a good return of nearly 30 yards. On first down Kim rolled right and hit Goddard for a 34-yard gain. We continued to move down the field but stalled on Burley's 36. We went for it on fourth down and Goddard grabbed a quick pass over the middle for a 17-yard gain and a first down. Kim moved the ball down to the five-yard line on a quarterback sneak, where on the next play he handed off to Revello over the middle of their line. When I say "over," I mean OVER! He saw the defense hunkered down and blocking any entrance into the end zone via the normal route so he vaulted over them into six-point land. All in all it was quite easy. We were up 7-0 after the extra point.

We lined up for the kick-off and Lords really put his foot into the ball. He could positively kill the ball on a kick-off, but his success at extra points was not too exciting. I looked over after the referee had blown the play dead since we'd tackled the run back man and saw Lords slowly getting up. He'd really taken a shot from someone.

Burley had gotten a good return out to the 32-yard line. We were still in our defensive huddle as they came up to the line of scrimmage so we scrambled into our defensive positions for the set that I had called. Horrors! They weren't in the shotgun formation we had practiced for all week; they were in a pro-set. None of us knew who or what we should be keying off. They hiked the ball and picked up a quick 11 yards thanks to our confusion. In the huddle we discussed what to do half-expecting Coach to send someone in with instructions. But nothing happened. No one was coming from the sideline. He was leaving the decisions to us. I could see Coach standing there on the sideline with his arms folded and, I'm convinced he had a sly little smile on his face. He was going to leave it up to us.

Burley broke the huddle and came up to the ball.

I yelled out, **"Play them just like Madison."**

We could handle that and were ready and stopped them cold. They moved the ball out to just about mid-field where they had to punt. They got a super punt and a good bounce to the eight-yard line where we took over first and 10 going back to the north.

We couldn't move the ball this time and we punted after the first three plays. Both teams struggled back and forth the rest of the first period with no one getting anywhere. In the second quarter, Burley gave up the pro-set and went back to the shotgun, but we were ready for that since it had been the object of our prior week's practices so were able to shut that down, too. However, they were moving the ball better than anyone had since Highland, and we knew we were in a football game. Right near the end of the second quarter they moved the ball down field to our 15. We were having a tough time, but this was where we always dug in and made every inch a hard fought battle for the opposing team. If they wanted to get into our end zone, they would have to really earn that feat.

They tried running into the line three times and we didn't budge an inch. It was fourth and 10 from the 15. Their quarterback dropped straight back into the pocket of blockers and lofted one to the middle of the end zone just shy of the end line. Don Johnson was all over the back of the receiver when he caught the ball on his outstretched fingertips. Even though it was a Burley score, it was really a very pretty pass and reception. Just as the receiver stepped across the back line of the end zone and the ref signaled a touchdown, the gun went off ending the first half of action.

Johnson was going crazy; yelling and jumping up and down, saying the receiver was over the end line. I didn't know, so I just kept my mouth shut. Johnson was really hot in the huddle and wanted to be the one to stop the extra point. The kick was a bit wide and the ball hit the post and bounded back onto the playing field. We all walked off the field with the score now 7-6, still in our favor. We took it very personally when someone scored on us.

In the locker room I noticed Lords over in the corner with Coach Jacoby helping him. Lords took a shot in the groin nearly every time he performed his kick-off duties. He had a bad habit of watching to see how well he had done on the kick and how far it went, all the while ignoring the oncoming blockers. Invariably one would get him unawares in that second tenderest part of the human body (according to my sisters and our "scientific" family vote). Lords was standing there with his pants down facing the wall in the corner.

He looked up and said plaintively, "I'm bleeding!"

We all cracked up. But he didn't think it was very funny.

Neither did Coach; the game thus far that is. He climbed all over us, saying we weren't playing up to our potential at all. We immediately came back to our senses and got focused on what we would have to do in the second half to win this thing. We all felt badly about the defensive unit's performance.. Even though six points scored against us wasn't the end of the world, we were very sensitive about any points being scored.

As we were going out for the second half, Coach grabbed me and told me to watch out for the guy who had hit Lords on the kick-off.

"Give him a good shot," Coach said.

We lined up for the kick-off. I was standing with my back to Burley to set everyone off, as I always did. I was looking around to see if I could figure out who it was that would come at Lords.

The whistle was blown and I sent everyone down field as Lords ran by to kick the ball. As he passed me, I quickly turned and watched Craig. I saw a player off to my right coming hard at Lords. He was concentrating on Craig so intently that he didn't see or expect me. I had to run hard to get to him before he hit Lords. I was going to hit him right in front of Lords, who had still not learned to defend himself after a kick-off and was admiring the flight of the ball, oblivious to the collision that was about to occur.

THWACK! I heard a moan and then Lords was standing over me, slapping me on the back and helmet saying, "Hey, thanks man, thanks—thanks a lot." I stood up but the Burley man was still lying there on the ground. The ref blew the whistle and their coaches came out, woke him up and carried him off the field. I didn't think I'd hit him that hard!

Burley was unable to move the ball and the defense stopped them easily. But our offense couldn't do anything either and we punted deep into their territory. They fumbled on the first play from scrimmage and we recovered at their 12-yard line. Terry Evans ran the ball in on the next play. Six points in very rapid order. We made the extra point and kicked off to Burley who elected to let the ball bound out of the end zone rather than try a run back.

Their offense came out and Burley began to move the ball on us. They got one first down and on the next play we were penalized for piling on. Coach Ravsten didn't agree and walked out on the field. Suddenly, another flag went up from the ref. Coach was really upset with him and he gave us another penalty. We had just received 45 yards in penalties! I was so mad I could hardly talk. The defense huddled on our 30 and we were all just boiling. Bauchman's eyes glistened with anger, he was so mad. In the stands, my father heard one man say, "Those refs shouldn't have made those calls against their coach. Look at those boys, they're fighting mad." You could even see it from the stands.

Burley came up to the ball. On the snap Bauchman literally picked his man up off the ground with a big grunt, threw him to his left and grabbed the running back in the back field, dropping him at the 34. The next play was much the same, with Bauchman stopping the back at the 35. On the next play Taylor dropped the fullback three yards deep on an option play for another loss. Our emotions were sky high and the entire team had been sparked. They would have to punt after they had been given nearly half the length of the field in penalties. We were vindicated.

We set up the return to the right. They punted and the ball came down to Rios. He came up the right side. I loved this procedure and saw a man coming at me, but he didn't see me. That's why I guess I liked these run-backs so much. The opposing team members were so intent on the ball carrier, they oft times didn't see a blocker coming. And I was that invisible blocker. I hit him at the knees and he did a complete cartwheel in mid-air, landing on his stomach. What a great feeling it was to execute a good block. As I hit the ground my facemask dug into the grass and my helmet pulled down on my forehead. I felt a ripping as the stitches were torn out. It hurt somewhat, but not too badly. I walked off the field as blood ran down the bridge of my nose. Coach Jacoby grabbed me, washed off the blood and pulled the gap together with some Band-Aids.

I could just hear Coach say, "Rub a little dirt in it!"

The offense couldn't move the ball and the defense went back in the game. Burley couldn't advance the ball either. The defense was doing the kind of job we knew we were capable of. But the blood kept running down my face and I had to go to the sideline for a quick wash up, new Band Aids (these new technology, super sticky ones we have now weren't available then) and then back into the game.

We scored again at the end of the third quarter and could tell we were beginning to dominate them. Second string went in and we scored twice more in the fourth quarter making the final score

28-6. The score doesn't always tell the whole story. It would appear it was an easy game for Skyline, especially in light of the fact the second string offense had scored two touchdowns in the final period, but we who had been on the field, knew it had been a very emotional and physical game.

As we were undressing in the locker room, Burley's coach came in and asked for a minute of our time.

He said, "I'd like you boys to know I have never seen a better coached team in all of my life. You boys have a wonderful man to lead and coach you. You are a great team and I will be listening with great interest to see how badly you beat Idaho Falls this next week."

A loud roar went up from all of us. I watched as the two coaches shook hands and talked for a minute. I didn't know what the problem had been between them in the past, probably was one of those supposed relationships that didn't exist except in the figment of someone's imagination, but I thought how good it was to see them talking and shaking hands.

After dressing we all went out and got on the bus for the long ride home. They had delayed the broadcast of the game on the radio. The bus had a radio on it-real high tech for the times-and listening to the game I found out my cousin had been playing for Burley and I hadn't even known it. It sounded funny to hear the announcer say, "And Couch tackles Couch." The bus ride home was a fun one. We were all in good spirits, telling jokes and having a good time.

On Monday we began practice for our last game of the season. This would be my last game and probably Coach's, too. I was not near big enough to go on to college football so I knew that this would be the last week of practice (which I wouldn't miss too much) leading to the last organized game of football I would play in my life.

The weather changes quickly in Idaho and had turned from Indian Summer to Eskimo Winter overnight. It was quite cold and the ground was frozen. It made full contact quite unpleasant. Emotions were running high because we all wanted to win this last game against our biggest rival very badly. One more victory and we would have given Coach his desire-an undefeated season!

On Wednesday, a few of us who played football and a few other friends decided we wanted to go paint the streets. Last year the same thing had happened, but it had gotten out of hand and some of the kids had decided to paint the school and some other very prominent buildings in town. We all decided we would stick to just one area of town and paint only the streets with slogans like "Beat I.F." or "GO Skyline.

Jim Hales got five one-gallon cans of white paint and we all met at my house.. My father asked me where we were going so I told him and he simply said, "You had better not, or you'll be calling me from the police station." I told him we wouldn't do anything destructive, just the streets with little sayings, nothing dirty, mean or destructive.

Out the door we went in high spirits and drove off in Delmar Gray's car. We drove over to 23rd Street and picked up Fred and Mike. We parked the car on 23rd and walked about 50 feet down to Boulevard and began to paint "BEAT I..F." in big, bold, white letters. Fred and I walked down past the Sacred Heart Hospital to the house of a girl he was dating. We talked to her for about 20 minutes and then walked back toward Delmar's car.

Suddenly, I recognized a cop car parked right behind his car. We looked at it for a few seconds wondering what to do.

All of a sudden I heard over a loud speaker, **"Okay boys, we see you. Now come on over here."**

Fred and I started running like rabbits back down Boulevard to 25th where we hung a left and started up the street next to the hospital. We were both holding onto a paint can in one hand and a paintbrush in the other. Paint was splattering all over both of us as we flew down the street. Unknown to us at the time, Delmar was sitting in the police car with the cops. He rehearsed all that happened in the police car that night as we later talked the whole experience over. They had followed us in the car and were all laughing as they watched us running down the street.

"Look at those guys go, spilling paint all over the place," one cop laughed to the other.

The cop sitting in the passenger seat grabbed the radio and said, "Unit 10, this is unit 16. Two kids coming your way up 25th Street."

Fred and I ran two blocks up the street, across the footbridge at the canal and hung another left along the canal bank and back toward 24th Street. There in the middle of the intersection, right under the streetlight, we saw Jim painting the road.

"**Hey**!" I yelled.

Jim jumped about six feet straight up and headed off in the opposite direction at at least 60 miles an hour. Fred and I just about died laughing at him as we called him back.

"Get rid of the paint," we told him. "The cops are after us!"

"I know," Jim said, "They've been chasing me, too." (I never did figure out why he had stopped to continue painting in the middle of a "hot pursuit" by the police and never did ask him about it later either.)

Just then we saw a cop car go by a block away with his lights turned off. He stopped as he saw us standing there under the street light-really smart on our part. We took off down an alley as fast as our legs would carry us. This was exciting and fun. We saw some garbage cans on our left as we were moving down the alley and slipped behind them to hide. There was a vacant lot between the alley and the street and we could see the cop car coming slowly down the street with his spotlight on, scanning every nook and cranny he could see. He stopped right across from us and shined his light across the vacant lot and onto the garbage cans we were hiding behind.

"Don't move and don't let the light hit you," I whispered.

They kept the light on us for about 30 seconds, but it seemed like hours. The cruiser went on down the street and we returned back up the alley in the opposite direction.

In the cop car the officers were having as much fun as we were, laughing at us as we ran all over the neighborhood. We ran down the street evading two black and whites by slipping into the bushes around the homes along the street. Fred jumped a fence and a large dog came charging at him sounding as ferocious as a mountain lion, so back over the fence he flew. His eyes were as big as basketballs as he looked at us and said, "Damn, I'll take my chances with the cops." I was laughing so hard I could hardly stand up.

"Come on, let's get out of here. The cops will hear that stupid dog and be here in a minute," I said.

We weren't too far from Fred's house so we ran down the alley, jumped over his back fence and slipped into his house. We talked for a while and decided we ought to go see what had happened to Delmar. Fred didn't want to go, so Jim and I headed out the back door and back to 23rd Street where we had left Delmar and his car. The car was sitting right where we had left it with the keys in the ignition. It was rare to even hear about someone stealing a car in Idaho Falls so it was not uncommon to see keys left intact with the owner nowhere to be seen. No one else was in sight.

We went home and got Jim's and drove down to the police station. We were scared to death to walk in, but decided we would just say we were looking for our friend and see what happened. Besides, we had been down there with the goose a few weeks before and had come through that experience unscathed. There was that lingering memory of the unwelcome noise coming from behind the bars of the cells that night, however, that we would rather not experience first hand.

We walked up to the front desk and told them what we were doing there and were referred to a man in a back room. We walked with the officer from the front desk back to the waiting room and sat down. He told us to wait for a minute and someone would be with us. He was smiling as he walked away. Another man came out of an adjoining room and asked us to come in. He was smiling, too. I was scared. I figured we had made a mistake coming into the police station, but it was too late now. I didn't want to get into any trouble.

As we sat down, he looked at me and said, "Are you Fred Finlayson, Jim Hales, Bruce Couch, or Mike Schafer?"

I felt sick, and Jim went white as we looked at each other. We both knew it was best to just turn ourselves in, rather than lie. So we fessed up and were told to call our parents and have them come pick us up. He complimented us for coming in ourselves and then said, "Now, if you guys want to do this tomorrow night, use some white wash."

"Oh, you won't pick us up if we use white wash then?" I said.

"Oh yes, we'll have to pick you up. But it will wash up much easier than the paint," he said. "Chasing you boys is about as much fun as I have had in a long, long time," he laughed.

I called Dad and simply said, "Dad, can you come pick me up?"

"Where are you?" he asked.

"At the police station, like you predicted," I replied.

He got there in about twenty minutes. He went directly to the front desk officer whom I overheard telling Dad not to be hard on us because we weren't being destructive and we had turned ourselves in.

On the he way home Dad said, "I hope you learned a lesson tonight."

I had, but couldn't really articulate it and had still had a lot of fun. I also had learned cops were all right and liked to have fun just as much as we did. In fact, I think they probably had more fun than we did. I got no real grief from my parents and the issue was as good as dead as far as I was concerned at the moment.

The next day at school we cussed Delmar for giving the cops

our names. But he said he had no choice because they were going to impound his car and it would have cost him fifty dollars to get it out.

"So we were sold out for fifty bucks," we all laughed.

Then he told us about how much fun the cops were having chasing us around while he was in the backseat watching and listening to their conversations.

Everyone at the school thought what had happened was funny. Everyone, that is, except Mr. Bigalow, the principal. He called all of us into his office, "cussed us out" really good and threatened to keep us from playing in the final game of the year. But he relented and allowed us the privilege of participating in the upcoming game.

Coach grabbed me in the hall and asked if we were all trying to get kicked off the team.

"We didn't think it was any big deal," I told him.

"Well, you didn't think much period. Because of what happened last year and the way it got out of hand, I had to talk like a Dutch Uncle to get permission for you to play and not get kicked off the team," he said.

Lessons Learned:

Example is a most misunderstood virtue in regard to its power and influence on the mind and will of man. When one is honored and respected and has achieved a position of leadership, the effect of the example that person provides to others who emulate those traits exemplified is probably never recognized for the impact it can and does have.

Many are in recognized positions of leadership and as such are aware of the impact their actions, words and deeds have on the lives of others. Others are not in universally recognized positions of leadership, but are looked to by peers to show the way and lead to better pastures.

It was said by Talleyrand, "I am more afraid of an army

of 100 sheep led by a lion than an army of 100 lions led by a sheep."

The leadership provided by one who recognizes the power of example will overcome all odds when proper and valuable goals are the objective and effort is at all times focused on the achievement of that end-whether someone is looking or not.

Because, most of the time, someone is.

Chapter 12

"Try not to become a man of success, but rather to become a man of values."
Albert Einstein

This was the week that was. There would not be another like this one for most of us in our later lives. Idaho does not produce many stellar college players to say nothing of the meager number of native Idahoans who have gone on to the ranks of the pros in any sport. Regardless, we were out there on the football practice field in weather that others would consider to be the dead of winter. We were loving it.

Practice went well all week long and on Friday we all dressed in our game uniforms because that day was mental preparation day, with no hitting. We ran through all the plays we were going to use in the upcoming game and reviewed specific assignments. It was all review and stuff for the head. Besides, if anyone got hurt on the last day before a game, there would not be any time to heal or to "rub a little dirt in it." So the day before a game was always a no-contact day.

We were all milling around outside, waiting for practice to begin and I.F. was having a pep rally in the gym across the practice field. We could hear some yelling and cheering emanating from the gathering. Actually, they were raising the roof! This was the last game of the season for them, too, and besides that, this game meant so much more than any other did. This was neighbor against neighbor, friend against friend, former classmate against former classmate. The schools had not been split long enough to have the demarcation lines so distinct as to eliminate all the relationships that had been forged in the years before when there had been just one school. We had beaten them in the last game of the season last year and started off this year with the victory over their varsity on the opening " exhibition game" of this year. There was some evening of the scales to be accomplished here as far as the Idaho Falls Tigers were concerned.

The winner of the game between Idaho Falls and Skyline had the honor of painting the goal posts in their school colors for the upcoming season-until the next conflict was over and victor crowned. It was then that it was determined whether the iron posts would be orange (as they had been since the dawn of time up until last November when they were repainted Skyline Blue) or blue. The current color of the goal posts was a real thorn in the side of the Tiger student body and if they had anything to do about it, the color would shortly change back to orange. If the volume of the noise coming from the gymnasium was any indication of the intensity of the emotion and tenor of the game, we were in for a good one.

Someone said, "Let's go warm up next to the fence down by the gym." So the entire team ran down to the other end of the practice field and we all lined up for our warm up drills. The only thing separating us from the gym was a narrow parking lot and that same wire rope that my brother was tenderly climbing over just before the midnight practice Coach had held after being beaten by the Boise Bruins four years before. Neither barrier mitigated any noise going or coming from the gym.

Struss and I came forward to lead the team. **"Okay, side straddle hops,"** I yelled.

"Ready!" "Go!" "Beat I.F.," we began to chant as we marked time for our warm-up drills.

I couldn't believe the noise we were making. We finished the first warm up and a huge yell went up from the team. We were having a ball. We started the next warm up and the noise was even louder. I noticed a bunch of I.F. students had come outside to see what all the noise was about. Suddenly, the assistant principal of I.F. came out of the back door to the gym and walked over to us.

"What are you guys doing?" he yelled. "We're trying to have a pep rally in there and you're making so much noise we can't hear a thing."

A roar went up from the team and everyone started to laugh.

"You guys have got to be quiet or go to the other side of the field where you belong," he yelled at us.

Everyone was laughing as Coach came out to the practice field. He blew his whistle and we all ran over to where he was sitting on his milk stool. We told him what had happened and I could see from the look on his face that he loved it. He was laughing and having a great time.

Practice went very well. We were ready physically, mentally and emotionally.. We would play tomorrow at 1:00 p.m.

Saturday morning I woke up and had a good breakfast. I was nervous as I got in the car and picked up Hickman and some of the other players in the neighborhood. There wasn't a lot of discussion or banter on the 15-block drive from home to the school. I parked the car next to the field house and we walked into the dressing room.

After we had put on the personal shielding of the day, to include taping and reinforcing some of the weaker areas of our anatomies, and were finally dressed, Coach came out and talked to us. He didn't need to pump us up and he could see that. It was obvious that we were very high emotionally and ready for the whistle to blow beginning the game. Yet, at the same time there was a somber, quiet, determined mood in the room. We had a lot of visitors in the locker room that day, the principal and his assistant, a newspaper reporter and a few others.

My brother, who had played for Coach four years earlier, was in the locker room and commented on what a difference there was between the two locker rooms in terms of demeanor and atmosphere. When he played football, Coach Ravsten was the head coach and Dale Leathem was the line coach for Idaho Falls and the second in command, so to speak. Now Coach Leathem was the head coach at Idaho Falls. Rob had mixed emotions about this game having been on the Tiger football team and wrestling squad and a recipient of the Sports Roundtable Athlete of the Year Award when he was a senior. Although he had great respect and admiration for Coach Leathem and the Tigers were "his" team, he was also drawn to Skyline only because of his great love for Coach Ravsten. I don't believe the fact that his brother was the captain of the Skyline football team made a hill of beans of difference to him in his allegiance to the two teams on the docket today. What made a difference was the man who was leading the Grizzlies in our quest for an undefeated season.

Rob had been over to the Tigers' locker room and talked with the coaches over there, all of which he knew well and liked. After a time, he came to the old, renovated auto shop building behind the backstop of the baseball diamond where we had our dressing room. The atmosphere in the Tigers dressing room was one of jubilation and noise. There was loud, heart thumping music playing and the players and coaches alike were very excited and urging each other on with overt action and vociferous urgings.

Coach Leathem was like that, it was his style and he was a great coach. Rob remembered him getting so involved in the challenge box experiences that had been the fare even back in the "old days" when Rob had been in school that Coach Leathem would get in the box himself! He would see a player messing up or not performing properly and he would jerk him out of the box and get in himself to show the proper way to execute the particular skill in question.. Now you may think that would be a downer and embarrassment to the player being jerked from the box, and it was, but the real brunt of the situation was felt by the poor kid who was doing what he should have done and was defeating the offending player.

He had to stand in there and be the opponent for Coach Leathem in his demonstration of the proper way to execute. And execute was generally the proper term. Coach Leathem, with fire in his eyes, would get down in his stance in the box and when the whistle was blown, mow down the player across from him with no regard for anything but making the point of how to execute. And he did this without any pads or helmet while the players, of course, were in full uniform. If you were so "fortunate" as to be his opponent you learned very early in the season to fire out and hit him with everything you had or you would regret it for the next week or so-the time it took for the pain to heal from the physical thumping you took in the box and the wrath he expended on you for "holding back" on him, he could tell.

The scene could not have been more opposite across the practice field. The players, like always, were lying down, sitting in a corner somewhere or quietly talking with another player. You could hear classical music that was softly playing from somewhere in the coaches' office. The intensity could be felt in both dressing rooms and the style of either could not be faulted. The proof would be in the result of the game to be played in very short order..

The principal talked to us for a minute while the coaches were huddling for their last minute preparations in their office, telling us what a great person Coach was. We all knew that.

He cut it short as Coach came out of the office and called out, "Couch, who is going to say the prayer?"

I stood up and asked Coach if he would pray for us. The light went off and we all knelt down. Coach gave a simple prayer, asking that each of us would do his best. He also prayed there would be no injuries on either side and that we would all be good sportsmen. He ended the prayer and we all stood up as the lights went back on.

Coach looked at me for a minute and there was total silence. He looked very tired and sad. I figured he knew that this was his last game. I felt sad because I realized this was my last game, too.

"**Take them out captains**," Coach yelled.

We warmed up via our standard drills and gathered together in the end zone to talk to each other for the last time as a team. It had all come down to this final game of the season, we couldn't let up now. We all had to give 100 percent if we were to win this game. If it took more than that, we would have to reach down and get it from whatever source we could. There would be no coming off that field after the final gun as losers.

The ref signaled for the captains to meet in the middle of the field for the coin toss. Struss and I and walked to the crown of the field at the 50-yard line. There were photographers from both schools and the local newspaper taking all kinds of pictures. We shook hands with the captains from I.F. and tossed the coin. We won the toss, elected to receive and ran to the sideline.

Rios took the kick-off at about the five and ran it out to the 25. On first down Fluke ran into the middle of the line and gained four yards. On second down Hall pitched to Revello and he turned the corner, streaking up the field 71 yards for a score. We all went crazy. This was going to be a fun game.

We kicked off to them and they punted to us after three plays. After a good return by Lords, Hall didn't waste much time. We were really flying high and the offense could do no wrong. Hall connected with Thomas in the flat and he scampered in for the score from the 48. The score moved to 14-0.

We kicked off to them and held them after they succeeded to get one first down. We forced them to punt to us and their kicker got some great protection, took his time and booted a great kick that put us deep in our own territory. On the 10-yard line Hall threw a quick pass out to Goddard on the 20 who moved the ball out another 10 yards to our 30-yard line. After two running plays, Hall hit Revello coming across the middle and he did some outstanding open field running to finally get down to the five-yard line. Fluke smashed into the middle twice and then Thomas flew over the top of the pile at the goal line for six more points. Lords missed the kick (two out of three wasn't bad for him) and halfway through the first quarter the score was 20-0. The rest of the first half was a defensive struggle with neither team moving the ball.

Not much was said in the locker room at half. We had handled them very easily defensively and the tension was eased. Coach looked happy, but tired.

We kicked off to start the second half and stopped them again. We took the punt and the offense began to move down the field like they had done in the first quarter. We got down to the four-yard line where we fumbled and an I.F. player jumped on the ball.

The Tiger offense then took the ball and very methodically and patiently moved down the field. It wasn't very flashy and exciting but they were making good blocks and executing properly and getting just over ten yards on every three plays. After consuming most of the balance of the third period, they were on our 18-yard line. I called for our goal line defense in the huddle, which turned out to be a mistake-we were too far away from the goal line and the compactness of that defensive alignment sabotaged us. Dave Mason, their quarterback, got loose and ran down to the two-yard line for a first down.. It was first and goal.

They had four chances to move the ball just 72 inches. But this was where we really got tough and we knew that we would have to be to keep them out of the end zone. They alternated running plays from one side of the line to the other for three plays but failed to score. On fourth down, Mason did a quarterback sneak and according to the spot of the ball, just barely got it over the goal line. I was really upset because I was right on top of the play and he hadn't really gotten in. But the wing official had called it a touchdown so there wasn't much that could be said. The defense just didn't like anyone scoring on us.

They kicked off to us but we couldn't seem to get the offense going again. After our fumble on the four-yard line, the momentum turned to Idaho Falls and they nurtured it. They had the ball early in the fourth quarter on their 45-yard line. Mason hit Kirn, a small halfback, but the fastest man in the state and suddenly he was running down the left sideline with no one between him and the goal line. Don Johnson came across the field and knocked him out at the three-yard line. How he ever got across the field and caught the fastest halfback in Idaho football, I'll never know, but he did. After two unsuccessful dives into the line, they gave the ball to their big 220-pound fullback. I hit him low at the goal line and he fell into the end zone. The score was suddenly 20-14 and I, along with the rest of the team, began to get really nervous.

Our offense still couldn't move the ball and we ended up punting to them. But the defense got back on track and we shut I.F. off completely on the ground or through the air-we weren't giving an inch. Toward the end of the game the offense got the ball back and began to roll down the field again but there wasn't enough time to score. The gun went off with Kim handing the ball off on an off tackle dive that came up short of the Tiger goal by a wide margin. But we had won 20-14.

We had done it! We were undefeated!

We had given Coach what he wanted, we had kept our promise. Everyone was jumping up and down, hugging each other. Coach grabbed Struss and me and we made our way to the center of the field for the presentation of the award of the game trophy. The photographers took a bunch of pictures as we received the awards. It was a great ending to a great season and I should have been happy, but it was a bittersweet time for me. I fully realized a very important part of my life had come to an end. I had just played my last football game and I didn't like the idea.

After the awards were given out, we all grabbed Coach and carried him into the dressing room. I was almost afraid of hurting him. Once inside, the showers were turned on and we ever so gently threw in Coach. He looked very happy and we were all happy for him. We had all learned so much during this past year.

I sat down on the bench with my helmet on my lap and watched the commotion around me. There were all kinds of people in the dressing room. Congratulations and adulation's were everywhere. I felt hot, sweaty and dirty, but I relished the feeling, it was my last game. I noticed that the seniors like me, who had just played their last game, were more contemplative than the rest. I sat there feeling the scrapes and bruises and not wanting to take off the uniform. I undressed very slowly; half-afraid I might start to cry. I walked into the shower and spent a long time letting the hot water run over my head and down my back.

I remembered that my parents and brother were in the parking lot waiting for me, so I quickly dressed and walked through the dressing room. The smell of sweaty, dirty uniforms and steam from the showers lingered in the air and the sounds of victory conversations from the lips of departing team members slowly gave way to silence as I, too, left the locker room.

I turned just before I opened the door and remembered the happiness that had been generated in that room by those who had spent so much time there. Yet at the same time there was a feeling of sadness. A sadness that only a senior could fully appreciate, for this was the last time we would enjoy the many happy times, trials, growth and pain that we had experienced over the years.

A very big part of my life had come to an end, but I didn't want it to end.

I walked out the door and my football career was over.

Lessons Learned:

To be driven by the winds from pillar to post with no safe harbor in which to shelter oneself from the storms that invariably blow, is indeed a perilous position to be in.

Values will always provide a haven from the storm that will protect one from the influences of the world that would otherwise drag one down and allow decisions to be made that in the end would cause damage beyond repair

A set of values must be defined and then adhered to as one travels through this life to reach the place where each one in his or her heart desires to be..

Those values need to be held to no matter the situation, no matter the influence, no matter the consequences. They will stand immutable in the courts that count when the books are opened and the actions of each one judged

A set of values is the guiding star that can be counted on to shine forth in all weather and all conditions. That star will not fail nor will it go out as long as we consistently fuel it with the power of commitment, integrity, loyalty, dedication, respect and responsibility.

Chapter 13

"...be thou faithful unto death, and I will give thee a crown of life."
Revelations 2:10

Football ended and wrestling started the next day. I had never been very excited about wrestling and had done it mainly for Coach. We began to get into shape and I again quickly found being in shape for football was nothing like being in shape for wrestling. But Coach Ravsten worked us hard and we quickly got there.

About three weeks after the football season, we had our Football Banquet. Coach took a few minutes and expressed the feelings in his heart. He was grateful for the efforts we had put forth during the season and for the outstanding, undefeated season we had achieved. We were all proud to be sitting there and happy for what we had done for Coach. True, it was a great accomplishment for us as a team but it truly had been for him that the season record was 9-0-1.

Wrestling was a great deal of work and Coach Ravsten was showing us some very good moves. While he was the head football coach at Idaho Falls, Coach Dale Leathem was the head wrestling coach and Ravsten was an assistant wrestling coach. Coach Ravsten (and Leathem, for that matter) were football coaches first and only filled the position of wrestling coach as a matter necessity and economics. Necessary because there was no one else to do the job and economic in that they were compensated for the extra duties in a small way. District 91 couldn't afford to hire a "real" wrestling coach as a separate position. That being the case, Coach Ravsten dove in and made a real effort to learn wrestling on his own so he could teach us the finer points of the sport.

One day he stood up in front and showed us a new move. He had his black-rimmed glasses on and I was kneeling there listening to him and thinking how bad he was looking. His skin was a green color; his face had lost so much weight he looked like he was starving to death. Yet his stomach looked like he was seven months pregnant.

Coach suddenly took his glasses off and said, "I've got to take off these danged glasses. They make me look like a cadaver."

He laughed but none of us did. I wondered how he could keep his sense of humor when he was dying and in such pain. He was truly a remarkable man.

One day I was sitting in my trig class and Coach walked by and stopped at the door. I sat at the first desk next to the door and he whispered to me from the hallway, "You need to lose some weight."

I was fine, within weight limits for my class but I would do anything to get out of class.

He looked over at the teacher and said, "Mr. Robinson, Couch needs to lose a bit of weight for the match this week. Is it okay with you if I take him down to the steam room?"

Mr. Robinson was a great guy and very supportive of the students in class and out. We called him "Uncle Robbie" out of affection and with no lack of respect. He could be a stern taskmaster when necessary but we all knew he was fair and honorable. He said it was fine, so off I went.

This same scenario was repeated many times over the next few months during wrestling season and these were times that meant much to me. Coach taught me many of the basics of life that helped me over the years in situations that I had to face. I relied upon the lessons learned from Coach Ravsten to get me through the tests of life. Parents, grandparents, church leaders, relatives and friends all had an impact on my formative years and I would not even think to minimize their impact on my progression. But I suppose the great trials Coach was facing were so visible and poignant at the moment, what he taught had an overarching impact on how his instructions and example were received by me.

We sat just outside a small shower on a wooden bench with towels draped around our waists. This was our "steam room." We turned on the hot water and let it run and sat there in a perfect steam bath. I still don't know where all that hot water came from but there was a lot of it.

As I mentioned before, at our house you had to get wet, shut off the water and soap up, then turn the water back on to rinse. And a short rinse at that.. Otherwise, those at the lower end of the shower schedule would be having a cold shower. Believe it or not, we had compassion on each other despite sibling rivalry because we knew the shock of a cold shower in Idaho-it was cold. At school there was a never-ending supply of hot water and we loved it.

Coach and I talked about many things, from wrestling moves, to football next year, to spiritual subjects, to relationship problems and the numerous gems of leadership he left with me, but never of death.

On that first day we had somewhat of an interview and recapped my attempt at being the leader of the football team. There were some things I had done right and many things I had done wrong. Coach then laid out for me some principles of leadership that have been very helpful in my life.

We started out with the weight training experience where we all sat down at the beginning of each year and set a goal for the efforts we would expend during our time on the weights:

"You have to know where you are going before you can ever begin to accomplish anything," he taught me. "Remember this.

Always begin a task with what you are seeking for foremost in your mind. If you know what you want to accomplish, you can then figure out how to do it. Set priorities in your life. Figure out what is really important to you and write it down. Then you can set your goal to be consistent with what you really believe."

He then taught me a lesson that has helped me manage relationships between others and myself:

"When you are in a group of people and someone begins to criticize another person who isn't there, stop the back stabbing by saying, 'You have a good point. I'm not sure he knows the mistake he is making. Let's figure out how we can tell him how he can overcome this problem.' Then watch what happens. Those without any character will slither away and avoid any confrontation. But you will do more than just help the person who wasn't there. Those who are there will realize you are loyal to those not present and they will know you will also be loyal to them when they aren't there. This will create great loyalty among your peers. Remember those who bad-mouth others in your presence will bad-mouth you when you are not around. Be loyal, and confront those who need to be confronted in a calm, constructive manner.

"Remember when dealing with people, you don't see the world the same way they do. We have all been brought up in a different way with different experiences. Just because you see a situation one-way, doesn't mean it is necessarily so. If you want to be an effective leader, try to put yourself in the shoes of the people you work with. Look at life through their eyes; discover how you fit into the situation and your role in it. Be sensitive to others..

"Don't ever blame others for your problems. You are a big boy now and if you mess up, then simply say, 'I made a mistake and I will do better next time..' Your circumstances, your temper, your mood or your intelligence may influence who you are, but they don't determine who you are. You remember that and you take control of your life. Don't let others determine how you act in a certain situation, you make that determination."

Coach taught us how to win, but he also taught us not to rub our opponents faces in the dirt. He taught us to have respect for those we work with and those we play against. He said:

"In sports, someone has to win and someone has to lose. Yet if you act properly and treat everyone with respect and fairly, everyone can win despite the score. In the world you will find much the same thing. Treat people with respect. You can learn something from every person in this world no matter how dull or uninformed they may seem. When dealing with people, don't take advantage of someone just because you have the ability to do so. Be fair, work out a situation where you both win.

"Now if you can master this next principle you will go a long way in this world as a leader, a friend, a father or whatever you desire to be. Learn to listen to other people. Now, I mean really listen. Put yourself in their shoes. Get out of your realm of life and put yourself into their world. Sympathize with them; try to understand where they are coming from. Don't do what everyone in this world does. That is, sit there and pretend to be listening to what is being said, but in reality, be formulating in your mind what you will be saying just as soon as they finish. Many times people with this attitude and manner won't even let you finish your statement. You need to listen and understand. Really listen. Then you are in a position to respond because you should now understand. If you don't understand, then ask questions until you do understand. That is the key; try to understand before you respond. If you will follow this simple principle you will be successful as a boss, counselor, husband or father. People will respect you because they know you care.

"We had something this year that I have seen a few times, but never to the extent I saw it this year. Whenever you get people together and are able to focus their attention on a goal, you create what is called synergism. That is, the efforts of two people both giving their all and working toward the same goal, equals the efforts of three or more people otherwise not so involved.

"We all saw this very dramatically on the football field. You are all different and you learn from each other. Each of you have your talents and weaknesses, but if you will all learn from each other and respect each other's abilities, you can accomplish the goals you have set for yourself as a unit. You will find this so true in the world. There will be differences of opinion. Listen first, contemplate, discuss, and form the team with a united resolve that will give you the synergy to accomplish much more than just you by yourself will ever be able to do.

"You are in great physical shape at this point in your life. Try to stay that way. Keep yourself in condition both physically and mentally. Spend an hour of each and every day in physical and mental training. Split it up however you want, but this will make you a more complete, well-rounded individual. Keep your life in balance and divide it up into four areas: physical, mental, spiritual and emotional. If you will do this you will find your life in balance and you will be a much happier individual as long as you don't let any one of these areas take precedence over the others. Set your goals in this area and then maintain integrity with yourself, as well as with other people. If you say you will do something, either to yourself or someone else, then do it. Keep your commitments. Help other people and always stay close to your family.

"If you are going to be a leader, you have got to set the example. Remember when you were elected captain of the team and I told you to be sure you were to each weight training session? That was because you have to be an example if you are to lead. You can't lead by pushing. You lead by being out front and showing the way.

"As a leader you can't do everything. You need to delegate to others tasks you may know you can do better than they. And sometimes you will even have the time to do the thing you delegate. This is not a time-driven exercise. If you are going to build a team and use synergism like we talked about, you are going to have to let some of the people you work with expand their horizons and possibly make some mistakes. They will learn from those mistakes and in the long run you will have a much stronger and better team. Be candid and forthright with those with whom you deal. If you see something that is bothering you, then sit down with the person and talk to him. This is always hard, but if you will do it you will be respected and everything will work out better than if you just let it slide. If you ignore improper performance or behavior, it will cause pressure to build and someday may explode causing more damage than if you had addressed the situation when the problem first appeared. This is especially true in a marriage. Talk to your wife when you get married and work out differences before they build up and explode..

"Remember when we had the weight lifting contests? There was a reason for those besides just having fun. That was kind of a reporting session where we could look at the results of the training you had experienced for the previous few months. I took those sheets and compared them with what you had done the time before and I could see the progress you were making. It was a time where you could realize progress, too. Reporting does more than communicate back results. It emphasizes and solidifies the benefits of efforts expended to the person doing the work and brings the realization of success to those who are laboring so diligently.

"As a leader you will need to hold your people accountable. Give them a task, then give them the authority they need to accomplish the job and finally ask them to return and report how they did. If they know there is an accounting time they will do a better job every time. Then give them the credit-sing their praises from the rooftops.

"One of the biggest mistakes I see leaders make is their

taking credit for results when, in fact, someone in their organization did the work. This is a huge mistake and you will never develop a team by doing this. Without a supportive team you will be one individual and will never accomplish much. The best way to encourage your people is to give them credit. Help them succeed and catch them in the act of doing something right. And then sing their praises. Praise in public, but always reprimand in private.

"We have talked a lot about leadership. Perhaps you look at me as the ideal leader. Don't, I have many faults and problems. But there is one leader I have looked to and tried to pattern my life after. He was the greatest leader this world has ever known- Jesus Christ."

"Let me give you this." Coach handed me a piece of paper which had a number of lines typed on it.

I read:

"But when we come to Jesus, we find ourselves in the presence of one without flaw and without peer. He was enthusiastic, blazing with enthusiasm, but he never became fanatical. He was emotional. Men could feel the throbbing of his heart, but he never became hysterical. He was imaginative, full of poetry and music, seeing pictures everywhere, throwing upon everything he touched, a light that never was on land or sea, the inspiration of a poet's dream. But he never was flighty. He was practical, hard headed, matter of fact, but he was never prosaic, never dull. His life always had in it the glamour of romance. He was courageous, but never reckless; prudent, but never a coward; unique, but not eccentric; sympathetic, but never sentimental. Great streams of sympathy flowed from his tender heart toward those that needed sympathy; but at the same time streams of lava flowed from the same heart to scorch and overwhelm the workers of iniquity. He was pious, but there was not a trace about him of sanctimoniousness."

Those were very special moments Coach and I spent

together. We spent many hours sitting and talking in that small little steam bath. The last time, as we dressed I looked over at Coach and realized he probably didn't have much time left on this earth. He was a real fighter and a winner who would never quit, but his earthly tabernacle was not cooperating and was wasting away.

One morning I looked for Coach and found him in the storage/resting room lying down on his cot.

"I come in here to lie down when the pain gets bad," he said. "I also come in here many times each day to pray for the strength to get through another day. If I don't pray four or five times each day, I just won't make it through."

I saw the glaze of pain in his eyes and wished there were something I could do for him.

Coach was there every day for practice over Christmas vacation and we had a couple of tournaments during the Christmas break where we did quite well as a wrestling team. Time marched on and after the holidays, classes began again in earnest. Santa had again ignored the wishes of at least a majority of the student body to make school go away and let us enjoy this wonderful time of our lives with out the trials of classwork and attendant drudgery.

One day at school I noticed Coach wasn't in class so I walked down to the storage room. He was lying on the cot and looked very tired. It was easy to recognize that he was in a great deal of pain. I felt devastated watching a man simply disintegrate into almost nothing. But would he give up? Never, no way!

Coach continually got worse and went into the hospital. We kept hearing rumors about him doing better and after a blood transfusion they said he might come home. Maybe Coach was right and he wouldn't die. Maybe he would beat this cancer after all.

Basketball season was in full swing and during his hospital stay the football stadium was renamed "Vernon Ravsten

Stadium" at a half time ceremony honoring a man beloved by his community, students and most of all, the athletes he led on the field and on the mat. And in life.

The people in the stands were very quiet out of respect and honor. I sat there on the front row of the gym watching the people politely clap and thought, "They didn't know, they don't have any idea of the story behind this man and the love a bunch of boys had for him and he had for them."

That night after the game, several men from the board of trustees went up to the hospital to tell Coach about naming the stadium after him.

His wife was standing by the side of the bed holding his hand and made the comment, "Honey, things like this just don't happen to common people."

Then one of the members of the board said, "Coach, you're definitely not a common man, rather a very uncommon man."

Coach was without words as he lie there in bed, just the shell of the man he had been not many months before.

With tears in his eyes, he simply said, "Thank you."

We went to practice every day, but since Coach was in the hospital, wrestling practice usually turned into weight training. On January 31, 1968, I went into the weight room to work out. I was sitting on a stool doing military presses at about 10:00 in the morning.

One of the guys walked in and said, "Did you hear about Coach?"

The room became completely silent.

Jamie Bauchman was lying on the bench doing bench presses and he sat up. "Coach died last night."

He had known but had said nothing. It was like if you didn't verbalize it, it wasn't true. No one wanted to accept the finality of the fact that Coach would no longer be there to encourage us, teach us, scourge us, laugh with us, cry with us, and just be with us.

A sick, empty feeling came into the pit of my stomach. Everyone just sat there and said nothing. I shook my head and looked over at Jamie and he looked at me. My eyes began to sting and tears began to form as I thought of this man I loved so much.

I thought back to the Highland game and walking off the field into his arms. I thought of watching him sitting on his milking stool with tears streaming down his face as we scored with seven seconds remaining and I pictured him standing at the front of the bus after that game as he fought to gain his composure. There was so much to think about and so much to be grateful for. This man had such an impact on my life, an impact I knew would never go away, but would grow from year to year, and every year of my life I have come to appreciate him even more.

I said, "You know, I was beginning to believe Coach was really going to beat it. He never quit, never."

The funeral arrangements were being made and I wanted to have the entire football team sit together and line the walkway as the casket was brought in and out of the church. Coach's father was there as I made the arrangements with the congregational leader, and I had a chance to meet him.

As we were introduced he had this very thankful and happy look on his face. He grabbed my hand and said, "I hope you boys know how happy you made Vernon and how much you did for him."

I looked back at him and said, "You will never know how much he did for each of us. In fact, I don't think anyone will ever know."

I went to the car after the short meeting and sat thinking of all the values coach had taught us. I knew these precepts would help us throughout our lives if we would simply apply what he had taught us.

The day of the funeral was beautiful. The sun was shinning and the team was dressed in our dark blue blazers. We all lined up as planned and then sat together in the church along one side of the chapel. We took up the entire left side. It was a long and touching funeral and it looked like about half the town was there. I had never seen so many people attend a funeral.

After the funeral the team lined up on both sides of the sidewalk all the way to the hearse. The pallbearers and family walked down between us and I had a tough time keeping my composure. I looked down the line of boys and saw a few crying and many staring at the ground. What an experience we had shared together. An experience I would love to have my own boys experience some day.

Coach's earthly remains were gently placed into the hearse and we all went to the cemetery. There was a short ceremony there and the casket was placed in the ground. I was with my family now and noticed as we left, a number of guys in dark blue blazers standing around by themselves or in small groups, all staring blankly.

People were heard saying as they walked back to their cars, "Oh, he was such a good man and such a good influence on the boys."

I thought to myself, "You don't know. No, you have no idea what kind of influence he had on us. You don't know the story behind this man called "Coach" and the boys who loved him so much."

I wondered if they ever would.

Brief Life History

Vernon Frank Ravsten was born December 14, 1930, at Clarkston, Utah, the son of Frank and Verona Ravsten. He received his early schooling in the elementary school in Clarkston. In 1940 the family moved north to Heyburn, Idaho. He experienced the normal days of a growing young man in the farmland of Idaho. He attended school in the Heyburn School District and graduated from Heyburn High School in the spring of 1949. He participated in many school activities and was an all around athlete.

His freshman year of college was spent at the Southern College of Education at Albion, Idaho. The school closed shortly after his arrival and he transferred to Brigham Young University in Provo, Utah on a football scholarship.

In 1951, after a year at BYU, he transferred to Idaho State University in Pocatello, Idaho. There he played center on the Bengal football team and was selected co-captain his final year, the same year the team won the conference championship.

On November 25, 1953, his senior year, he married Jean Anderson in the Idaho Falls Temple of the Church of Jesus Christ of Latter Day Saints. The next two years were spent in the service of the United States Army at Walnut Creek, California, after he was drafted.

Discharged from the Army in January of 1956, he moved to Rigby, Idaho, where he assumed the duties of head football coach at Rigby High School. He remained in Rigby for three years and then returned to BYU for graduate studies in psychology. While completing the course work for his Master's Degree, he helped coach the freshman football team and taught health at the university..

In 1961, he returned to Idaho and the city of Idaho Falls. He was hired as head football and track coach and assisted in the coaching of other team sports at Idaho Falls High School. Academically, he taught health, P.E. and psychology. He was also a school counselor.

Always active in stimulating and inspiring his students, he received many accolades, one of the most memorable to him being selected to return to Rigby High School to deliver the baccalaureate address. Just before passing away, Vernon received a letter from then Governor Samuelson of Idaho, commending him and expressing gratitude for his long and valuable service to the youth of Idaho.

Skyline High School was formed in 1966, from a division of Idaho Falls High School due to the growth of the city. Vernon decided to accept the head football and wrestling coaching positions in the new school.

His life was filled with service to others-both youth and adult alike. His family was of utmost importance to him and he counted family experiences as most memorable the last year of his life. The birth of his son Deric, baptizing his youngest daughter and ordaining his oldest son to the priesthood in his church were the highlights of his last year of life.

His wife Jean, two daughters and three sons-Kimberly Ann, Christopher Frank, Kendi Kae, Darren A. and Deric Vernon, survived him.

He also had two brothers and two sisters-Janell, Lynn, Trena and Curtis